Writing!

OTHER BOOKS BY ADRIAN WALLER

Theatre on a Shoestring
Adrian Waller's Guide to Music
Data for a Candlelit Dinner
The Gamblers
Soulikias: Portrait of an Artist

Writing!

An informal, anecdotal guide to the secrets of crafting and selling non-fiction

by Adrian Waller

M&S

Canadian Cataloguing in Publication Data

Waller, Adrian, 1936–
Writing!

Bibliography: p.
ISBN 0-7710-8794-2

1. Authorship. 2. Style, Literary. 3. Self-employed. I. Title.

PN147.W34 1987 808′.025 C87-093915-7

Printed and bound in Canada by Webcom Limited

McClelland and Stewart
The Canadian Publishers
481 University Avenue
Toronto, Ontario
M5G 2E9

For Irène, Nathalie, and Zoë,
who have come to understand
that writing is not just a profession,
but a way of life.

Contents

Acknowledgements

I am indebted to my colleague Joan Naimark, who copy edited and helped clarify important points in a bulky manuscript while feeding it into a word processor against fast-approaching deadlines. She kept my spirits high when the road seemed rough. Nor can I possibly overlook the professionalism, enthusiasm, and understanding of Dinah Forbes, my editor at McClelland and Stewart. Her studious assessment of my manuscript and the changes she suggested helped make for a far better book.

Thanks are also due to the following editors, librarians, friends, magazines, and publishing organizations for their encouragement and help with research: Sandra Bell of the National Library, Ottawa; Robert Fulford, editor of *Saturday Night*; Alan Walker, managing editor of *Maclean's*; Jerry Tutunjian, editor of *Leisure Ways*; Ann Rhodes, editor of *Empress*; *Reader's Digest* both in Montreal and Pleasantville, N.Y.; Mebbie Black, editor of *Homemaker's*; Bart Robinson, managing editor of *Equinox*; Christopher Dafoe, editor of *The Beaver*; Lindsay Crysler, Director of Journalism, Concordia University, Montreal; *Toronto Life*; *enRoute*; *Quill & Quire*; *Select Homes*; *Dogs in Canada*; *Empress*; *Chatelaine*; Judy Lord, editor of *Nature Canada*; Nicole Rault; Association of American Publishers; Magazines Canada; Canadian Booksellers

Association; Canadian Book Publishing Council; Association of Canadian Publishers; Canadian Periodical Publishers' Association; Canadian Business Press; Maclean-Hunter Ltd.; Southam Communications; *Harrowsmith*; Fran Oliver, editorial assistant of *The United Church Observer*; Rose Robart; Ioana Teodorescu of the Côte Saint-Luc Public Library, Montreal. I would also like to thank the Estate of the late Sonia Brownell Orwell and Secker and Warburg, Ltd. for permission to reprint from *Animal Farm*. Finally, my thanks to N. William Ross, LL.M., who carefully checked my chapter "The Writer and the Law."

Introduction

I've built this book out of a passion for writing and a joy for explaining it to those who want to listen – what it is, exactly, and how it works.

Writing has probably been invaded by more riddles, misconceptions, and quirks than any other vocation I know, incessantly inhibiting all who seek to try it. During thirty years of applying the craft and lecturing on it, I've met hundreds of enthusiastic freelancers who want to write articles for our best magazines and books for our largest publishing houses, but who worry constantly about the wrong things in the wrong order.

They agonize over copyrighting their work, for instance, long before they have even written the first word, which is rather like drafting the introduction to a book when the manuscript is nowhere near completion, or putting up a front door, then erecting the house to fit it. Far too many of those same writers select ideas that are either dead or beyond their capabilities. All too often they toil blindly on a manuscript hoping that when it's finished, it might – with luck – sell, a futile exercise at best, and one which can be dreadfully dispiriting. Neither do they know how their work is affected by the law or who are the editors, those silent back-room people who fine-tune thoughts and words. Writers are all too frequently overwhelmed by the task of researching, intimidated by setting out their information for all to see, bemused by recycling, and ignorant of the market. The tragedy is that many are imaginative, perceptive, and resourceful people who have understood little about the kind of equipment a serious writer needs for the long journey, or even the measured steps that must be taken to enter the business as a professional. They have never been shown the way.

Thus, as best I can, I've tried to do this by addressing *all* major aspects of non-fiction writing, not to tell how people would *like* the craft to be, but as it really *is*. The chronological system I explain adheres to standards required by our top magazines. The simple assumption here is that, if you can consistently write articles well for them, you can satisfy almost all good magazines and even eventually produce books for our better houses. I've touched, however, on some smaller magazines so as to present a cross-section of the scope of a successful freelancer's work. To round out the picture and show it from many sides, I've also spoken to scores of colleague writers, professors, editors, and publishers, to whom I'm eternally grateful for their time and expertise.

The early chapters are intended to spell out the foundations: the nature of writing, what the freelancer requires to enter it, how to get started, and what quality magazines expect. Here, I've tried to explain the multi-faceted character of the magazine piece itself, what makes it, and what doesn't. Much of this detail falls into fuller perspective in chapters dealing with searching out ideas, refining them, then proposing them – quite frankly the most crucial piece of writing the freelancer ever undertakes.

Since brilliant ideas are useless without research to support them, I've devoted much of the middle of the book to just this: chapters on both digging up information and interviewing, primarily for biographies. To demonstrate how a writer must control an interview, I've reproduced selected segments from recorded conversations I have had with such widely contrasting celebrities as Country singer Wilf Carter, opera tenor Luciano Pavarotti, and a former Chicago Black Hawks hockey player named Gary Platt. What goes into an interview, I feel, is best shown by actually inviting readers to sit in on a couple.

Separate chapters on constructing the article and the book speak for themselves. They are fuelled, however, by another observation: that when most people write badly, they do so because they're unable to organize facts and ideas logically or pick the simplest, clearest words to make themselves understood.

This, in a nutshell, is what writing really is. A constant tussle with emotions, facts, and language, it has never come easily to me or anyone else I know, hence a chapter on writer's block and ways to cast it off. Chapters on applying words to paper, polishing, and editing are intended to reinforce one of the book's main themes: that crafting a text well requires considerably more effort than merely hammering it out in one or two sessions.

Finally, the idea for this project came from a student at the University of Montreal, where I spent a year teaching written English. She enjoyed my classes, she said, because they were spiced with stories that informed while evoking infectious laughter. "You should try writing a book the way you lecture," she added.

Actually, she wasn't quite right. I may have made the students chuckle from time to time, but I don't give lectures. I organize seminars so that everyone can speak. I relish the possibility that one student's thoughts or impressions might be of value to another – and to me, too. Having information flow in all directions in a book, however, is impossible. An author can only hope for his ideas to be taken to heart, mulled over, and be made a part of someone else's conversation. And that's what I wish now.

So read – and enjoy. Share what you can with friends, and remember that every word, sentence, and paragraph has been written with one earnest desire: to inspire writers and help even those already active in the business to turn out better articles and books than they ever thought they could.

Adrian Waller
Montreal, 1987

1. The Nature of the Beast

The work / the variety / the discipline / the need for versatility / the adventure / the slowness / the writer's reasonable sights / writing's appeal

"Writing is easy: all you do is sit staring at a blank sheet of paper until the drops of blood form on your forehead."

GENE FOWLER

A few years ago, while returning to Canada from France, where I had been collecting stories about our longest-serving governor general, Georges Vanier, for a posthumous *Reader's Digest* profile, I visited my grandmother in England. She was ninety-six then – a spry little Cockney who read three romances a week and walked at a half-run in a flurry of apron strings.

"Well, dear," she asked as we sipped tea against a backdrop of lupins and hollyhocks in her garden in Sheerness, Kent, "what are you doing with yourself these days? How are you earning your living?"

"I'm a writer, Nan," I answered, a trifle bemused. "I've *always* been a writer. I thought you knew that."

In a momentary silence between us, my grandmother reached for a cookie and dipped it in her tea. I used the time to think back to France – to the dusty village of Trosly-Breuil, twelve kilometres east of Compiègne, where I'd spent an entire day interviewing Georges Vanier's widow, Pauline, in her greystone farm house. That had gone well. But later, during a brief trip to Genova, Italy, my luggage had been stolen from the trunk of my rented car in a restaurant parking lot. Losing my clothes wasn't important because they could be easily replaced. My tape recorder, too. But the cassette in it? And my research file, which had taken me several weeks to build? Except for what information I could remember, I was telling myself despondently in that garden, my work was completely lost.

"I know you've done a lot of writing through the years," my grandmother went on, "but I don't mean that at all, dear. I mean, what do you do from nine till five each day? Where do you go? Don't you have a normal, *regular* job?"

"Yes, Nan," I answered, now with agitation. "I write. I regularly put words on paper, shuffle them around, play with them, change them – then sell them."

"You do what?"

"I write. I sell words – in magazine articles and books."

"But is that *really work*?" my grandmother asked.

Such assessments of the writer's craft are by no means uncommon, even from those who one day aspire to master it. All too often they perceive putting words on paper as far too romantic an occupation to be work in the ordinary sense of the word. Nothing, I can assure you, could be farther from the truth.

In fiction, the writer is a free bird who retires at will to an attic, pours himself a scotch or two, then dictates his pearls of wisdom into a tape recorder in a flood of the deepest, most tragic nostalgia. Sometimes, he summons his secretary to take them down in shorthand, type them, then rush them off to the publisher. He is waiting eagerly, of course, because these pearls are "money" pearls that will make both him and his author rich.

In reality, however, things are very different. Admittedly, the writer is still a free bird who may come and go at will, but since there's probably not a person alive who can produce a polished piece of writing of any respectable length without researching it, angling it, focusing it, tailoring it, agonizing over it, then changing it endlessly to try to make it better, he's more of a *rare bird*. In this sense, he does work that is far from ordinary, and certainly not romantic at all. And if quality is his goal, it promises to be incessantly hard into the bargain.

The most oft-published writers you've seen between book covers or in our better magazines, would doubtless agree. Theirs, they will tell you, is a tough, arduous profession in which idle dreams or silly notions have no place at all. Writing is made of intricate details, sprawling complexities, long, fatiguing hours of research and typing, and a relentless pursuit of saleable ideas. "Every writer, without exception," the eminent American psychoanalyst Dr. Edmund Bergler once said, "is a masochist, a sadist, a Peeping Tom, an exhibitionist, a narcissist, an injustice collector, and a depressed person constantly haunted by fears of unproductivity."

I wouldn't go that far. Nor, I think, would my colleagues. Most, though, would probably confess to having anguished a lot from time to time. The intensity of their job is one thing; wondering how, when, or if their next assignment will eventually arrive, is another. When writers are sometimes narcissistic, then, it may well be to camouflage their masochism. What else but masochism would cause them to follow a profession that is precarious at best, and that demands resilience, optimism, and stamina to fight constantly diminishing odds?

But writing is much more than this – with a decidedly happier side. It is also rewarding and interesting, offering an abundance of challenge and variety. One Vancouver writer I know makes a respectable income from planning and producing company newspapers and selling articles on Canadian and American history, nature, and conservation. Occasionally she writes on pet subjects, too: sports, health, and handicrafts. A friend in Montreal, meanwhile, works successfully on a desk in her basement laundry room, of all places, producing trade paper pieces, fillers for larger magazines, and items for various government pamphlets – all between helping two companies prepare reports and public relations handouts and write speeches for their senior executives. She gets enough jobs to keep her afloat from one year to the next.

I, on the other hand, prefer to concentrate on fewer but larger assignments that take more time and pay considerably more. Occasionally I might write a corporate speech or a short piece for a specialized magazine, but most of my work entails crafting articles of between 3,000 and 5,000 words for large consumer magazines sold on the newsstands.

To do it, I've needed to be versatile. Long ago I recognized that writers who specialize rarely ever make steady livings from their work. Those who do are usually highly regarded experts in politics, consumer protection, personal finance, or law. They are both knowledgeable and so intensely hooked to their fields that they rarely need to step into another. The most successful, however, are industrious men and women eager to apply their natural curiosity and need for diversity to numerous different topics, thus considerably increasing their chances of being published in almost as many different places.

Over the years, I've grappled with countless important social issues without knowing any more about them initially than what I had read in a newspaper or heard on radio: the tragedy of teenage suicide, the plight of the unemployed, the anatomy of labour unrest, the dreadful scourge of illicit drugs, the ugliness of prostitution, and the values of parole, all of which have touched hearts and minds in every corner of our land. I've written articles, too, about animals, inventions, music, and crime, not to mention essays on rivers, mountains, death, and sex, and have ghost-written for members of Parliament and academics on such varied topics as their life experiences and great moments in sport, and their views on television violence and the inadequacies of IQ testing in our schools.

Like others who have chosen a similar path through writing, I've built up a prodigious bank of personality profiles on the way. This includes pieces on the photographer Yousuf Karsh, the jaunty, Irish flautist James Galway, actor Donald Sutherland, opera tenor Jon Vickers, and actress Kate Reid. I recall sipping whisky-sours in a Toronto hotel with ballet dancer Rudolf Nureyev one week, then nursing an orange juice backstage at Nashville's Grand Ole Opry the next, while researching an article on Canadian-born Country singer Hank Snow. Bandleader Guy Lombardo spoke to me in an Italian restaurant on Manhattan's 46th Street, boxer Sugar Ray Robinson in a London pub. And that wizened old Indian, Chief Dan George, granted me a five-hour interview in his Vancouver hospital room following major hip surgery.

Within only eight days, I once flew to balmy Los Angeles to interview singer Paul Anka, then went directly to snowbound Sault Ste. Marie, Ontario, to talk to an electronics expert for a piece about citizens-band radio. Just as rewarding was a 300-kilometer drive from Thunder Bay to remote Geraldton, Ontario, to profile a seventy-year-old garage clerk named Ted Tarkka, who had spent nearly half his life as his town's Santa Claus, volunteer fire chief, and unpaid "veterinarian," tending neighborhood pets, and wildlife struck by vehicles on the Trans-Canada Highway or left injured by indiscriminate hunters in the woods. And how could I ever forget travelling to

Truro, Nova Scotia, to interview a twenty-three-year-old school teacher named Maura Cameron who gave up her summer to drive sixteen severely handicapped teenagers, nearly all of them confined to wheelchairs, on a cross-Canada camping trip?

As appealing as they may instantly seem, however, journalistic excursions like these should never tempt anyone to quit a full-time job and plunge obliviously into the business. There is too much to consider first. Being a self-employed writer – a freelancer – means being your own boss, with both the advantages and the problems this can entail. On the one hand, of course, freelancing is being free to work when *you* want to, when only *you* feel the time is right; on the other, it requires the judicious scheduling of assignments so that working time is always properly apportioned and never lost. Time, after all, is the freelancer's most valuable commodity. Used well, it can make writing enjoyable and reasonably lucrative; applied badly, it makes writing a thankless chore, a drudgery, and this inevitably shows in what the editor gets to see.

In the course of coping – or trying to – some freelancers have become rare breeds, let alone free birds. The most successful, it seems, are those who have adapted. Those who have not, struggle. "I don't love writing like you do," says one disillusioned writer I've known for many years. "I simply like writing because it saves me doing other things I've tried and hated, like teaching school and selling encyclopedias."

He talks with incessant fervour about producing articles for small magazines, the bulk of his output, and threatens one day to reveal himself as an earth-shaking novelist or playwright. But he does little to realize either. His greatest talent is inventing the most diabolical excuses for not writing at all. In so doing he has become walking testimony to the tongue-in-cheek confession of American comic novelist Peter De Vries – "I love being a writer. What I can't stand is the paper work."

Every morning, my acquaintance jogs to keep fit, does crossword puzzles to expand his vocabulary, and plays chess with a retired physicist to sharpen his mind. He then suddenly remembers that the blank paper he fed into his typewriter the previous night still awaits the beginnings of his magic touch. So, at around midday, he returns to his office to work. No. Wait. That's wrong. He then goes for lunch and, to avoid facing the blank paper on his return, decides a little more research is in order and saunters to the library to do it.

On his way back, he stops off for a drink, ostensibly to help him put his life in order, gather his thoughts, and plan his story.

So it goes. Several days later, as his deadline looms, our disorganized, jaded freelancer musters up enough steady heat to write in one long, frantic burst through the night, biting his fingernails, chain-smoking, and swearing at his cat. For the most part, his stories are clear and informative but uninspiring to read. And no sooner has his name appeared above them, than he goes for another drink – to celebrate. "You wanna know something?" he says to friends. "There's this tremendous egotism about writing something so good the editor can't resist printing it! But I sure wish he'd pay more. Writers work for peanuts, for godsakes. It's one helluva buyer's market!"

On that score, he's right. In one given year, the busy, self-motivated freelancer is very lucky to dream up and sell twelve articles at an average fee of $1,200 for each. Considering that these pieces would run to between 2,000 and 3,000 words and generally take a month or so to produce, the magazine writer deserves every cent he or she makes. All too often there is no payment for preliminary research to develop ideas or "kill fees" for stories that don't pan out. And while large consumer magazines pay considerably more, reimburse phone bills, and cover travel expenses, competition to make their pages is so high that they remain beyond most freelancers' reach. To exist, then, and afford vital fringe benefits like health insurance and pensions, most writers must grab whatever assignments they can and hope that these will quickly lead to others.

But that's not all. The business is notorious for its slowness, often to send cheques and nearly always to acknowledge ideas for articles or books, however good they may be. Reasons for this vary. On small magazines, the editor might be the lone in-house writer, frequently expected to leave office work undone while he goes out on assignment. On larger magazines, where decisions are made by groups of editors at monthly story meetings, the reasons are similar. If too many editors are vacationing, attending seminars, busy doctoring manuscripts, or travelling the country to recruit new contributors, those monthly meetings are convened bi-monthly. Sometimes, particularly during summer vacation time, they are postponed indefinitely, leaving the writer dangling, wondering, and waiting. Thus there's irony in these sample letters which, believe me, are by no means uncommon:

> Dear Author: I'm so sorry we kept you waiting nine weeks for a response to your two latest suggestions, but we're short-staffed. Now we're in a bind. Can you stop what you are doing and tackle one of them for us by the end of this month so we can slot it into February's line-up?

Or:

> Dear Author: We regret having kept you waiting six months while we sent your book proposal to market research. I'm pleased to say, however, that this appears to be working in your favour. We will have more definite news soon. Meanwhile, can you take on another project? We have a book for which we must find a writer by the end of next month.

All is never lost, though. As a University of Toronto Press executive once wrote to me, "Publishers move with the awful solemnity of the elephant rather than the lithely leap of the dikdik, but, thank God, they get there in the end."

They do, and this is one more excellent reason why serious writing is far too fulfilling to be shunned. As long as there are magazines and publishing houses there will always be chances of work, whether it be for full-time writers, specialists in one given field, or occasional contributors happy to take on the odd piece that may come their way. "If you really believe in something, dear, and think it's for you," my grandmother used to tell me, "take time off and do it. But try not to starve."

To ensure that they don't, the majority of freelancers combine writing with other jobs. The woman in Vancouver, for example, is a part-time nurse. A writer I met on assignment in Kenora, Ontario, also pilots an Ontario Provincial Government helicopter. I know freelancers who are doctors, lawyers, librarians, and clerics. Many others, like myself, teach – not always for the extra money, but so they can legitimately escape those long, reclusive hours at the typewriter.

Yes, writing can be intensely lonely, too. It is "a solitary occupation," the prolific American author Laurence Clark Powell once told a Yale University audience. "Family, friends and society are the natural enemies of a writer. He must be alone, uninterrupted, and slightly savage if he is to sustain and complete an undertaking." Needing quietness and solitude is one thing; it's another, however, to toil endlessly behind closed doors with only yourself to talk to. If you were working in a busy office, of course, you would find other people are constantly around to assist you by making a phone call on your behalf, helping you add a column of figures, or by checking your files. But when you write, no one can help out. Only *you* know what you want to say and how, and with what kind of texture and tone. Only *you* know the direction of your research and how it can be used to its most potent effect. Fleeing the typewriter to exchange thoughts and ideas with other people, then, becomes a welcome diversion indeed.

Not long ago, while teaching an evening course on magazine writing at John Abbott College in Ste. Anne-de-Bellevue, Quebec, I made a point of asking why each student was there. Many, it transpired, had never written before but sought the encouragement to try. Some were newspaper reporters, public relations executives, or technical writers who wanted to broaden the scope of their skills. A few, however, were young, aspiring fiction writers shrewd enough to know that the novel, with its themes, plots, sub-plots, and parade of finely etched characters, is such an intricate art form that it cannot be taught. It relies almost exclusively on natural, in-born talent.

Like the poets, librettists, song writers, and playwrights who filled the hall with them, they were wise enough, too, to extol the virtues of the magazine article as being, perhaps, journalism's most exacting form – and an excellent start for larger writing projects to come. One man, a former reporter-photographer who had spent many years in Africa, knew this all too well. He had written for numerous magazines but now wanted to know how to marshal his research and refine his prose so he could write his autobiography. Aged and etched with deep, hard lines, he contrasted sharply with a wide-eyed young woman of seventeen, fresh out of school.

"I'm here, sir," she said, "because I want to write for *Chatelaine*."

Tactfully, I like to think, I told her that writing for *Chatelaine* was a worthy goal. For the moment, however, it was a shade too ambitious – she would be wiser starting on a smaller scale by producing five- or six-paragraph pieces for a local paper or a small magazine, building up credibility and a portfolio of tear sheets, and graduating to more challenging work later. All good writing, I explained, appears so deceptively simple, particularly the short article in our better magazines, that a lot of amateurs are lured into thinking they can craft similar pieces without experience, practice, or skill. Since each of these is usually learned on the job, it's always better for beginners to write as much as they can so long as it's within their interests or abilities – something they can handle with relative ease and see published on one or two attempts.

"Please don't try to make *Chatelaine* until you're really ready," I told the young woman. "That way, the rejection slips you're almost certain to get won't dispirit you before you've even begun. Try to understand the high standards a good magazine imposes on its writers and meet them so as to build your reputation. But don't aim work at top editors until the time is right, until you can really consider yourself a pro." I'm glad to say that she heeded the advice.

From that course's two-way discussions emerged one fundamental philosophy: Our best writing is usually accomplished when we enjoy doing it – when it's fun. For me it generally has been, and there are numerous other freelancers who marvel that they've carved livings from something that would otherwise have been a hobby.

Most memorable to us all are the people we've written about. Characters are to writers, after all, what actors are to theatres. They will forever amble through our lives by the scores, each with a message or some special advice, or as attestation to an achievement that will never cease to inspire. Through writing, we get to know how others live and what urges them on. From Ted Tarkka in Geraldton, I learned the real value of our wildlife and how much emptier we would all feel without it. In his slow, measured cadence, Chief Dan George explained the real issue of native rights. In Pincourt, Quebec, a school principal named Henry Wohler, who devised a rig so he could teach a boy born without legs to ski, showed me selflessness and kindness at its best. With his wheelchair marathons, through the poetry he tapped out on a word processor, and from his determined academic studies, Paul Legault, a young Ottawa man rendered quadriplegic in a high school football accident, gave me insight into the authentic meaning of courage.

The most applicable perception of all, though, emerged from a casual chat with the lean, callow man I met while waiting to interview The Beatles at Toronto's Maple Leaf Gardens in 1966.

"Have you been here before?" I asked him.

"Yes," he said. "Once."

"And do you like The Beatles?"

"Yes," he said. "I have to like them. I'm their manager."

His name, of course, was Brian Epstein. Not only had he discovered the group, but he had refined it, packaged it, and marketed it worldwide. Like many people of my generation, those long-haired boys from Liverpool's drab, forbidding back streets appealed to my musical senses only when the years had rolled by and some time after that conversation. So standing in that corridor, normally the lone territory of hockey players, my questioning was not entirely out of place. "Can you please explain to me, Mr. Epstein," I asked, "what exactly it is The Beatles have got?"

"Yes," he replied quickly. "Discipline. Discipline must form the basis of all creative endeavour. Without it, all the entertainers, artists and writers in the world would be totally lost. Their labour would be utterly useless."

By writing's very nature, with its contacts, wide-ranging subjects and feedback, it opens doors, deepens knowledge, broadens horizons, creates visions, forges opportunities, and makes writers infinitely more sensitive to their surroundings. We become astutely aware, for instance, of when the world works well, and also when it doesn't. Often, perhaps too often, we presume to possess magic powers to promote change. There are times, maybe, when we might all heed the advice of Isaac Bashevis Singer, the old, Polish-born master of Yiddish prose, who said that a good writer was "basically a story-teller, not a scholar or redeemer of mankind." For all this, we tend to roll boldly ahead, airing pet peeves and exposing truths because, as people – as one of Edmund Bergler's injustice collectors – we feel, think, and care.

Wherever we are, though, those of us who write for a living unhesitatingly agree on one thing: Our sustained, painstaking research, the permanence of words, and the toil and frustrations of setting them down, all combine to give writing a unique character and enduring appeal.

2. Reaching for the Best Magazines

Newspaper reporting vs. magazine writing / the news / the magazine article's multi-faceted character / issue pieces / profiles / wrinkles and warts / what magazines expect of the writing

"The great art of writing
is the art of making people
real to themselves."
LOGAN PEARSALL SMITH,
AFTERTHOUGHTS

Writing is one of the most portable professions there is, needing only a typewriter, some paper and a place to hang your hat. With these, and a few bright ideas, the beginner is fully equipped to surge ahead. But wait. I've leapt ahead of myself again. Writers starting out need the security of a regular job, or a cushion of cash to tide them over – and a full knowledge of what the business is all about.

First, they must, above all else, recognize that the gap between the quick, slight newspaper story and the solid article top magazines generally demand is as wide as the Grand Canyon. Most unsuccessful non-fiction writers I've met have consistently been so because they have wasted far too much time trying to sell the editor of *Toronto Life* entertainment stories that really belonged in *The Toronto Star*, or cooking columns to *Homemaker's Magazine* that were suitable only for Montreal's little weekly newspaper *The Downtowner*. They haven't properly understood that newspapers and magazines want entirely different things since they aim to please different audiences.

Newspapers, of course, exist by publishing stories that *must* be told that day if they are dailies, and that week if they are weeklies. Their reporters are expected to gather the most pertinent facts on, say, a state visit, an industrial accident, a fast-breaking political scandal, or the death of a prominent figure, then write them down as quickly, concisely, and accurately as they can, all in a matter of hours. Sometimes, to beat a deadline, they must do what they can in minutes.

Since news loses its value the moment it's spilled, experienced freelancers tend not to chase it unless specifically assigned by a news editor to do so. Staff reporters, on the other hand, spend their days hunting down stories that can be sufficiently well told in one given day, and the scope of their work is broad. A good news story must, before all else, have impact. But it also requires such other elements as timeliness and proximity. The best stories, used at the top of each page, are usually the most important to emerge that day. But reporters also deal in incidents of lesser news value, or those that may earn a place purely by being novel, ironic, or just plain comic.

Man bites dog, news editors tell us, is definitely a story because it's unusual, if not downright bizarre, but that dog bites man is worthless because dogs are often known to act that way. There are exceptions to every rule, however, hence this hypothetical incident which, I predict, would make an instant front-page brightener anywhere:

> Dog bites man as man begins scaling a museum wall to steal enormously valuable Oriental art treasures. As man tumbles to the ground, he grabs a drain pipe for support, pulling down a large section of guttering, which is somehow ejected over a high wall surrounding the property, spilling across a main road and backing up traffic for several blocks. The police arrive to sort out the chaos and our would-be thief, a gaping tear clearly visible in the seat of his trousers, willingly helps out. His volunteer work done, he slips off into the night, never to be seen again.

The point of this little bit of nonsense is that here, the dog-bites-man story has an extension, an extra dimension. It's a story that would be told briefly, then be forgotten – a "one-shot deal." Whether or not it could be carried into another day would depend on what other "extensions" ensued. Rest assured, however, that reporters assiduously monitor stories like these for further developments. Between churning out their big, hard-news stories and their flimsy little "brighteners" – the comic relief for which both editors and public constantly yearn – they keep careful records of everything they write, hoping to be able to update it later. They reach out for what reporters the world over call "the latest angle" in on-going stories like juicy court cases, government inquiries, or collapsing money markets, knowing that whatever they may miss or get wrong in their rush today can always be included or surreptitiously corrected in a follow-up piece tomorrow.

Sometimes, a story's magnitude automatically lends itself to far bigger treatment, with more explanation and background. Here, newspaper feature writers appear on the scene, who are often allowed as much as one week per story. They produce work which, with photographs, diagrams and charts, may fill an entire page. But time is always their enemy, too. They must work so quickly that, when they hand in their copy, the topic is still piping hot.

With less pressing deadlines, however, and any number of skilled freelancers on whom they may call, magazines generally cover large stories more comprehensively than do newspapers. They avoid reporting incidents, and when they jump on issues, they make sure they're durable, current, and of national or international significance – the power of organized labour, for instance, human rights, the state of our national pension scheme, Middle East tension, or the pros and cons of capital punishment. They angle, focus, and document the wide implications of these stories with anecdotes, case histories, and expert opinion from across the country or around the globe. For magazines, there *is* no tomorrow or second chance to right inaccuracies, because they don't do follow-ups. However awesome national or international stories may appear at the outset, magazine editors and their writers work hand in hand to report them accurately – first time.

Among writers, then, those who sell to magazines occupy a fortunate position. They have much more time to plan and craft their stories than do reporters. Accordingly, magazine editors expect articles with design or shape, anecdotes to help transport readers and make the subject better understood, and a crisp, fluid writing style that sparkles and shines. In this respect, one top Canadian editor with whom I have worked for many years, strongly maintains that, rather than being a long newspaper story, the kind of sculptured, full-bodied article sought by most mass-circulation magazines is more like a short book.

Such an analogy is an over-simplification, of course, but nonetheless well worth exploring. Some magazines, particularly trade journals, read very much like newspapers. Their main stories are imbued with an ever-present hurried quality and, certainly, a lack of warmth. This is *not* to suggest that newspaper reporters can't write well. They can and often do, developing other skills besides. They become experts on their "beats," learn the power and need for strong anecdotes, and develop both a keen eye for the unusual and finely tuned dramatic sense which they put to excellent use every working day. But time and space, they argue, justifiably, rob them of chances to show their real literary talents.

For all this, relatively few reporters ever successfully master the jump to magazines because they have become experts at nibbling at the news rather than sewing up a story in one tidy package. True, newspapers have proved to be an invaluable training ground for anyone wanting to write; reporters generally agree, though, that carefully crafting magazine articles as opposed to hurriedly writing news stories, is a completely different skill. Thus they content themselves with the excitement of dealing with the newsroom's day-to-day pressures, recognizing that magazines – particularly those that have built up loyal advertising and a faithful readership – strive for a healthy balance between good literary prose and stalwart, informative journalism that reporters cannot consistently provide.

Besides length, shape, anecdotes, and sensitive writing, magazine articles require other ingredients that will justify their prominence and length. To some degree, the news editor's criteria apply. He seeks stories that are timely, prominent, different, and to some degree unusual, all set mostly within the paper's circulation area. But here the similarity ends. For the magazine editor, such saleable elements as the unlikely, the tragic, the comic, or the bizarre can never stand alone. Neither can a story be merely interesting. It must earn a spot in a magazine's pages by having infinitely more to commend it.

The magazine article, you should know at the outset, is a multifaceted organism composed of many things all so inextricably entwined that they often cannot be separated. One element that *can* stand alone, though, is significance. In fact, it towers high above all others.

"Why don't you write something on the number of kids getting killed at railway crossings?" a friend asked. "There were two deaths last year and one this. It's getting serious!"

Is it? One child dead, of course, is one too many. But is this a problem so serious and large as to deserve nation-wide attention? More children die in swimming pools or from influenza than by wandering in front of trains. Since the three victims my friend had mentioned were the only ones in Canada that year and were all from Montreal, the story was of local significance, yes, but not nearly important enough to develop for a national audience.

Nor, by way of another example, was a student's idea to write a survey-type piece on agoraphobia, which he planned to sell to *Homemaker's*. Editors there, I explained, had probably already touched on the illness as part of a larger article on phobias in general. If, however, the student still wanted to go ahead with the piece, I told him, he would need to establish that agoraphobia, the fear of open spaces, was significant enough to write about in the first place.

"Can you prove there are enough people suffering from it – that it's reached epidemic proportions?" I asked him. "You'll need this to make the entire country care."

"No," he said.

Another would-be writer contemplated a story on giants! He phoned to tell me he was asking Statistics Canada if by chance they had a record of the number of Canadians who stood more than seven feet tall. Armed with this information, he said, he would then find "two giant people," interview them on the telephone and write a story for *Saturday Night*.

"But Saturday Night doesn't use tall stories," I quipped, "only large fat ones that tell us how our country works. They're only interested in the nuts and bolts of our social and political systems. They use big sprawling pieces that take many weeks, sometimes months, to put together. What on earth would they want with giants?"

"Why not?"

I took pains to explain that *Saturday Night* features in-depth profiles of the men, women, and institutions that shape and run Canadian society. Its insightful reporting goes far beyond explanations of events, focusing instead on why things happen, who makes them happen, and how they may affect our future. Besides this, I said, the only institutional giant I knew was Pierre Berton. But he rose only to a mere six-foot-six!

"I'm sorry," I said, "but I don't think giants are a good idea for a magazine piece at all. Your suggestion has a horrible believe-it-or-not ring to it."

"Okay, fine," was the reply. "So if *Saturday Night* won't take it I'll sell it elsewhere!"

Examples like these of what *isn't* a magazine article, help us come closer to what *is*, or what may be under a certain set of circumstances. Two other elements of the article with which the writer must come firmly to grips, are interesting people – and enough of them – and the fascinating background a subject has. Both are important in varying degrees, depending on the topic. Take talented, eccentric musicians out of a piece on the Montreal International Jazz Festival, for example, and you would be left with a bland report belonging in that coming-events pamphlet you've so often seen in hotel rooms. Remove the dramatic day-to-day setbacks and triumphs from a mountaineer's quest for a summit, and his adventure would read like a Girl Guide hike. And if by chance you consider it pointless to show the ups and downs a young woman experiences as she finally conquers leukemia after a long, painful ordeal that so often threatened to defeat her, then don't bother writing the story at all. It will find no good market.

By far the most effective way of getting acquainted with the magazine piece is to listen to those who commission it – editors who know what their stories must say and how they want them said. Admittedly, they all have varying needs, but what each editor wants sheds more light on what a good article is made of.

Launched on a kitchen table in the rural Ontario town of Camden East in 1976, *Harrowsmith* is now a national, award-winning, bimonthly magazine published for a highly thoughtful, critical audience interested in the concept of self-reliance. The subjects it most frequently explores rather than covers are country life, food gardening, solar and wind energy, folk arts, ecology, small-stock husbandry, owner-builder architecture, and alternative lifestyles – subjects newspapers and trade papers rarely touch upon. It expects "thought-provoking writing, a creative use of anecdotes and a clear demonstration that the writer knows what he or she is talking about."

So does its sister publication, *Equinox*. Started in 1981, it has since risen to become a world-class magazine of science and geography with a circulation fast approaching a hundred and seventy-five thousand. This magazine deals with geography in its broadest sense, encompassing biology, astronomy, earth sciences, the arts, architecture, industry, travel, and adventure – again, topics needing too much explanation for newspapers to do justice to, and those they generally only nibble at. It has carried articles on wildlife painting, cerebral scanners, the forgotten Dogon tribe in Mali, north-west Africa, and a backstage look at the equally world-class Royal Winnipeg Ballet.

While its range of subjects is diverse, however, *Equinox's* main theme is narrow and specific – discovery and, in numerous instances, rediscovery. "Readers should finish an article," says managing editor Bart Robinson, "with the impression that they've shared the writer's experience. To this end, the writer should use clear, specific details, avoid generalities, and where possible, stories should be rich in personal impressions and anecdotes. We always want principal characters introduced early and expect them to be very fully developed."

The *Reader's Digest*, the mass-interest magazine DeWitt Wallace and Lila Acheson Wallace began in February 1922, and whose nineteen editions are now bought by nearly thirty million people worldwide, sheds extra light. In Montreal, the *Digest's* Canadian editors, who cater to more than a million and a half subscribers, admit to providing an eager, even hungry market for top-notch stories, but a demanding one that can be hard to break into.

Like *Saturday Night*, *Harrowsmith*, and *Equinox*, the venerated old *Digest* wants topics that are of lasting interest. That's not to say it likes stories that will wear nicely only until Christmas. Far from it. It seeks pieces that will be as gripping and satisfying to read several years from now as they are today, further reinforcing the necessity for serious writers to stake out the important part of life and leave the trivial alone. Thus the *Digest*, or any other highly professional magazine come to that, would definitely *not* be interested when dog bites man, or even if man were to sink his teeth into a Great Dane! Editors there might smile at the comic implications of both stories, even pin them on the editorial notice board and chuckle as they pass by to the coffee machine. But they would recognize them as being slight, without substance or human value, and lacking another part of the article's complex character: action, action, action – and an abundance of it.

Usually, a magazine piece requires action distributed over a reasonable time span so the story can develop – a year, perhaps, a night, even an hour if it contains enough. I've seen especially fine stories, however, that have been confined to a much shorter amount of time. Britain's Dr. Roger Bannister once successfully wrote a magazine article on his strategy and thoughts as, in May 1954, he became the first man to run a mile in less than four minutes. More often than not, though, a lack of time erases the kind of movement good writing needs to sustain itself. Yet sometimes, says *Digest* editor Alexander Farrell, "stories about dramatic or unusual events are suggested in which the action is over in the first paragraph – an individual who's hit by lightning, for instance, and survives." In other words, that story could conceivably be completely told in just one or two sentences, the only action being a single bolt of lightning. After that? Nothing. And for a magazine, our dog-bites-man piece would slip into the same useless category.

Wisely, general-interest magazines like the *Digest* leave special-interest stories for special-interest publications, electing instead to use those that can in some way reward their readers emotionally by sharing a powerful experience that combines human drama with practical information. With this in mind, its editors might well be interested in the girl who fought off leukemia. It would have to be properly told, though, and this means that all those ups and downs – the peaks and valleys or the climaxes and low points – would all need to rise and fall in a swift, lean narrative to make the piece heart-rending and dramatic. Through masterful writing, the goal would be two-fold: to capture the young patient's intensely emotional experience and terrible suffering, and use it as a vehicle to explain the type of medical treatment that saved her, then to provide a deep excursion into the kind of human determination that can justifiably be held up as an example to us all.

Complex? Of course it is. But who said writing a magazine article was simple, particularly one about a human drama?

Issue pieces also put heavy demands on magazine writers. Merely reciting facts to illustrate the topic's magnitude is totally insufficient. This kind of article needs examples – and many of them – plus an ending that suggests solutions. Often, though, a topic is far too complex to be handled in one piece and the writer is wiser to deal with only a corner of it. But what corner? The magazine article, after all, is not a book and can never hope to be. The answer: the best and most powerful corner. The corner that is on most people's minds. The interesting corner.

Grandiose notions of what the magazine piece can achieve have never ceased to amuse me. One example which immediately springs to mind came from a young writer who phoned asking me to help him market a story he had thought of over Hanukkah. "Professor," he said, "I'm writing about the history of the Jews."

"When?" I asked.

"Some time next week."

"But isn't that story going to be rather long?" I asked. "Isn't it an epic book that needs to be written by a team of scholars? You've got a few centuries to deal with, not to mention some figures that'll need quite a bit of fleshing out. And what about all those battles and achievements? It sounds to me like a string of a million issue and human-interest stories all rolled into one and spread over many centuries."

"Don't worry," the writer assured me. "I can cram it all into about ten pages – double-spaced, of course. I know magazines like their stories double-spaced."

"Well, if you can find a way of doing it," I said, "let me know. I've been struggling to tell big stories in a few words all my writing life!"

A few weeks later, the writer realized his idea was far too ambitious for a magazine and, on my advice, wrote a little story about a prominent Jewish family's art collection, which he gleefully saw published in his local paper.

Suffice it to say, then, that large stories must frequently be narrowed down for magazines. Example? Don't write a piece entitled "What's Wrong With Our Prison System?" You'll need to produce a book to cover that. You and the magazine piece will both do far better with "Are Halfway Houses Really the Answer?" or "Are We Doing Enough to Rehabilitate Ex-Convicts?" Both would be much more manageable.

For their profiles, consumer magazines want stories on people with proven track records of achievement, whose lives are rich in struggles and conflict and the anecdotes that these inevitably bring. They open their pages only to those who, in the process of getting their wrinkles, have also accumulated their warts.

Wrinkles and warts? They sound more like the property of plastic surgeons and dermatologists than of writers, don't they? They are, of course. But such imperfections have editorial functions, too, as reflected in novelist W. Somerset Maugham's instructions to a visiting photographer. "Take whatever photographs of me you like," Maugham said, "but refrain if you will from doing what others have done before you and washing out my wrinkles. I want them left in. I have spent many years earning them."

On magazines, the wrinkle doesn't denote age so much as long, outstanding service in one given field, which helps explain why editors steer well clear of stories about up-and-coming stars, leaving them instead to newspaper entertainment pages. And the wart? That's an editorial device aptly demonstrated by Oliver Cromwell's annoyance on seeing his portrait painter carefully covering up skin blemishes. At that, the story goes, Cromwell roared, "Remark all these roughnesses, pimples, warts, and everything as you see me!" Unless this was done, he added sternly, he would not "pay a farthing" for the poor artist's painting.

In much the same way, good editors expect warts to add dimension and flavour to profiles. They know that by touching upon a subject's occasional faults, the article is indirectly enhancing his or her good points and credibility. The piece is also displaying a sense of journalistic objectivity that will make it more believable to the reader. The warts, then, cast a shadow of skepticism by providing a momentary glimpse into the subject's darker side, making him real, even more human, a splash more lovable, definitely more plausible, and infinitely more interesting.

Knowing this, Paul Anka willingly gave me an editorial wart: When he was a fourteen-year-old drop-out, he said, he borrowed his father's car without permission and, not knowing how to drive it, made the 460-kilometre trip from Ottawa to Quebec City in second gear. On the return journey, and less than two kilometres from the Anka home, the car's engine seized up on a bridge during rush hour. Police charged the boy with taking a vehicle without the owner's consent and driving without a licence. In context, this story shows that Anka was as vulnerable as any other teenager in his neighbourhood, and that his adventure taught him how foolhardiness doesn't pay. It prepared him for what he is today: a highly successful entertainer and a respected, law-abiding businessman.

Magazines that run first-person pieces often receive manuscripts in which the writer is the central character or the narrator of a personal experience that happened many years ago. The first questions that spring to an editor's mind are, "Why run this piece now? Does it still have relevance?" The editor also must ask whether the article is so personal that any larger meaning within it will be lost on an equally large audience. What's vitally important to us or our families can't always be made relevant or significant to other people.

Again, there are exceptions. With careful thought and a deft, sensitive hand, first-person pieces can be made to work very well – like a Toronto woman's moving recollection, in *Legion Magazine*, of how she was able to grant her dying father his final wish, taking him from a hospital so he could spend his last days in the security and comfort of his home.

Stories like this are testimony indeed to the old dictum that says we usually write best what we think, know, or like. They are successful because, despite their appealing, personal nature, they strike a common "chord," that unpredictable, ephemeral dimension which somehow embraces a lot of what ordinary people enjoy reading about. Music has always achieved a similar feat. You don't have to be German to feel the mighty force of Richard Wagner's Romanticism any more than you need be French to comprehend the complex harmonics and rhythms of Claude Debussy's Impressionism. And look how successful The Beatles were in Japan! In purely journalistic terms, the "chord," which can't be orchestrated at the best of times, makes a story satisfying to all manner of readers across all manner of borders, be they geographical, demographic, ethnic, or economic. It is a story most people relate to because it either satisfies their need for special information or simply provides an outlet for emotion.

First-person stories, or those revolving around one central character, often present another dangerous trap. "Does the protagonist win by his own efforts and hard work or merely by luck?" editors will ask. If the answer is luck, the magazine article might be flawed beyond repair – just as it would if the central character, the reason for the piece in the first place, were undone by stupidity or dishonesty rather than by an outside force beyond his or her control. A businessman rendered bankrupt through foolishly mishandling money, for instance, will never command the same compassion as a Prairie farmer who has been defeated by hard economic times. Any newspaper reporter will tell you that.

3. Getting Started

Contributors' guidelines / studying magazines / the reader / the writer's mind / magazine sense / the writer's social responsibilities / the rewards

"Reading maketh a full man,
conference a ready man,
and writing an exact man."
FRANCIS BACON
(1561-1626)

Understand at least some of the magazine article's spectrum of components – we'll cover more as the ride continues – and you'll almost be ready to write. The next step is to contact editors, asking them to send their contributors' guidelines. From these, you will get to know what kinds of pieces they buy for what sections of their magazines, and how much they pay.

In part, guidelines from the highly esteemed *Toronto Life* say:

> Articles should have a strong Toronto orientation. Length: 200 to 6,000 words or more, depending on subject and treatment. Freelance contributions are accepted for feature articles in *Toronto Life* and its supplements: *Epicure*, *Homes* and *Men's Fashion*. Fees for feature articles vary according to length from $800 to $2,000. Occasional fiction is accepted at $800 per short story.

Canada's world-class women's magazine, *Chatelaine*, expects its major pieces to be between 2,000 and 3,000 words, for which it pays $1,200 and up. Its guidelines explain in part:

> We look for important national Canadian subjects examining any and all facets of Canadian life, especially as they concern or interest Canadian women. For example: "Porn: Does It Incite Violence Against Women?"; Personalities: (Chatelaine's Woman of the Year) Maureen McTeer; Lifestyles: "Baby Boom Women – High Hopes, Uncertain Prospects"; Health: "Progesterone – The Answer to Severe PMS?"; Relationships: "Real Women/Real Men – Role Free at Last?"
>
> For all serious articles, deep, accurate, thorough research and rich detail is required.

By way of further example, *Nature Canada*, published quarterly and distributed to about twenty thousand members of the Canadian Nature Federation and to selected newsstands, says:

> Feature articles on a broad range of natural history topics make up 55 per cent of our editorial material; our regular "departments" make up 20 per cent. The departments consist of:
>
> *Discovery*: sharply-focused one-page explorations of the quirks of nature and the passion of naturalists.
>
> *Notebook*: first-person accounts of naturalists, scientists, artists, film-makers and writers working in the field.
>
> *Uprising*: profiles of major conservation battles from the perspective of those in the trenches.
>
> We pay modest honorariums for manuscripts we accept – 20 cents per word of the final, edited text. Any photographs used are paid for separately. We give each author five copies of the issue in which his or her article appears. Extra copies are available at cost price.

Guidelines will quite often also tell you about the most important people of all, without whom your work and mine would be totally futile – the readers. Many years ago, I conveniently formulated a concept of my own typical reader. She was a person I would aim to please at every turn of the craft, from selecting ideas to putting them on paper. A woman of seventy living in Middle Musquodoboit, Nova Scotia, where she once taught school and was still active in her community, her interests spanned everything from pop art and archeology, I decided, to scientific advancements and the most hard-hitting issues of the day.

One night, while I was appearing on a television talk show, the interviewer, who was playing the proverbial devil's advocate, suggested that for a writer wanting to spread his wings, this hypothetical reader was more of a hindrance than a help, a decidedly limiting factor.

"She might be a nice, spunky old lady," the interviewer said, "but she's no more likely to pick up *Trucker's World* than *Artistic Tattoos*. And supposing you got your chance to write for *Playboy*? Would she be enthralled by that?"

She wouldn't, of course, which blew my formula askew. Since then I've become increasingly aware that one magazine's readership is completely different from that of another. This is why many magazines spend a lot of money on surveys to find out who their readers are, where and how they live, what they earn, how much they spend and read, and what interests them most. Guidelines will sometimes explain what editors and publishers have so far found out – a compilation of data that helps give freelancers useful directions before they begin to write. The wise ones take this information to heart. They compare guidelines from one magazine to another. They try to visualize various publications' readers and equate them with people they know. Without setting their sights too high, they then decide for what magazines and what audiences they feel most competent to write.

Not all magazines have compiled guidelines, however. "My own feeling," *Saturday Night* editor Robert Fulford says bluntly, "is that those writers who possess enough intelligence to read a few issues of a magazine before trying to do business with it, don't need any such guide. Those who lack the intelligence to do that – an astonishingly high number – won't be helped by anything."

He exposes an aspect absolutely integral to the craft. The best way to discover what magazines *really* want and who they aim to please, is by reading their back issues, and lots of them, from cover to cover. Studying their advertising will tell you at whom they are targeted. Note what their writers say and how they conform to a journalistic style or a point of view. Analyse the kinds of leads and endings different editors like, their preferred style of prose, vocabulary and sentence lengths, and the overall wordage of published pieces. Do this consistently well and, with mounting experience, you'll begin to think like a professional writer and develop such prerequisite tools as intuition and instinct, without which it's pointless to carry on.

Newspaper reporters term this combination "news sense"; magazine editors call it "magazine sense." Some talk of the writer's "antenna," a sort of built-in detection device that feels out a story and what slant will best make it work. Other journalists take it all for granted as part of their innate psychological make-up: a gut feeling that although an incident may appear to be simple and straightforward on the surface, there lies below a facet of greater magnitude which, when properly explored, will create a story so good that it will come to rest on a loftier plane.

One magazine editor describes the intangible coagulation of all the story-gatherer's forces as "a spark signalled by a bell that sounds in the brain the moment your heart says you could be onto something good. From then on, brain and heart work hand in hand, compelling you to pursue, dig deeper." For newspeople, the process works incessantly, which is why they hold their jobs. But for the magazine writer who must seek topics of greater value and with wider implications, it may happen only a couple of hundred times in a lifetime. When it does, he or she will be shuffling, reshuffling, and filtering the pros and cons of yet another story in one corner of the writer's very intricate mind.

It is intricate, indeed. Karl Kraus, the Austrian poet and satirist, who carved an entire career out of attacking the middle classes and the Press, once observed that a writer was someone who could "make a riddle out of an answer." It's a somewhat sardonic view, but not totally without foundation. Writers think constantly in possibilities, probabilities, perspectives, and variables. Their fixations are statistical evidence, concepts, analogies, and "damn-good quotes." They contemplate the minutest fragment of information or the tiniest anecdote most other people would dismiss as being worthless, wondering how to apply it to its most powerful effect.

As if this isn't enough, writers also ponder the power of their criticism and the weight of their words, anguishing constantly over the challenge of revealing a troubled world positively so they may somehow spread hope. And in this mire, they are forever rummaging for angles, vistas, directions, and solutions. "There is only one trait that marks the writer," says novelist Morley Callaghan. "He is always watching. It's a trick of mind and he is born with it."

Born with it? Perhaps. No one pretends that thinking makes writers or even that writing can be taught. But a voracious craving for thoughtful expression never hurt anyone, not the least those who yearn to see their words in print.

Success in writing comes largely from being curious, inquisitive, and broad-minded. We must possess a strong sense of argument but always be ready to recognize both sides of an issue fairly and with a natural compassion born of an appreciation and understanding of life. "How vain it is to sit down to write," said Henry David Thoreau, "when you have not stood up to live." Writers need to hold their own views firmly, of course, but they should develop the skill of setting down other people's without letting theirs intrude. These are qualities that, like magazine sense, can be acquired by assessing our best, most objective journalism on radio, television, and in print and appreciating the contemplation and planning behind it.

As writers, we should never forget that our two prime functions are to entertain and to inform. Both must be tempered by rigid, professional ethics and keen social responsibilities. "A writer," said the suffragette Nellie McClung, "must have the pores of his heart open." When we are honest with ourselves, our readers will be the first to benefit. Using that intuition and instinct as best they can, then, good freelancers ferret out the worthwhile and quickly shed the irresponsible.

They learn this by trial and error, mainly. As an exuberant young *Toronto Telegram* reporter incessantly looking for "scoops," I wanted to tell the public how mail thieves had devised an ingenious way of removing cheques from the corners of sealed envelopes. "Why?" my editor asked quizzically. "There's no point telling readers about a problem unless you can suggest a defence. In this case, there isn't one. So why waste time writing something that'll titillate the curious and leave half the population worried sick, wondering what in God's name they can do about it?" I had to admit he was right.

There's far worse to guard against, however. Mature, conscientious writers always find stories rooted in racism or aimed at inciting crimes, absolutely repugnant. A Canadian book published in the 1970s told how salaried workers could cheat on their income tax. A bookstore in Washington, D.C., boasts the world's largest collection of how-to pamphlets – many of them professionally written – on making explosives from ordinary household chemicals. One gives step-by-step directions on ways to assassinate a public figure, from staking him out and breaking through his ring of bodyguards, to planting a bomb or using a crude but lethal firearm which can quite easily be assembled in the most rudimentary basement workshop.

A satirical book on, say, bringing down the government or methodically fiddling corporate expenses, is something completely different. Satire is humorous criticism, invariably making its point by planting stereotypes – particularly of those people we know – in uncharacteristic or improbable situations. The skill in writing it is lordly, indeed, requiring a light hand and an impeccable knowledge of the subject being ridiculed. Above all else, however, it demands that the writer make his audience fully aware that it is reading or watching something intended to be tongue-in-cheek. If this mission fails, both humour and message are lost.

Writers who care about their work see no value whatsoever in dispensing horror for horror's sake. Stories about gruesome mass murders or monstrous hostage-takings are in the public interest and *must*, therefore, be told. But beyond this, there is an abundance of atrocity that need not be. You'll readily understand, then, that when a Miami-based tabloid telephoned me some years back for a story on a horse that had been dismembered by a snow plough, I was not at all pleased.

"We got great pictures!" an editor enthused. "All we need now is some fantastic copy to go with them!"

"I'm sorry," I said. "I don't write about squashed horses – only those that are alive and kicking."

Not long afterwards I rejected an offer from another American tabloid to write about a pregnant woman who had survived a spiteful winter's night trapped under a parked station wagon. My reasons were simple. While quickly recognizing the story's value for a good daily newspaper, I questioned the tabloid's motives. I immediately envisioned its editors changing the focus of my story to give it a sensational slant and an attention it didn't deserve. I even anticipated that they would bend the facts to suit their readers' insatiable appetite for gore. General-interest magazines like the *Reader's Digest* handle dramas like these sensitively, accurately, and in exquisite taste, showing a fuller dimension that usually embraces such human elements as courage or bravery. But generally speaking, tabloids – members of the so-called "yellow" press – have neither the skill nor the conscience for this. Their stories are too often inaccurate by omission, or just plain overblown.

Be conscious of the size of your role, and a reputation for care and integrity will precede you; acknowledge writing's skills and you will be well poised to grasp them and find yourself published. As a reward, you can be reasonably sure that, unlike that of the newspaper reporter, your work will not be used to wrap garbage or line cupboards – not, at least, until it has spent a respectable length of time on a coffee table or in a briefcase. Your articles will be listed in all manner of periodical indexes on library shelves, proof to posterity that once upon a time you actually existed and did something eminently worthwhile.

"Magazines," says the *Report of the Special Senate Committee on Mass Media*, published in 1970, "constitute the only national press we possess in Canada. Magazines add a journalistic dimension which no other medium can provide – depth and wholeness and texture, plus the visual impact of graphic design. Magazines, because of their freedom from daily deadlines, can aspire to a level of excellence that is seldom attainable in other media. Magazines, in a different way from any other medium, can help foster in Canadians a sense of themselves."

As you progress, you will discover you are something of a unique attraction. Writing, after all, has always fascinated the young, the old, the rich, and the poor – all hoping one day to spill out their life stories for the world to read. "To be a well-favoured man is gift of fortune," says Shakespeare in his comedy *Much Ado About Nothing*, "but to read and write comes by nature." The most well-favoured individual I know personally is a real estate developer who has amassed a tidy investment in art and real estate on three continents. "You're doing something," he is forever telling me, "that I've always wanted to do myself, but can't. I'd give my right arm to write."

"Maybe you would," I tell him with a chuckle. "If you did what I do, you'd probably have fun all right, and you'd learn something new every day. But you wouldn't be one-thousandth as rich."

People will approach you at parties with an air of uncontrolled fascination. "You're a writer," they'll muse, typically. "That's interesting. What do you write?"

"Magazine articles," you'll say.

"Oh? You mean short stories."

"No, no," you'll explain quickly. "Short stories are fiction. I write fact. Non-fiction. Fact. Journalism. The truth."

"Oh, that's *very* interesting. And where, may I ask, do you get your ideas?"

4. The Writer's Ideas

Sources, unusual and otherwise / scanning the media / unlikely places / personal interests and intuition / ideas for specific magazines / refining the idea

"Writing is no trouble at all:
you just jot down ideas as they occur to you.
The jotting is simplicity itself –
it is the occurring which is difficult."

STEPHEN LEACOCK

All writing, be it a huge piece of fiction or the shortest, most compact magazine article, starts with an idea, usually only a simple one. When it enters our mind as a casual notion or a "hunch," it is nothing more than raw bones. By giving it a context, putting it into a frame with other facts, we install the flesh that makes it saleable.

As a rule, magazine editors are too harried to dream up ideas for writers. Sure, they study their own back issues to see what topics can be updated or resurrected, or what personality profile might trigger another, but generally, they expect suggestions to flow more profusely the other way. For the most part they do – the silly, impractical, unsuitable, and sometimes even the nonsensical. Our magazines thrive, however, because enough freelancers understand only too well that publishing's lifeblood is good, fresh ideas that are not only important and fascinating, but timely and unique.

Your ideas will stem from the same sources as the seasoned professional's. That is to say, from anywhere – and at any time when you least expect them. There are no magical powers that can be attributed to the creative notion. Ideas come in a rudimentary or fragmentary form in a variety of ways and, more often than not, in a completely unpredictable manner. Your interest could be sparked by a tip-off dropped casually by a friend; your curiosity might be piqued one night by what appeared to be bothering a succession of callers to a phone-in radio show. You might also overhear a tidbit of a conversation on a bus or at the local store. Whatever it is, your intuition for a story will suddenly click into action and instinctively you'll want to check it out.

Other ideas may assert themselves gradually over a longer period of time – a local newspaper story growing steadily to such importance, for instance, that it can almost certainly be expanded and developed to appeal to a much wider audience. A chain of stories appearing regularly on one subject might indicate a national trend. An intense, action-filled hunt for a convict may, when he's finally apprehended and dealt with by the courts, make a compelling detective story – fact or fiction, magazine article or book.

Newspapers provide by far the most fertile sources for magazine articles. Let's put that to a simple test by glancing at two give-away weeklies I picked up at the cash register in a restaurant in Sugarbush, Vermont. One, the *Country Courier* (its August 22, 1986, edition), contained an advertisement which said, "DON'T MISS OUR YARD SALE! OUR JUNK IS YOUR TREASURE." To me, this cliché immediately suggested a serious story on the ever-growing number of neighbourhood garage sales and flea markets that have grown into summer attractions throughout Canada. And the cooking column, which introduced "a breakfast even the kids can prepare," sparked an idea for a piece on the unprecedented number of "latch-key" children forced to fend for themselves while both their parents work to cope with tough economic times.

Perhaps the best idea of all was contained in the *Country Courier's* competitor, *The World* (its August 20, 1986, edition), which published this reader's letter:

> I am a 65-year-old widower. My beloved wife of 40 years recently died, and I miss her terribly. Since her death, her friends, most of whom are widows, call me (constantly) and hound me to go to dinner, parties, church functions, teas, etc. I get a call from one or the other of them at least once a day. I appreciate their concern for my loneliness, but it only aggravates me. I don't want to go out and force myself to have a good time when I don't feel like it. I just want to be left alone and grieve in private. They don't seem to be getting the message. What can I do?

To me, this hints strongly at an article demonstrating what is or isn't being done at the community level to help senior citizens deal with grief. "But aren't we all afflicted in this way at some point in our lives?" you might ask. "So why confine this idea to the aged?"

You would be absolutely right. By weighing the topic against the times in which we live, a better story emerges with an even wider appeal – how people in *all* age groups sometimes need help to start life again following the loss of a loved one. If ever you decide to pursue it as a human-interest piece for *Homemaker's*, or in a more analytical way for *Psychology Today*, remember the germ of the idea was culled (cross my heart) from a little Vermont paper that neither you nor I would ordinarily think of reading.

Many ideas I eventually sold came just that way. Small regional newspapers introduced me to both the school principal who helped the boy without legs and Geraldton's amateur "veterinarian." One of my most lucrative projects, however, leapt from a mere fifteen-second report which concluded the CBC's nightly newscast, "The National." Two women RCMP undercover agents had posed as drug couriers for an international narcotics-smuggling syndicate, carrying $20-million-worth of heroin through Asia into Europe, where they helped arrest eight men. "Why is this report so short?" I remember asking myself. "There's *got* to be more to the story than this."

There was – quite an adventure, I found out. Under instructions from senior RCMP officers, the women frequented a Toronto hotel bar where the syndicate was known to hang out and worked carefully to get themselves "hired." They were, and then were flown to Hong Kong for a briefing and on to Penang, Malaysia, to be given luggage containing the drugs. Several times their "bosses" made them switch hotels in case the police were watching. They were: six hand-picked RCMP Drug Squad detectives assigned in Canada to trail their colleagues to the job's conclusion.

It was a magazine writer's dream: a story of car chases, bugging techniques, tears, threats, seedy hotels, posh hotels, big money, and suspense. There were peaks and valleys all right, plus conflict, tension, and a sizeable parade of characters all bobbing in and out of non-stop action spanning five weeks. I developed it into a *Reader's Digest* special feature, which swept into world editions as a superb example of ingenious police undercover work.

Shortly afterwards, an editor's curiosity was aroused by an obituary in *The United Church Observer*. A fifty-one-year-old Winnipeg man had died four years after being paroled from Manitoba's Stoney Mountain Penitentiary. He had been there for more than twenty-six years, the story pointed out, as an habitual criminal. That in itself was of little interest to a top magazine, but there were other vital elements. When freed on compassionate grounds, the man, a reformed alcoholic and drug addict dying of cirrhosis of the liver, vowed to spend his last days helping juveniles in trouble on Winnipeg's streets.

When I checked the idea out, talking by phone to prison officials, probation officers, clergymen, lawyers, and parents, I discovered the ex-convict had counselled run-away adolescents with so much success that local judges had committed dozens of them into his care instead of sending them to a juvenile detention centre. A good story? Of course it was. Human nature being what it is, nearly everyone likes to hear that a man once condemned is finally able to make restitution. In this case, a one-time burglar was able to pay his debt many times over.

Conventions, company bulletin boards, and scientific reports are all sources for possible magazine ideas, too, as are circulars, trade-journal stories that can be popularized, and literally scores of pamphlets available free from museums, exhibitions, and government offices. Public relations people anxious to promote their products can be useful as well. A CN public affairs manager suggested I travel from Montreal to Vancouver on a freight train, then made all the arrangements for the five-day trip. Once, after a taping for a CBC television music show, an RCA publicist poured me a drink and suggested: "Hey, why don't you profile James Galway? He's coming to town next month – golden flute and all!"

Galway had certainly earned *his* wrinkles, I found out, plus warts and barnacles. So I went off to Toronto to see him. "You're lucky," he told me. "I've always wanted to write. By the way, where do you get your ideas?"

"Everywhere," I said. "Everywhere."

The most novel came from a photocopying centre's waste bin, in which I was rummaging for scrap paper. What the bin contained was typical of the kind of cast-offs you'd expect to find near photocopying machines anywhere – documents that were too blurred to read and those aborted efforts that had ended up as black as tar. Among all this, however, I discovered a letter from an electronics firm to a pest control company, lauding citizens-band radio as an effective way of boosting business. "Your exterminators," it read, "could be directed from one job to the next without having to report to head office for further instructions."

Zing! A trend story on CB radio! With its special lingo and beams stretching far afield to save lives and help the lonely – and by enabling truck drivers to warn each other of dangers on the road, even police radar traps – CB could make a fine piece, indeed. And it did.

Some stories might be right under your nose. It's reasonable to assume that most of us have some knowledge that will be useful to others. A simple way to find out is to ask yourself these and other questions like them: What is my background? (Consider your family, ethnic roots, religion, socio-economic place in society, and where you live or hail from.) What have I done? (Don't forget even the smallest things can be expanded.) Where have I been? Who do I know? (Don't forget the acquaintances who've given you something or helped you see a different point of view.) Who has taught me something important – something that has helped me improve the quality of my life and that I can now pass on to others? Who are, or have been, my friends and where are they now? What's wrong with my life? What do I want? What are some of the emotional landmarks I've experienced? Skip down that list. I'm sure it will jog something worth developing.

Very often, you'll find, people close to you have useful information they would be happy to share. In the late 1970s, my closest friend, a dentist, suffered anxiously as his brother lay dying in a Seattle hospital from a blood disease called aplastic anemia. Only a sibling's bone marrow would save the man, doctors said. So my friend flew off instantly to donate it.

The ordeal was really just beginning. To prevent their patient from rejecting the marrow transplant, doctors drastically lowered his immune system, then raised it to its normal level. In effect, they were taking him to the edge of death, then bringing him back, a treatment that would last several weeks. At one point, the patient's chances of survival were less than fifty per cent.

Happily, my friend's bone marrow became a brother's gift of life, and one night he and I sat recounting all the events that surrounded it. It dawned on me then that they had the makings of a powerful human drama set against advancing medical science. No one likes to exploit friends for stories, but the patient wanted to see his in print. "I'd like to talk some of the trauma away," he said, "and help give hope to others enduring a similar, solitary nightmare like I went through."

The article, "A Brother's Gift of Life," was written and sold. So was a piece on my grandmother shortly after she died at the age of ninety-nine – a *Reader's Digest* "Unforgettable Character," which was widely published abroad. This idea descended one lunchtime while speaking to an editor about her. "I would've liked to have met her," he said. "She sounds terrific!" Throughout her life, she had displayed unswerving resilience through shocking adversity – three decades of poverty, bringing up a mentally handicapped daughter in an age when treatment was virtually non-existent, surviving an explosion at the ammunition plant where she worked as a security officer during World War I, coping with the Depression and later the Blitz over London during World War II.

What made my grandmother particularly "storyable," however, was an extra dimension: that through it all, she came out smiling and showing heart-rending kindness and compassion. She fed tramps on London's streets, set up a second home for off-duty soldiers during the second war, and in later years, instead of retiring, opened a little seaside boarding house to give low-income workers the first holidays they had ever been able to afford. Through good times and bad, she had remained determined, active, and optimistic – a lesson for us all. But was there conflict, action, a cast of colourful characters, pathos, humour, and adventure in all of this? Of course there was. That's why I was ultimately able to market the idea. And when tenacity triumphs over tragedy, remember for all your ideas on people or institutions, it gives a story a built-in, upbeat finale that helps make a central character indelible.

As a general guide to ideas, entertaining articles are made of romance, suspense, pathos, and humour, by far the toughest thing to write. The unexplainable, the chaotic, and the mysterious have wide appeal, too, as long as they have other ingredients that will combine to make a story with substance. Sex is one of our strongest drives, love our most popular emotion. Both are as timeless as writing itself.

Most of my suggestions over the years have come with a specific audience in mind. So will yours. But you'll stumble on many more for which you may have to comb through the market until you find their proper place. Let's take a quick look at the contrasting needs of three magazines and see how they can be filled:

The Toronto-based *Canadian Doctor* claims to be our only non-clinical medical publication. Instead of defining diseases and explaining new treatments, it examines how the medical profession is affected by legal, ethical, social, and political issues. It seeks to guide doctors through "the myriad non-clinical considerations that accompany clinical decision making," says its contributors' guidelines, and "presents all possible perspectives, defines risks and proposes expert solutions to common dilemmas."

Most ideas for this magazine will obviously come from well within the medical profession itself – conventions, medical papers, or from doctors. Some ideas, however, may well be provided by social workers, lawyers, or people in para-medical professions. When I think of medical ethics, I immediately wonder how or if a doctor should report child- or wife-beating cases to the police. How does the doctor feel about prescribing the pill to minors? How and when should a doctor tell a patient he is dying? I'm curious to know how doctors – including my own – feel about patients' rights, or what they can do to protect themselves from those hard-to-please people who constantly threaten to sue for malpractice.

On the social or political level, I suspect that in a lot of cases government medical insurance schemes may have turned doctors into civil servants. How has the government changed the quality of medicine? How has the profession come to be perceived by the public? If not too well, what can doctors do to change it? And, by the way, whatever happened to the "old family doc" who dropped in for a cup of tea now and then just to see how we were? He's gone forever, maybe. But is this really a bad thing? Or do we miss him? In each of these questions there are probably one or two good *Canadian Doctor* articles – and a way into the editor's heart.

Founded in Winnipeg in 1920 as the Hudson's Bay Company staff magazine, *The Beaver*, published six times yearly, has become one of the pre-eminent journals of Canadian history. It buys lively, informative pieces on such related topics as exploration, development, native peoples and their art, and displays them so well that it has won numerous awards, including certificates of merit from both the Canadian Historical Association and the American Association of State and Local History. Although many of its regular writers are historians, scholars, and folklorists, the magazine is designed for the general reader.

Good. Just as the background of anything tends to fascinate readers, so does its history. A lot of people enjoy reading about new insights into the past, with its heroes and their struggles, conflicts, and adventures. Though relatively short when compared to Europe's, Canada's history is comprised of an abundance of these.

When I think of *The Beaver*, then, a lot of ideas flood my mind – great rivers that helped forge our cities, fur trading, logging camps, the Gold Rush, old hotels, and the embryo of our transportation system with its canals, locks, barges, and steamships. I think, too, of our first railway, born in 1836 with wooden tracks – and the earliest settlers who welcomed it.

Stories like these, of course, have already been done. But when writing for historical magazines, there is always a chance to offer a topic a new slant, a different point of view. What was Louis Riel *really* like? What went through Calixa Lavallée's mind as he penned our national anthem after a tune so clearly reminiscent of a moment in Mozart's operatic masterpiece, *The Magic Flute*? How did that pugnacious French Canadian soldier Charles-Michel de Salaberry repulse those determined Americans wanting to capture Lower Canada in a battle near Lacolle, Quebec, during the War of 1812? What a market *The Beaver* could be for writers who revel in history!

In Toronto, the trade journal *Hardware Merchandising* is constantly looking for shortish pieces from various regions of Canada on unique outlets, merchandising techniques, and the application of new inventions. Since I'm an inveterate fix-it-yourself freak fascinated by pipes, putty, and spray-on lubricants, I would have little difficulty coming up with ideas for this magazine. I spend about a third of my free time browsing through hardware stores anyway, looking for the latest in hardware technology. If I wanted to convert this into cash, I would attend hardware shows and talk to exhibitors about store lay-out, markets, trends, and staff hiring, always, however, with one eye open for the retailer worth profiling for having done something unusually well, like displaying the latest in bathroom fixtures, saunas, bicycles, or using computers for ordering, costing, and inventory control. I would need to remember the magazine's specialized readers, of course, and get merchants to talk only about what those readers want to know – customers, store sizes, the communities they serve, not to mention sales, profits, inventory turnovers, and future plans. If I were starting out as a writer, I would have literally dozens of ideas for *Hardware Merchandising*.

Always remember that while the writer's job is to inform and entertain, it is also to *help*. Ideas for articles telling readers how to do something, such as enjoying a hobby, travelling to a place they've yet to see, or generally improving the quality of their lives, are always welcome. So are suggestions for profiles of people who have made a significant contribution to society or have shown us that, like them, we can attain what was once considered impossible.

Readers love heroes: men and women they can identify with and look up to. All of us possess a yearning to know that what we can't do ourselves can be accomplished by others. Through them we experience our own adventure, whether it be travelling through the Alps on a bicycle or penetrating a cult. We enjoy reading, too, about unusually courageous children, plucky senior citizens, and intelligent animals that may have somehow come to understand the human race. More than anything, readers want to know about themselves, where they live now, and from where they were once uprooted. They want to be told of all the latest developments and receive advice that will help prepare them for their future.

Many smaller publications, like city magazines or trade papers, invite stories that conform to a specific theme coinciding with the seasons: holidays, for example, the opening of a new building, or events like Expo 86 and large rural fairs. Ideas for these may come from calendars, public notice boards, and flyers handed out in shopping malls. But whatever you find, confusion will doubtless reign. Your worst ideas will sometimes be well received. Your best will not. Never despair, though. Nearly all of us in the business have experienced this.

When I first asked the *Reader's Digest* if they were interested in an article on the deepening tragedy of teenage suicide, an editor shrugged, "It's a bit of a downer, isn't it? I suggest we leave that one for the newspapers." A year later, one of his colleagues collared me in a hallway and said, "How about doing a good, strong piece on all these poor kids who've been killing themselves. It could make us a fine, hard-hitting story."

I once suggested that the big, extroverted Italian tenor Luciano Pavarotti would make a superb profile, to which an uninterested editor responded, "Pava-*who*?" A year later, after Pavarotti's round, smiling face had adorned the covers of *Time*, *Newsweek*, and *Businessweek*, another editor agreed to the idea. "I'm really surprised we haven't done him before," he said.

Ideas may spring from a sentence or two in a television documentary – the hint of a growing social dilemma, perhaps, or the beginnings of a portrait of despair. A lot more will come as you read those magazines, not so much now to find out what kinds of pieces their editors buy, but more to ascertain what subjects they have recently dealt with. The quickest way to peeve an editor is to suggest a topic he or she has used within the past two or three months. Conversely, the quickest way into a magazine's fold of writers is to ply its editors with a steady stream of top-notch, written suggestions and to follow up each with a manuscript requiring the minimum of in-house work.

As time moves on, you'll find there are other questions you should ask yourself: What do I know? What am I most interested in? You'll discover that by far your best suggestions will, ideally, be on subjects you like or know something about: consumer protection, perhaps, sports, cooking, art, entertainment, or personal finance. Conversely, there'll be times when although you think an idea is solid, it won't excite you. The trick here is to turn it around and view it from all angles, automatically thinking of its place in the market. Will it appeal to children, young adults, or senior citizens? Will it interest small investors, people trying to save money from moderate incomes, or those hoping to start second-career businesses on large investments? Do you want to reach factory workers, office employees, or university professors? The greater your knowledge or feel for both the subject and its potential audience becomes, the more your enthusiasm for writing about it will grow.

Another fascinating characteristic of ideas is that once you've given birth to one, it usually starts multiplying by itself. Sometimes your original idea won't sell – but the spin-off will. You'll then be able to fan it to creative flames. But there is one proviso: Whatever you conjure up must not only be fresh and interesting, but strong and opportune. "Nothing in this world is so powerful," novelist Victor Hugo said, "as an idea whose time has come."

5. Breaking In

Usefulness of the query letter / the story proposal or outline / the "pulse points" / outlining books / the story that can't be outlined

"The editorial job has become, unlike the ancient age when one judged what one read, a job of making judgements on outlines, ideas, reputations, previous books, scenarios, treatments, talk and promises."

SAM VAUGHAN,

EDITOR-IN-CHIEF, DOUBLEDAY & CO.

Almost without exception, professional non-fiction writers never produce anything on speculation. It's a gamble they're not prepared to take. Having studied those magazines for which they would like to write, they earn their commissions by putting an idea into a query letter first and then, if it takes an editor's fancy, following it up with a full story proposal. That is to say, they refine and expand their suggestion hoping it will win an assignment.

This is an element of the craft that shouldn't be taken lightly. The well-prepared proposal, you'll find, is a sales tool. You will use it to sell both your idea and yourself as the one person best equipped to write a particular article for a particular magazine. Needless to say, it quickly distinguishes the amateur from the professional – or the ardent up-and-coming freelancer worth encouraging from one who isn't.

Magazine editors, more than newspaper editors, tend to nurse their writers along, returning manuscripts with all manner of questions and suggestions in the margins. They often write long letters explaining why an approach should be changed or certain information omitted. Only as a last resort do they ditch stories, because they're forever looking for good ones that fit their needs. Besides this, editors consider that a writer who has come this far is well worth having around. In return, they want ideas in written form so they may give them the serious consideration they deserve.

Basically, the proposal is a nicely crafted overview of the actual story, touching upon all the major points it will include and demonstrating how it's likely to be written, with tone, colour and scope of language. Magazines that opt for anecdotal journalism invariably need a sampling of anecdotes throughout. Either that, or case histories, examples, or analogies – anything that will show editors how the topic will be made easily understood to the uninitiated. The onus here is on the writer to prove that he or she can make an idea meaningful and palatable to the magazine's readership.

Small magazines are happy to decide a story's merits from a proposal that is merely a couple of paragraphs long, like this little thumb-nail sketch which enabled me to sell an article to the inflight magazine, *enRoute*:

> There he sits – tuxedo-clad in a pool of stage lighting, his fingers cavorting across the keys of the concert grand like tireless gazelles. Oscar Peterson, born into poverty in Montreal in 1925, has been performing like this since becoming a star virtually overnight aged only 24. I have wonderful stories of him making his debut at New York's Carnegie Hall in an old raincoat over a midnight-blue suit, going on tour with Ella Fitzgerald and generally carving for himself a career as probably the finest jazz pianist of our time.
>
> Today, Peterson lives quietly in Mississauga, Ont., where he collects pianos and art. He earns nearly $300,000 yearly performing in supper clubs and concert halls – a far cry from the days when he played for peanuts and was refused admission into Deep South restaurants because he was black. I have collected a lot of research material and have a five-hour conversation with him on tape.

Or this brief proposal that led to a sale in *Chimo!*, a now-defunct Montreal corporate magazine:

> I recently spent a month travelling through Greece by bus, to retrace the footsteps of Homer and Sophocles, about whom I had read in boyhood. I do not propose a traditional travelogue,

but one full of personal impressions, anecdotes, and nostalgia. Going to the beginning of our civilization was like visiting a mysterious, weatherbeaten old man in black who had survived earthquakes and wars, but who could still spin a happy yarn.

Experience followed experience, most of them good. As my plane left Athens, I caught my last glimpse of the glorious mountains, copper in the morning glow – and thought of my Greek dry cleaner back in Montreal. "Say hello to my cowntry," he'd told me. "Just tella them Constantino said to say big hello."

Larger magazines and book publishers, which pay infinitely more, require fuller outlines in considerably more detail. "Queries regarding non-fiction," says *Saturday Night*, "should be long enough to give us some idea of the focus of your proposal, your preliminary research, and your writing style." Adds the *Reader's Digest*: "Your outline should be a brief version of your story, opening with the lead you plan to use, developing the story line you propose to follow, and giving a taste of the kind of detail that will bring the story alive."

Usually, a couple of pages is sufficient for a self-evident story; for a complex issue, the writer must produce something extra in as enticing a style as possible. To propose an article on the primitive painter Maude Lewis, who sold her works for between three and eight dollars each by the roadside near Digby, Nova Scotia, and never lived to see them earn nearly a thousand dollars apiece, I wrote twenty-four manuscript pages. An idea to profile the Vancouver-based Irish Rovers took twenty-seven pages: what editors call "the hard sell." For this book, by the way, I submitted fifty-four pages – 12,500 words – showing editors how I envisioned each chapter would be focused and what it would include.

"That's more than a sixth of the final manuscript!" my secretary said.

"I know," I told her. "But if I want a contract to write it, I've got to prove my worth. Now I'm wrestling with a bloody octopus!"

In moments of gloom, when the words fail to flow and my ideas are hopelessly jumbled, I remember an acquaintance's plight. While a senior writer for *Time* in New York, he had to write a sixty-eight page outline on United States defence spending for an essay that would run to only sixteen manuscript pages. "And they promptly slashed my finished piece to seven," he recalled. "But that's the way it is." Indeed, those magazine and book publishers faced with large financial outlays often want outlines on complex topics to be as long as necessary to convince them that there *is* a story there, and it really *is* for them.

But the outline has another function. Editors like to pass it to colleagues so they can each add their touch, all helping the writer refine the idea and gain a "sharper fix," always with the reader in mind. This extra input can be extremely useful. If, for example, you wanted to profile a prominent industrialist or an athlete, an editor might have a good anecdote to contribute. When *City & Country Home* accepted my suggestion to tell how Heritage Canada has fought so hard since 1973 to save many of our fine old buildings from the demolisher's bulldozer, an editor felt the story might benefit from politicians' tributes, an aspect my proposal didn't touch upon. Another editor astutely pointed out that, since the magazine sold mainly in southern Ontario, most examples of Heritage Canada's work should be drawn from there.

My outline on Toronto's Massey Hall for the same magazine, however, was accepted without question. It's not great writing, nor is it intended to be – just a clear exposition of what distinguishes this concert hall from others and why *City & Country Home* should bother featuring it:

> She's old in the tooth now, and not very pretty, but Toronto's venerable old Massey Hall – the Grand Old Lady of Shuter Street, as Gov. Gen. Vincent Massey once called her – has provided a showcase for the world's most celebrated personalities, performers and speakers for 92 years.
>
> Indian runner Tom Longboat was married there. Melba, Chaliapin, Gigli, Robeson, and Gracie Fields often sang there. So did Enrico Caruso, who plastered the men's washroom with self-drawn caricatures of himself in various operatic roles. Explorers Shackleton, Scott, and Amundsen spoke of their expeditions in Massey Hall, Charles Laughton entertained eager audiences with readings from the *Bible* and *The Hunchback of Notre Dame*, world heavyweight boxer Jack Dempsey fought an exhibition bout under the huge chandelier.
>
> I have many anecdotes showing what the hall meant to both public and performers alike. Caruso sang to adoring fans on an old, iron fire escape overlooking Shuter Street. During Prohibition, members of the Philadelphia Orchestra filled drums with

> liquor to smuggle back to the U.S. The great diva Adelina Patti disliked the women's washroom so much that she insisted the manager buy her a chamber pot. He did – for $3 from the T. Eaton Co. It is now known as "Patti's potty."
>
> Union meetings, typewriting contests, suffragette and Evangelical rallies are all part of Massey Hall's long and illustrious history, too. After Monday-night rehearsals of the Toronto Symphony (for 59 years the main tenant), the staff cleared the stage for Tuesday night's wrestling card, which introduced the Old Lady to grizzly men like the head-butting Gus the Goat and the fearless Count Zarinoff.
>
> A few years ago, German physicist Fritz Winkel tested the acoustics by blasting three blanks from his .38 revolver. "They're among the best in the world," he declared – then compared Massey Hall to such contemporaries as London's Queen's Hall and New York's Carnegie Hall.
>
> Once threatened with demolition, Massey Hall has not only survived – thanks to public campaigns led by singers Maureen Forrester and Lois Marshall, who often performed there – but it is still going strong. I can write a bright, tight, informative piece full of history, humour and warmth. Interested?

How could this outline have been better? First, it needed some indication of how I would start the article: whether my lead would be anecdotal or general, based on some intriguing material I'd already uncovered. Second, although it revealed some interesting facts, it failed to show my strategy for actually setting them out. Had I been a beginner, the proposal might have been rejected, but fortunately, the magazine trusted me sufficiently to let me write it – as did the Imperial Oil *Review*, a corporate current-affairs journal, when I outlined a profile on the internationally revered Rehabilitation Centre of Montreal.

Above all, a proposal of this kind needed to show the editor how I planned on taking the reader into the Centre. I began it:

> Shortly after noon on October 7, 1973, Gilles Landry was helping a friend install a 25-foot metal television aerial on a metal-roofed shed in a trailer park in St. Amable, Que. Suddenly the wind carried the aerial to within inches of an overhead power line. The fog in the damp air that day was enough to conduct

> the electricity. For about 30 seconds, Landry, then a 30-year-old corporal in the Canadian Armed Forces, was held rigid in 250,000 volts – until the breaker blew at the local hydro plant.
>
> He then collapsed and was taken to Charles Le Moyne Hospital in nearby Greenfield Park where doctors confirmed what he had already decided for himself: that his hands and feet were so badly charred, they would have to be amputated.
>
> The surgery over, Landry, a father of two, went to the Rehabilitation Institute of Montreal – to begin life again. "What a patient has lost," a doctor told him, "isn't important. We develop what's left."

That lead, by the way, was the one I ultimately used for my finished story – a little more polished, perhaps, but basically containing the same information. And the remainder of the proposal? It documented how successful the Centre had been, with its impact stretching abroad, and ending with the man in my opening case history walking into the medical director's office on artificial legs and lighting a cigarette with artificial hands. "Thanks for what you've done for me," he said. The outline was fairly complete. It had come full circle.

Before writing story proposals, you'll have to recognize yet more components of the magazine article's character, what I call the "pulse points." These are aspects it's *absolutely* imperative to touch upon and document so as to make the piece work.

The pulse points are the story's key elements or main topics within the broader subject itself. They address questions the serious reader invariably ponders subconsciously and the writer should ask instinctively: "Is this thing really happening? What evidence is there of it? How important is it? Who has been affected by it and how? What is this thing's background? Why and how did it happen the way it did in the first place? Will it continue? If not, why?" The story proposal should answer all of these.

Let's suppose you were writing one of those entangled social stories: an enigmatic national debate, a public outcry, or a disturbing moral issue. Your first job would be to distill it, analyse it, then, as straightforwardly as you can, show the editor:

- The problem in process, with case histories, examples or anecdotes.

- The magnitude of the problem, with statistics, more case histories, anecdotes, and expert opinion.
- The root of the problem.

By now, the editor will be ready to accept that what you are saying is weighty. You've reduced your idea to the basics and given some indication of how readers will ultimately understand it when it arrives in story form. The editor is ready to read on and be told:

- How the problem arose, its background, its history, how it is the result of the way we have chosen to live, and the impact it will continue to have.
- How we, our politicians, and our laws may be able to solve it.

Now let's assume you are contemplating a profile of a notable person. The pulse points will be much the same. You must show the editor:

- The person in that role for which he or she is deserving of an article in the first place.
- His or her credibility and accomplishments, through anecdote, example, or through experts' impressions.
- A smattering of the struggles and triumphs in his or her life.
- How, exactly, he or she became successful or "storyable."
- How he or she works to maintain a stature, a disciplined life style, a dedication to whatever made him or her worthy of your proposal.

Of course, if you plan on writing a popular story for a large readership on an important, colourful personality known only to a relatively small number of people, the editor might ask you for a little splash of physical description to show how you'll bring that person to life. Here's how I tempted the *Reader's Digest* to buy a story about the late Canadian drama critic, Nathan Cohen:

> He was a familiar sight in theatres across the land, a shy, lumbering six-footer weighing 200 pounds. Opening night audiences actually craned their heads to see if he was there, and usually he was – halfway back in an aisle seat, leaning ponderously on his walking cane. "He's out there!" actors would say as they costumed and made up. "He's out there!"

As the theatre darkened, Nathan Cohen of *The Toronto Star* sat erect, his huge square head and black hornrims aimed at the stage. During intermissions he refused to talk about the show, declaring, "I haven't written my column yet. Wait until tomorrow."

When tomorrow came, however, he had often outraged theatre-goers and players alike, with his tough, relentless criticism. In 1962, the New York cast of Brendan Behan's *The Hostage* burned him in effigy outside Toronto's Royal Alexandra Theatre. Threatened with physical violence and banned from theatres, he was called "the most cussed and discussed man in town," by a CBC producer, "an imitation intellectual," by a Toronto professor – and Canada's *only* critic by himself.

Often criticized for being heartless, Cohen would reply, "I don't work for the theatre company, I work for *The Star*. It's not my job to lie." Even when the public thought a show was good, Cohen remained bolted to his views. A manager at Toronto's O'Keefe Centre once asked: "Do you really think that hundreds of thousands of people who love *Brigadoon* are wrong and you are right?"

"Yes," replied Nathan Cohen.

For an institutional portrait, the pulse points hardly differ. If you were writing about, say, Canadian Tire, the Royal Canadian Air Force, even your local medical clinic, surely your job would be to try to draw a picture of a fine, old friend, loved and respected by everyone. Of course, with so little research done, it would be impossible to show the institution's full impact on the people it serves, but you would still need to catch it in action, describe it, prove its value to the community or the country, tell the reader how it came about, and so on. Back in the days when I edited books and doctored manuscripts, an editor handed me a writer's attempt to profile the Twin Otter. "It's a dead piece," I mused. "Why does it have to be so bloody dull?"

"A workhorse of an airplane like that, a real institution," the editor said, "should come across to readers as a person they've grown to care about."

In dramas, the pulse points are all those natural peaks and valleys in the action. Take for example, a man who gets lost in the woods. The first point that comes to mind – though this wouldn't necessarily be where you would want to start the story – is when, where, and how he got lost. Others would, quite naturally, be the ups and downs of his total experience: the escape paths he finds open, those he finds closed, the pinnacles of his optimism, the depths of his despair, and that final moment when he realises he's about to be rescued.

If you were doing a story on a disaster, the pulse points would, again, be the important events that led up to it and caused it, what actually happened, the broad implications, and the clean up. Here, for example, is how I described the Halifax Explosion in an outline I wrote for the *Reader's Digest* some years ago and later, during recycling, for *Equinox* – the bare bones of one of the biggest man-made disasters in history.

> At around 8 a.m. on Thursday, December 6, 1917, in Halifax Harbour, the 3,121-ton French freighter *Mont Blanc* carrying 35 tons of benzole, 2,300 tons of wet and dry picric acid, ten tons of gun cotton and 200 tons of TNT, ploughed ten feet into the side of the 5,043-ton Norwegian tramp steamer *Imo*, carrying relief supplies to aid Europe's World War I victims. Fire raged out of control. Finally, at 9.06 a.m., as schools finished their morning hymn, the *Mont Blanc* blew up.
>
> She disappeared in a thunderous explosion and a ball of gases that were sent skywards for more than a mile. The sea parted, exposing bedrocks 60 feet below. A massive tidal wave surged shorewards, smashing concrete jetties in its path. Ships broke moorings; 276 loaded freight cars were carried from the Intercolonial Railway Co. sidings.
>
> In Truro, 60 miles away, windows rattled; at the Learmonth Hotel, a clock was ripped from the wall and hurled across the dining room. Plates moved on breakfast tables 125 miles away in Prince Edward Island. Two hundred miles north in Sydney, N.S., houses shook. Ships well out to sea watched the sky turn red and a pall of black smoke rise above Halifax like a gigantic mushroom.
>
> Night, lit by torches and lanterns, fell with utter desolation. Now the statistical litany could be recited: nearly 2,000 people were dead, and another 10,000 injured, 200 of them blinded.

> Two square miles of Richmond had been totally levelled – 1,600 buildings, including 600 homes. Another 12,000 homes within a radius of 16 miles were damaged, many beyond repair. The cost: $50 million.

No one pretends that the key to an exquisite outline lies in four or five pulse points. Obviously, the more labyrinthine a story is, the more there will be, and you won't be able to include them all. Other pulse points will rear their heads during research later, and you will need to document them all. My little lists, and the excerpted outlines I've offered, are merely intended to show the basics. In essence, these are examples of what the editors of better magazines would automatically look for.

There are some stories, however, that even the most polished, well-thought-out proposals will *never* sell – those that are so personal to the writer they rely exclusively on how they're written. Novels and poetry are perfect examples. So is that student's intimate encounter with agoraphobia. Another was the profile of my grandmother. I could have given the editors an endless list of those qualities that made her unforgettable and "storyable," but from experience I knew it would have been to no avail.

Stories like these depend on how well, through good prose and a feeling for nostalgia, you can resurrect the person inside them for all to meet. They rely heavily, too, on your ability to link the subject with yourself. What did my grandmother mean to me? How did she shape my life? What lasting piece of philosophy did she leave me? What did she teach me by example through her actions: her kindness and compassion for others? How could I bring all this to bear through warm, enlightening anecdote? "It's all in the writing," editors will say. And I can assure you that it is.

If writing query letters, proposals, or outlines implies a lot of thought, so it should. Proposals also need preliminary research: enough to prove to yourself, if nothing else, that you're onto something worthwhile before passing it on for others to judge. I'm always grateful that I didn't pursue a story on genital herpes, even after reading numerous medical papers and talking to a lot of doctors. Even though *Time* had done a cover story on herpes, I couldn't for the life of me find sufficient evidence that it was so severe a problem. Sure it might be uncomfortable and a nuisance, but no one has ever died from it. So I abandoned the idea, just two months before a more serious sexually transmitted disease came to public attention – AIDS.

It's not always easy to penetrate a magazine's fold of writers. Magazines quite often have a sufficient number of reliable people they can assign to a story at a moment's notice, without needing to recruit more. A full, rich proposal from someone they haven't yet met, however, can lead to lasting rewards on both sides – a precious contact for the writer and, for the editors, a new byline, plus the beginning of a string of fresh ideas that will keep their editorial philosophy alive. It's worth repeating here that a good, intelligent, and suitable idea deftly explained in a well-thought-out proposal is the *only* way into the business. This nearly always involves a lot of work, and for this, I assure you, there are no short cuts at all. There really is no other way. Your very first story proposal, it may well transpire, could be the most important piece of writing you ever undertake.

Bear in mind, too, that if your story is commissioned, all the effort you invested in preparing your outline will not have been wasted; much of this writing is likely to end up in your final draft. If, on the other hand, an assignment is not forthcoming, you will have been spared the heartbreak of a rejection – and considerably more work had you tried selling the piece "on spec."

6. Research

The importance / the pitfalls of over-researching / charting the course / libraries / reference books / useful organizations / research leads / unusual sources

"I keep six honest serving men
(They taught me all I knew)
Their names are What and Why and When
And How and Where and Who."

RUDYARD KIPLING

All serious writers will tell you that the most fascinating, challenging, and satisfying part of their work is digging up information. It is their excursion into previously unknown territory, that method by which they become mini-experts in their assigned topics. It is also the way they build up huge depositories of general knowledge which stay with them for life. For all this, though, research is too often done haphazardly, too hastily, or left only partially completed.

Contrary to yet another popular myth, *all* writing cries out for some kind of research, be it a short story, novel, speech, play, magazine article, public relations handout, even a song or a poem. Nor is it fully understood that when writers actually sit before their typewriters to apply crisp dialogue, lucid description, and lean narrative (writing's three main parts) they are really only making the final onslaught. They are at last starting the beginning of the end – the wind-down – of a project that was conceived several weeks, if not months before, by committing to paper words that express what they have found out.

But it's the creative process, *away* from the typewriter that absorbs most of the writer's time and, ideally, nearly all of this is spent on research. Exactly how much depends on who you choose to ask. One Toronto freelancer claims that for an average magazine article she spends three weeks gathering information, four days sorting it out – and only a day or so actually turning it into copy. For me, however, these proportions would be exaggerated. A day to write a 3,000-word magazine piece tends to underestimate the effort required to shape words and polish them until they shine. For an average assignment, I probably spend 10 per cent of my working time thinking, 30 per cent on actual writing, and 60 per cent on unearthing the facts.

Generally speaking, the bigger and more intricate the article, the more research it will require. I, and others like me, have all too often wrestled with issue pieces containing as many as one hundred sources: from people actually being quoted as experts to those who have merely substantiated a line here or a word there in the finished job. Rarely, you'll find, does a well-researched piece contain fewer than thirty sources, particularly one aimed at a national audience. Conversely, some stories may have only a dozen or so – profiles, for instance, when the prime source is obviously the person about whom you are writing. But even these stories require a lot of research, if only to verify those dates, times, places, or events your subject might have told you about.

Suffice it to say, then, that while we rarely ever develop a voracious hunger for leafing through newspaper clippings, dry academic studies, or dull government reports over several hours for days on end, it's a chore that just has to be done. This, in a nutshell, is what research is, and serious writers will also confirm that what they produce ultimately lives or dies according to how well they research it – to cover their tracks, plug the holes, or touch all the bases. No amount of clever writing later, they know, will ever camouflage a digging job done erratically or skimpily.

Good research is rich, solid, full, and totally relevant to the story you're writing. Another Toronto freelancer tells me she's so excited to receive an assignment that she instantly explores it with a passion, "halfway across the Atlantic and back." By this she means that her well-tuned writer's mind causes her to be intrigued by virtually everything she uncovers, even when it's only remotely connected to her story. "I go haywire," she confesses, "and collect everything." What she really means is that she allows herself to be side-tracked, and this has disastrous results. Several weeks later when she sits down to write, she's unable to decide what material among the huge piles she's assembled is important to her task, and what is not. In other words, by habit, she researches too extravagantly, and too far afield.

While digging is definitely better done profusely than meagrely, it must always be narrowed down to the specific task at hand. There is, however, one warning to heed: A story that is strongly national needs to reflect this uncompromisingly with what editors call "geographic spread." That is to say, no self-respecting magazine will ever publish a piece with wide implications – such as one on abortion, women's rights, or missing children – when all the case histories and people quoted within it are rooted in the author's home town. Since these stories touch every part of the country, each region needs in some way to be represented. There are, of course, those of national interest that are indeed confined to one small area, and sometimes the research can stay right there. But for most pieces, digging goes considerably farther afield. When I wrote about how carrot-topped Anne of the old farmstead Green Gables in Avonlea had run away with the hearts of young girls the world over who wanted to be just like her, my research had to mirror that, too. Following a trip to Prince Edward Island, I spent many hours finding material that showed Anne's impact on other cultures. A lot of well-documented information on this came from historians and museums, some from books and travel brochures. At one point I phoned Toronto to speak to a former director of the *Anne of Green Gables* musical. My Chief Dan George profile had me telephoning across the United States to ask film directors and fellow actors, like Dustin Hoffman and Clint Eastwood, what they thought of him and whether they had good anecdotes that showed his commitment to his new-found acting career.

Where does research actually start? I usually begin it by planning a strategy. No wait. That's wrong, too. I invariably *resume* research with a concerted effort because I've already done a fair amount of it for my story proposal. To continue it, I first review all the story's pulse points, jotting down possible sources of information for each, and those likely to lead to others more prolific. Depending on the nature of the assignment, these could be organizations that have done studies or collected statistics that I'll almost certainly need to demonstrate the story's breadth. Sources could also be institutions that are custodians of case histories, or ordinary people with observation, impressions, or anecdotes.

Given that time is always an important consideration, especially when faced with a deadline, you must chart a course that will lead from one source to the other naturally and fruitfully. If, for instance, you were doing a story on the plight of Prairie farmers, it would be far better to research the geography and intricacies of the issue first, then see the farmers last so you would know what to ask them. In much the same way, a serious piece on our thriving fashion industry has less to do with models and more to do with designers, manufacturers, exporters, and customers. At some point, however, you may want to talk briefly to a model or two to add a splash of glamour to your story. By way of further example, an article on oil exploration would require you to read about the topic's political, economic, and sociological elements, then speak to company officials, politicians, and drillers afterwards.

Jobs like these are nearly always best launched in libraries, which come in three main types: public libraries, those on university and college campuses, and those set up to meet the specific needs of industries or government departments. Wherever they are and whoever they serve, librarians are much more than mere guardians of books. They are purveyors of facts on every subject imaginable and are trained to help you find them. What information they can't locate in their own library, they will usually find elsewhere and then direct you to it.

Within arm's reach on the shelves of a library's reference section lies the best research start of all – such tools as printed, bound indexes listing what articles have been written, by whom, on what subjects, for which publications, and when they appeared in print. There are literally dozens of bibliographies like these. They include the *Canadian Periodical Index*, the *Canadian Magazine Index*, the *Canadian Business Index*, the *Canadian News Index*, even the *Canadian Legal Periodical Index*. If ever you need sources south of the border, there are such American counterparts as the *Reader's Guide to Periodical Literature*, the *Humanities Index* and the *Social Science Index*. I'll bet my life that in recent years, tons has been written on farmers' plights, fashion, and oil drilling. All will be there for the looking in all its many forms – the economic, sociological, political, even the human-interest.

Eventually, if you were to go ahead with one of these stories, you would probably need to contact specific key organizations: the Fashion Council of Canada, perhaps, a remote branch of the Saskatchewan Farmers' Union, or oil drillers' associations and regional offices of Energy Canada.

Some of the most valuable sources are usually contained in any one of several directories that list every club, government agency, or institution that ever officially existed. The two most widely used are *The Directory of Associations in Canada* and the *International Directory of Associations.* Despite their bulk and the greyness of their pages, they can be an enlightening read. Preceding the Trail Riders of the Canadian Rockies and the Roofing Contractors' Association of Nova Scotia are the New Brunswick Chess Association, the Toronto-based International Save the Pun Foundation, and the International Federation of Tiddlywinks, in Silver Spring, Maryland, which, I suspect, you may *never* need to contact.

I was particularly glad of these books when researching a story on soccer in North America. They helped me find the Canadian Soccer Association and the North American Soccer League, both of which mailed me articles, newspaper clippings and the names and addresses of clubs and amateur and professional players. In *Who's Who* and *Artists in Canada* I was able to find the name and address of Oscar Peterson's publicist, who sent me a press kit and then arranged an interview.

Large city libraries sometimes have hook-ups, computerized or otherwise, with others. By sitting before a monitor and pressing a few keys, a helpful "on-line" librarian can find her way into huge lists of books on every subject imaginable, from obesity, photography, and stamp collecting, to insects, grass, and plastic. With a little extra work she can narrow a subject down from, say, bees, to queen bees, to African bees, to hives, to how to treat bee stings, to who treats bee stings best in Manitoba!

Try the system some time. Still at her computer keyboard, a librarian can also produce lists of books on libraries themselves: from general information about them, to different types of libraries, to how to build libraries, to selecting books for libraries, to selecting non-fiction books for libraries, to choosing reference books, to how to properly use a library, to how a library can be the writer's best friend. And although she may not have the book you want on her own shelves, her "on-line" search will tell her where there's a copy she can borrow for you.

Research is considerably more than libraries, however. Broadly speaking, it's *anything* you can find out for your article – either facts on the printed page or what you may hear and see. Indeed, some of the most reliable sources of all are your ears and eyes, particularly when, like me, you've stood behind the scenes at a Stratford Festival production of Gilbert and Sullivan's *Iolanthe*, watching, waiting, and taking careful note of how backstage workers co-ordinate their efforts to see their show mounted.

To write about computer dating for my book *Data for a Candlelit Dinner*, and later to produce an article for *Maclean's*, I actually enrolled for three months with a Montreal agency. The data was provided by the answers to 120 questions on a form I completed, which asked me to describe myself and the kind of woman I had in mind. Then I sat back and waited for lists of dates to arrive by mail. I also researched the computer dating trend, how it was started as Operation Match by a group of fun-loving Harvard University students back in 1965, and contacted other similar agencies across North America. Most of the material for that book, however, came from the women I eventually met. I learned from them what kinds of partners *they* sought, and what they heard, felt, and saw while dating. This research method is all part of a process journalists call fact-finding from the inside looking out rather than from the outside looking in.

For another book, *The Gamblers*, an idea given to my by a man hooked on horse betting, the research was largely done by attending Gambler's Anonymous meetings over a period of several months. With members' permission, I recorded their stories and wove them throughout my text.

Research on my grandmother, carried out for several months shortly after her death, came largely from what I and others could remember about her. If you were writing a similarly nostalgic or personal piece, a lot of information would emanate from your memory or thoughts, leaving you to consult – as I did – reference books or historians for place names, spellings, and dates of important events, all so necessary to give the finished work its authenticity.

Documenting the achievements of the eminent Canadian psychiatrist Heinz Lehmann was considerably more gruelling work. On reflection, it was typical of the digging necessary for any medical or scientific story – information that's not so much hard to gather, as difficult to interpret. I compiled details of Lehmann's achievements from a lot of reading and by talking to both him and his colleagues. In 1953, he introduced to North America the science of psychopharmacology – the treatment of the mentally ill with medication. This followed several small tests of a major tranquilizer called chlorpromazine, first on six volunteer nurses at Montreal's Douglas Hospital, and later on seventy of his sickest schizophrenic patients there. After observing them over several weeks, then increasing the dose to five times that recommended by the manufacturer, Lehmann was overjoyed to find the so-called "mad" people, who had been irrational day in and day out for many years, behaving normally virtually overnight. Instead of spending their lives in an institution, they could at last go home, as long as they continued treatment with their family doctor. It was a major medical breakthrough.

Instinctively, I recognized all the pulse points: Where did Heinz Lehmann first hear of the new drug? How? Where did he test his patients? How did he cope with the inevitable criticism from within his profession, much of it accusing him of being naïve and rebuking him for taking risks? How was he able to do good clinical research and maintain comprehensive files and charts at a time when governments spent little money on treating and rehabilitating the mentally ill? How did he react when his initial tests appeared futile? How did he feel years later when published assessments of his discovery estimated that he had been able to slash the number of institutionalized patients across North America from 560,000 to 170,000, a figure that remains constant today?

I found answers to all these questions in medical papers, psychiatry journals, magazine articles, speeches, and lectures that Lehmann himself had given, or in those delivered about him. Drug companies were able to plug holes, as were other psychiatrists, several of them now in private practice in New York City and London, England.

There was a pulse point, however, which was painfully difficult to cover properly. (There's usually at least one of these in every intricate piece.) If, according to Lehmann's untiring trials and tests, chlorpromazine was such a "wonder drug," which heralded psychopharmacology and completely changed the face of psychiatry, *how did it work*? Sure, the medication could be injected or taken orally with a glass of water like Aspirin. Sure, it didn't induce such side effects as drowsiness, commonly associated with other tranquilizers. But what exactly were the *physiological* changes it made to quieten the psychotic down?

Back in libraries at three Montreal hospitals, I read eight different books and several medical papers on neurology, because I was unable to find a doctor who could explain these physiological changes in language I felt either myself or my readers could understand. For all his talent, even Heinz Lehmann could not initially do this. Like most of his psychiatrist colleagues, he assumed I knew more about medicine than I did. So I decided to research the effects of tranquilizers on the brain independently and return to the experts later with greater knowledge of both their territory and the terminology they use among themselves. This work helped me considerably. Understanding I was in earnest, a young neurologist at The Montreal General Hospital obligingly drew a series of diagrams on his office blackboard. With what he explained and what I had found out for myself, I could compile the following paragraph which, I think, adequately addresses the question:

> The psychotic's brain undergoes a chemical change. Cells produce too much of a substance called dopamine, considered to be the most important of several natural chemicals that help transmit thought processes across tiny gaps – the synapses – separating one nerve ending from the beginning of another. With a normal dopamine flow, we think clearly and remain in contact with reality. But when this fluid is over-produced – either genetically or because of a sudden, traumatic experience – the synapses become clogged. Thoughts and movements are then jumbled. As a result, a person becomes erratic, irrational, and "hears" noises or "sees" visions. In medical terms, the patient becomes psychotic.

All I needed to explain after this was that chlorpromazine and numerous more-refined medications that have been developed since, *control the dopamine flow*, though doctors still aren't exactly sure how. This research required many hours of work – first to understand fully the chemical changes myself, then to find the words to explain them. Indeed, the Heinz Lehmann story was one of the toughest I've ever been assigned. I knew I was on the way to doing it reasonably well, however, when a few weeks later I sat before Lehmann himself with a tape recorder to fill in all the gaps. I suddenly discovered I could discuss the functioning of the brain with an internationally acclaimed expert! "You've learned a lot," he said. "You should quit writing and go into neurology." He was joking, of course.

Stop and think about it. The fountains of information are as endless as sources for article ideas. All you need do is ponder them, then hunt them out. The *Yellow Pages*, that seemingly endless kaleidoscope of professions, products, and services (also good for ideas), rarely fails to give a lead or two. While researching Quebec's Richelieu River for the Imperial Oil *Review*, I telephoned local sports stores until I found one that sold diving equipment, which could put me in touch with a diving club. The manager there gave me a list of several, one of which had recently found 200-year-old artifacts on the Richelieu's bed – shipwrecks, cannonballs, swords, gunbolts, and pieces of porcelain. One contact led to another. Through a second club, I met an archeologist who was given a $30,000 Quebec government grant to explore the river in a sixty-foot boat once used to fish lobsters off Nova Scotia. He gave me an article he and two colleagues had written about their "finds," then steered me to folklorists, fishermen, boat owners, inn keepers, and farmers – all of whom owed their very survival to the Richelieu River.

In Federal government directories, I found phone numbers of lock-keepers and Parks Canada administrators of two forts that attract more than a hundred and fifty thousand visitors annually. Transport Canada led me to experts who monitored the river's flow and kept records of its 109 different species of fish; various provincial government agencies sent maps, diagrams, and photographs. All proved invaluable when I came to bring the river to life for a national readership.

Government researchers, who are among the very best we have, helped me prepare an article on our parole system, how it worked and when it didn't, and plied me with statistics, case histories, and phone numbers of parole boards across the country. Transport Canada sent background material when I profiled Air Canada president (later chairman) Claude Taylor. So did the airline itself, of course, through its public affairs department. Such departments in both public and private sectors are manned by journalists, remember, who are quick to assess and respond to a writer's needs.

Some of the best research help I ever received was from a CN public relations manager who arranged for me to travel on that freight train. He understood from his own journalistic experience on newspapers and magazines that this story was a way of showing the reader how the railway system worked. So, before actually setting out in a caboose CN installed especially for me near the rear of a freight train nearly a mile long, I was grateful for the chance he gave me to see railway technology in action: computerized signalling systems and safety devices, humpyards, traffic control offices, and the enormous amount of manual work that goes on day by day to ensure our freight moves smoothly.

When convinced that a story is truly worthwhile, public relations people can be invaluable. When writing my book *Adrian Waller's Guide to Music*, I gathered anecdotes and interesting historical information by writing to the piano firm Steinway & Co. in New York City. Almost by return mail, I received a hefty parcel of magazine and encyclopedia articles, plus photographs of some of the earliest keyboard instruments in museums around the world. RCA sent me invaluable material on the history of the phonograph. Other recording firms, orchestra press departments, and opera companies scattered throughout North America and Europe were only too pleased to forward photographs and biographies of those modern-day musicians I wanted to mention and interesting comments from internationally known conductors. The biggest package of all, however, came from the Consulate General of Austria – books on Beethoven and Mozart, maps of Vienna, old programs, and an essay (which I later had translated from the German) on the Waltz King, Johann Strauss.

Ultimately, whatever you research, and in whatever order you choose to do it, it will nearly always require some kind of library back-up. There was plenty of time-consuming library work for me on my Halifax Explosion piece. Tracing survivors who could remember it – many of them in their eighties – was especially hard. Here, the Mayor's office helped, as did people I met in the street. Everyone, it seemed, knew a resident who had in some way been touched by the disaster. To my delight, I discovered that the Halifax Public Library had a "Great Halifax Explosion" file, which contained pictures, clippings, documents and a complete list of all the dead and injured. From then on, armed with names, I was able to do a lot of my research by telephone.

The hardest part of this assignment was piecing together what *really* happened during the disaster. Museums, I discovered, had much of the story, as did several books, magazine articles, and newspaper clippings of the day, which I read on microfilm, carefully taking notes and making photocopies when I needed them. The most valuable information, though, was at the Archives of Nova Scotia – twenty-two volumes of transcripts from five different court cases. Two of these were civil suits; three involved criminal manslaughter charges, later dismissed, against the Halifax Harbour traffic officer and the captain and the pilot of one of the ships involved in the collision. I spent nearly two weeks studying those transcripts and found in them *all* the pertinent details I needed about the actual explosion and much more. They contained a full chronology of the events that preceded it, the exact weight of the ships involved, what they were carrying, and how, through human error, they had collided. In a transcript of the British Admiralty's Wrecks Commission inquiry, which sought to apportion blame for the disaster, there was some stunning dialogue which I couldn't resist using.

From the assignment's outset, a major concern was how I could unearth good conversation to brighten the narrative. Survivors would provide some of it, I anticipated, and they did. But I wanted words that reflected some of the ensuing bitterness in that mass of litigation, marked by blizzards of horrible insinuations and false accusations. Leafing through the transcripts, I found it!

> "You are a considerably hard drinker?" lawyer C.J. Burchell asked one of the pilots.
>
> "No," was the reply.
>
> "A man who frequently gets drunk?"
>
> "No."
>
> "*Sometimes* you get drunk?" Burchell persisted.
>
> "Not lately. I have, sometimes – a long time ago."
>
> "You drink quite a bit? What is known as a *constant* drinker?"
>
> "No, Sir," the pilot said again. "Not a heavy drinker at all."
>
> "Do you know that there were some hundreds killed and many thousands more injured and wounded for life?"
>
> "Yes"
>
> "And you know that at this very hour the bells are ringing for this funeral?"
>
> "I have not heard them."
>
> "I want to ask you now, knowing that this is the hour of the funeral," Burchell said, "if you are willing to admit frankly that you have been deliberately perjuring yourself for the past two days."
>
> "No, Sir, I haven't," the pilot replied.

Whatever your strategy, there are more aspects of research to consider. First, art directors are always grateful for pictures, drawings, cartoons, old advertisements – anything you can pick up from libraries, newspapers, or photo agencies that may suitably illustrate your work on its own, or give ideas to an artist assigned to illustrate it. The source for material like this should always be listed, particularly if it is copyrighted. The art director will not only want to trace a cartoonist or a photographer to ask permission to use his work, but also to pay him. In magazines, this extra cost is met by the editorial department. Most publishing houses, however, particularly smaller ones, expect authors to pay for art work needed to illustrate their books. This may help explain why, when I wrote *Theatre on a Shoestring*, I illustrated it myself.

A second point to keep in mind is that those written words you photocopied from the library or had sent by public relations departments may not all be correct. Intuitively, you'll feel you want to check them out, and as you do, you'll encounter the inevitable: that some sources, even those considered among the most reliable, will on occasion be inaccurate. While doing an *Equinox* story on the eccentric Canadian inventor Reginald Aubrey Fessenden, who discovered radio in 1900, almost a year before Marconi did, I noticed that several encyclopedias said that he had died of influenza in 1932 in Hamilton, Ontario. They were wrong. Fessenden had died from a heart attack in Hamilton, Bermuda.

You are also likely to discover that anecdotes, which at first appeared to be just what you wanted, had originally been badly or only partially told. Your job will be to complete them. Finally, as you prune, splice, and sift your information – through your hunches and that emotion already invested in the project, which drew you to it in the first place – you'll quickly find that by far the best information of all will come from people with first-hand knowledge: what they think, feel, know, and remember.

7. Interviewing

The pitfalls / the technique / taking control / interviewing for profiles / interviewing "cold" / why busy people see us

"A good listener is not only popular everywhere, but after a while he gets to know something."

WILSON MIZNER

(1876-1933)

Good oral research is predicated almost entirely on how well the writer understands that the spoken and the written word are two entirely different things. Psychologists tell us that people hear about one word in five, but read virtually everything they see printed, if not the first time around, certainly on the second or third, because it is always there for another look. If, then, you were to take a tape recorder and try to use a television interviewer's technique on someone you were profiling for a book or magazine, you would find when you played back your tape that you had fallen hopelessly short of the task. Your recorded conversation might indeed be interesting, comic, or sad when you listened to it, but it would probably contain insufficient detail to commit to saleable words.

That's not to say that television interviewers don't do their homework. They do, or have researchers do it for them. By the time they go before the camera, they know exactly what questions to ask and can usually anticipate the responses to each. Obsessed with minutes, even seconds, they want interviews tailor-made for an allotted time, or those that can be adjusted with a minimum of editing. Writers, on the other hand, who are absorbed instead with getting enough hard facts to make a story full and broad, should persist with questioning until they get exactly what they want – if it takes hours, or even days. Like their television counterparts, they must do their homework first, but be prepared to delve into their topic more deeply.

The ultimate success of your interview will depend almost entirely on how much you've found out before you talk to the characters or experts involved. People warm naturally to writers they think have done their share of the work but tend to be infinitely less cooperative with those who haven't. They become distracted, confused, irritated, or downright bored – and certainly not receptive to intense questioning. When interviewing for profiles, it's a good idea for writers to have their research with them, either in the form of carefully prepared notes, or as a rough draft. This will enable them to check the accuracy of what they've already dug up, flesh out anecdotes that may not have been properly told, and spark plenty of fresh information hitherto unpublished.

I discovered all this the hard way back in 1965, when the *Toronto Telegram* assigned me to talk to Sir Roy Welensky, about whom I knew absolutely nothing other than he was the former prime minister of the Federation of Rhodesia. For some time we sat staring at each other in a room in Toronto's King Edward Hotel, wondering why each was there. Newspaper reporters racing against deadlines often find themselves interviewing "cold." But for me, with ample time to research Sir Roy's background before shooting off to meet him, my inadequate preparation was inexcusable. Had he not been kind and understanding, I would not have got a story at all. Think how much richer my piece could have been had I dug up something about him! I vowed then that such a tawdry piece of journalism would never recur. Since I've worked almost exclusively for magazines in the intervening years, and have made considerably more time for research, I'm happy to say it hasn't.

Above all else, interviews need to be orchestrated so that questioning follows a logical sequence, helping the subject recollect clearly and answer fully. Simply stated, the writer's job is to ask those questions that will elicit answers about what is vivid, interesting, or most important in the subject's life. This means always being in control – or at least, appearing to be – and instinctively feeling out how best to question different kinds of people in varying situations without being brash, pedantic, or aggressive.

Of paramount importance to all writers' interviews are the mundane questions their television colleagues never *need* to ask because the responses will have no entertainment value – "What was the date of that?" for example. "Have you only got four children, because some sources say five?" Or: "How do you spell it?" Indeed, a properly planned interview rather than a loose, informal chat, can – after the basics have been taken care of – have the subject dropping anecdotes like apples falling from a tree in a hail storm. When a magazine has dispatched you far afield, hoping the expense will yield an abundance of good material, this is a prime consideration.

Not long ago, I flew to Orlando, Florida to interview the Canadian-born Country singer Wilf Carter in his mobile home in the nearby, dusty town of Tavares, knowing more about him than he could remember for himself. He had started adult life as a hobo, I had already ascertained in libraries and from impresarios, often travelling across Canada by stowing away on freight trains with nothing but his eight-dollar, mail-order guitar. His entertainment career began in 1933 when a record company executive heard him singing and yodelling a song called "Swiss Moonlight Lullaby" on a Calgary street corner, and signed him to a contract. Carter later became an idol, selling more than four million recordings, and was soon rich enough to buy a home in New York City and a cattle ranch (he called it a "spread") on Calgary's outskirts. Then, at the peak of his fame, he suffered a severe setback – a pulse point in my story.

Sit in on part of the interview:

"So you finally shed your rags for your well-earned riches," I said to him. "Then what happened?" I knew, of course, but wanted him to tell me *his* way, as *he* remembered it.

"I was taking the wife, on April 30, 1940, back from the U.S. to Canada."

"From where to where, exactly?" I asked.

"From New York back to Calgary to see the spread," said Carter. "At Shelby, Montana, we'd just filled up with gas and was headed outa town when a man in a two-ton truck blew a tire and crashed in the side of me. We ditched the car and rolled over three times. They put me into hospital in a steel brace."

"Back injuries?"

"They first said it was broken, but it wasn't."

"What was it then?" I asked.

"Severe whiplash that kept me in bed nine years," Carter said. At that moment, the conversation appeared to be winding down to a premature end. During a slight pause Carter, a robust, leather-faced man standing well over six feet, gave the distinct impression that he would've been happy had nothing more on the matter been said. But for me, it was far too dramatic a moment in his life to let pass unexplored. "What happened then?" I persisted. "Something *must* have happened. What did your fans feel for you?"

Carter brightened. "They announced over CBS I was dead. One station read my obituary. I *was* damn-near killed – critically injured, smashed-up real good."

"Then what?"

"They brought me back to the ranch, dressed me up in a brace, but couldn't do nothing for me. Then I went back to singing."

"But we can't just cut nine years out of your life like that," I said. "In any biography this material is imperative. How did you feel being away from entertainment? Did you miss it? Did you worry that the fans might forget you? Did you get well again? Did you need the money?"

"I didn't need cash," Carter went on, "because the ranch was paid for. I was raising cattle and doing very well. The kids were borned and doin' well, too. But when the wife saw me better but depressed and missing singing and worrying about the folks that bought my records, she said, 'I think I'd like to go back to New York.' So we went and I started all over again."

I was curious now about Carter's first public appearance after his accident, obviously a peak and – since it was the resumption of such a colourful career – *another* pulse point. Was the old zip still there? Had his fans forgotten him? Did he still perform well? Was he apprehensive about his future? The questions cascaded one upon the other. All were designed to keep him talking, and get more good stories.

"In 1950," I reminded him, "you were at the Canadian National Exhibition."

"Right."

"You were pretty nervous, I understand, to face Toronto again."

"Yes, I was just getting back. I didn't think I had *it* left. I'm gonna tell you, they had a great guy on *The Toronto Star* that really got me on there. But others in the show were asking, 'What's this guy Carter got? Whatever it is, it ain't music!' The producer said, 'It doesn't matter. Whatever it is, the folks out there'll love it.' So I went out and did quite well."

Carter's response was too flat for my liking. He'd underestimated the importance of the occasion. Besides this, "did quite well" didn't satisfy my instinct for the dramatic. And I knew differently about this public appearance, anyway. "That's not *really* what happened, is it?" I reminded him, checking my notes. "You presumably went out there with a fluttering heart to see all those faces, then you took the gum. . . ."

Carter's eyes sparkled like fireworks. "That's it! How did you know that? I took the chewing gum outa my mouth, stuck it on the microphone and sang my song!"

"What song?"

"I sang 'Swiss Moonlight Lullaby' and yodelled my head off! And they liked me so much they waved me back on. I was really nervous. Nervous like crazy. In fact, the only thing I could say was, 'Folks, thank you very much. I've just come back for my chewing gum!' That did it! The place went wild. I sang 'There's a Love-Knot in My Lariat' and when the people didn't stop clappin' and shouting for more, I did six encores including 'They're Gonna Tear Down the Mailbox.' They wouldn't let me off the stage! It was a wonderful night. I spent about three hours after the show dressed to kill with my stetson and this pale-blue sharkskin suit on, signing autographs. That was the beginning of my career all over again."

Instinctively, interviewers must recognize those moments when their subject *wants* to talk – like Carter did then. They must listen intently and jab in the odd question to keep him or her on course or to illuminate something just glossed over.

"I couldn't believe it!" Carter went on. "Finally they dared me to jump down off the stage."

"Who are *they*?" I asked.

"The promoters. The people running the show and the people in it." They said, 'Go on down, Wilf. Go see your fans. They love you.'"

"So, did you jump down?"

"I did, and damn-near broke my ankle. And there was people for as far as you could see just piling into me, wanting autograph after autograph."

"How long were you doing this?"

"About an hour and a half. But that doesn't make any difference to me, you know, because the people made me. That's the way I look at it. If it wasn't for the people, I wouldn't be where I am today."

I had managed to open a floodgate. The anecdotes poured out. I enjoyed it, and so did Carter, who was now a lot more comfortable.

Note the picturesque language he used to detail his reminiscences. Dialogue like this is a profiler's delight!

"I got a standing ovation at the Opera House in Seattle and I'd never even been there before in my life! I stood there with tears in my eyes. People were going up the coast to Vancouver and buying my records by the hundreds. I never believed anything like this could happen. Then people who owned this Seattle radio station asked me to put my feet and hands in wet cement so they'd remember the visit. They said they'd never seen anything like it! They said my feet and hands were like elephants' paws, too big for the steps! Then four years ago I went to hear Johnny Cash. I was sitting there in my stetson like a bug on a pin and Johnny was playing the stage. Then he started talking about a man he knew very well who'd been to Australia and all over America."

"That was you, wasn't it?" I asked Carter.

"Sure, it was me! And Johnny was saying, 'Everywhere I went they were playing his records in juke boxes and on the radio. Everywhere I went you heard nothing but this man's records.' Then he said, 'He's one of you, a dyed-in-the-wool Canadian. He lives in the States. He's a great friend of mine. He's a great friend of yours. He's not only a tradition in Country music, he's a *giant*. I want him to stand up. Wilf Carter!' I stood up in this spotlight, tipped my stetson and damn-near died. Then Johnny said, 'There he is right there! C'mon back Wilf afterwards. You and me's gonna have a real big feast!'"

"And did you?"

"Sure I did. I ate him outa house and home."

"And what about the audience who presumably gave you a round of applause? Did you thank them, too?"

From Carter's instantaneous response I was delivered the obvious and most natural closing for my piece. "Sure I thanked the audience," he said. "I turned round, still with my hat in my hand, my face streaming with tears, and said, 'Thanks a million to you and to Johnny. And remember, so long as you need me, folks, I'll always be here.'"

My encounter with Wilf Carter illustrates, I hope, the necessity not only for pre-interview homework, but the need for a sociable atmosphere. It goes without saying that interviewers should be friendly, polite, most certainly unpretentious, and should never appear with the inflated idea that they're important writers. Celebrities dislike being fawned over, remember, leaving that for the throngs of admirers they never really get to know. Entertainers like Carter need good media relations to help enhance their public images. To them, the best interviewers are those who can put them at ease and draw them out.

In a similar atmosphere, I had been told, Luciano Pavarotti could be equally as sociable and forthcoming, except that he occasionally needed to be "pinned down" and sometimes "drawn out." It had less to do with modesty and more with a preconceived notion of what he thought all writers wanted from him. He tended to rely persistently on a repertoire of stock answers to equally stock questions, most of which he had answered in *Newsweek* and *Time*: "What's it like being a superstar, Mr. Pavarotti?"

"Well, I still go to bed the same way – without pyjamas."

I met Pavarotti in his efficiency apartment in Chicago. A huge block of a man – 300 pounds and rising – with no neck, an immense girth, and a round, boyish face topped by a smudge of black hair plastered to one side, he had moored himself in a dusk-blue tracksuit on a pink sofa, one leg on the coffee table, the other stretched out at right angles. A useful way of putting people at ease is to explain the kind of information you expect from them, and that's what I did.

Pavarotti, I suspected, was so used to talking to musicians and critics about his art (when he could afford to get technical) that he would surely do so with me. His fame, we should acknowledge at this point, stemmed from his larger-than-life image, his sense of fun – and a beautiful voice able to explore the very highest reaches of the tenor range. One of his most successful roles is in Bellini's *I Puritani*, with its excruciating string of high notes and marathon duets with the lead soprano. The role is largely remembered, however, for its tough first aria, "A te o cara."

"The high D in this aria is not a question of the D himself," said Pavarotti in his inimitable, newly learned English. "It is a question of the entire aria and the approach."

To the layman, of course, this means little. He doesn't know what "approach" in this context means. He may not even know the opera, let alone the aria and the way it needs to be sung. So, remembering the reader and checking my notes, I helped Pavarotti find some useful analogy that would make his point understandable.

"You've likened hitting the high notes," I said to Pavarotti, "to walking the tightrope when, with one mistake, you can fall off and crash to the ground. Is that still the case?"

"Well, it is," Pavarotti replied. "It is more like attempting a champion high jump when the bar is set impossible high, and if you don't run up with proper steps you will knock him off. I tell you that at the end of *I Puritani* you feel to be a dominator, a gladiator! You feel you have done a conquest. It is so impossible written for the human throat, so for one minute when it is all over you say, 'God, I did it!' I never say this after any other opera."

"Do you tape every performance?" I asked, returning to my research.

"Not me," Pavarotti said with a little giggle that came from well within his belly. "But I know a lot of people that does!"

That prompted several fine anecdotes about fans trying to sneak tape recorders backstage while he was singing. After a Metropolitan Opera performance of *La Bohème*, a well-known music critic accused him of a flat high C and Pavarotti was quick to prove him wrong by playing back a tape of that performance and comparing the note in question to the corresponding one on his newly tuned dressing room piano. "You see!" the singer declared jubilantly, "Pavarotti never cheats!"

He doesn't. But he sometimes tries to dominate an interview by steering it his way. I recall him shrugging off one of his most extraordinary accomplishments of which I needed a precise, chronological account – the afternoon of Sunday, February 12, 1978, when he gave the Met's very first live television recital before an audience of some five million people. What went through his mind? How did he cope with it? How did he prepare for it? What did it mean to him? Again, thanks to my research, I had a lot to put to him.

"More people watched you that day than will probably hear you for the rest of your life," I observed, hoping it would prompt a story or two.

"Yes," Pavarotti said. "That is true. And when I walked onto the stage I told myself, 'Well, I'm going to do a normal recital and television will be there.'"

"Fine," I said, "but I want a step-by-step account of the events leading up to it. Now I'm going to try to *lead* you. I'm going to help you. You were watching a war movie on television when your manager, Herbert Breslin, arrived to pick you up. Right?"

"Yes. I like war movies."

"And you were staying at the Navarro Hotel."

"Yes," said Pavarotti.

"What time did you go to the Lincoln Center? About two-thirty?"

"Yes."

"And you presumably put on your hat and coat and . . ."

"Yes, and put my tuxedo in a plastic bag like I always do."

"Did you? Not tuxedo, surely. Tails."

"Yes, tails," the tenor said.

"And you said to Breslin, 'Don't make me nervous.'"

"I didn't say that," Pavarotti insisted, "because I was already nervous!"

"Okay," I said, "we'll leave that out."

"Well, I don't know why I say that. Probably I say it."

"Fine. Now when you got to the Lincoln Center you must have seen people already lining up to get in because the recital was starting at four-thirty. Right?"

"Yes," Pavarotti went on, "there were some people waiting to go in and some people waiting for me. And I have a rule since I begin to make recital than I always try at least half of the recital in full voice. I try the lights two hours before the concert. So I did that at that time. We tried the high points of the concert and the voice seems to answer very well. And then I went to my dressing room and begin little by little to be dressed."

"At three-thirty, the lobby began to fill up."

"Yes."

"Was this at the point where you actually began to put on your tails?" I asked.

"Yes, and then I try to rest. I try to make yoga respirazione . . ."

"Breathing exercises."

". . . to make the oxygen go to my brain and to feel a little more relaxed. It was very interesting. I sang the first part of the . . . ."

"You're jumping ahead, Mr. Pavarotti," I said, "because according to what I've found out, a Met official found you slumped over a chair wanting to cancel."

"That is true."

"You were petrified, I understand."

"Who wouldn't be in a time like this?" asked Pavarotti, somewhat defensively.

"Then you apparently said something rather interesting to your secretary – 'If I die, make sure I'm buried in the ground.'"

"Yes," said Pavarotti quickly. "I always say it when I am so scared than I think I am wanting to die."

"Good. Now, four minutes before air time – and remember I've compiled all this information I'm putting to you from many, many sources – you went through the cavernous backstage area, past the *Eugene Onegin* props . . ."

"Yes."

". . . into the wings. There was a little card table set up there with a blue and white towel, a bottle of club soda for you, and a pot of tea for your accompanist, John Wustman."

"Yes," said Pavarotti. "Absolutely right. Perfect."

"Good. And six cameramen out in the auditorium were as taut as their cables, feeling for you. Suddenly a producer said, 'One minute to go, Mr. Pavarotti. Is everything all right?'"

"And what did I say?" Pavarotti inquired of me.

"You nodded and said, 'Yes.'"

"That's exactly right," Pavarotti confirmed.

"Your nervousness now appeared to be well under control. 'Don't forget the ground,' you reiterated. Then you were gone. You'd walked out into a pool of stage lighting – and to a tumultuous welcome. Am I right?"

"Yes," Pavarotti said. "You found out a lot of things. You make me relive this agony all over again!"

Now he was free to give his account of how he felt the recital went and what the fans' adoration meant to him. It's true to say, I think, that without preparation and, perhaps, the audacity to take full control, I wouldn't have had such a vivid, first-hand account of that auspicious musical event. I don't think for one moment that Pavarotti would have volunteered it.

Like Wilf Carter, he was relatively easy to interview. Actor Donald Sutherland was, too, except for odd lapses into esoteric metaphors that readers unfamiliar with the film business wouldn't have understood.

"How do you prepare for a role?" I asked him simply. He'd answered all other questions well, so why not this one?

"Well," he replied pensively. "It depends. I usually see a little screen in my mind's eye with people moving across it. And on this screen there are . . ."

At that very moment, a crane swung past the window of the Manhattan office block where he and I were seated in a lounge on the nineteenth floor.

"Mr. Sutherland," I said. "How would you tell that crane operator how you prepare for a part in a film?"

"Oh," he said, stirring from his metaphysical image. "Oh, I see what you mean. Well, I'd tell him I read the script about six times trying to get to know the character I'll be portraying, his physical characteristics and what's inside his mind and how he relates to the people around him. I make notes of how he moves, thinks, talks, and what motivates him, and stuff like that. I get to know why he's there, in the script, and I spend hours when I'm walking, swimming, driving, sailing, even watching baseball, putting myself in his shoes, his skin. Then I learn the lines the way I think he'd say them."

The most frustrating job, you'll find, is having to interview someone who is not particularly talkative in the first place, and suspicious in the second. Gary Platt was like that. He was a Chicago Black Hawks hockey player who had been demoted to a farm team, the Flint Generals, when his game fell short. While there, he discovered through the team doctor that he was suffering from leukemia. He fought that successfully in a Montreal hospital, dreaming of one day rejoining the Black Hawks. He did, but didn't stay. He couldn't make the team. Nearly three years of chemotherapy had sapped his strength. He was no longer the muscular, six-foot-two defenceman who once held so much promise as the great Bobby Orr's successor. Nonetheless, giving the NHL another shot was his way of convincing himself that he was finally well.

Instead of playing professional hockey, Platt joined an amateur team, opened a sporting goods store, jogged, trained as a trader at the Montreal Stock Exchange, and became a Chicago Black Hawks scout. His was a story that had a lot of the natural ingredients: time, characters, tenacity, spirit, drama, and – since Gary Platt married his childhood sweetheart while under his "sentence" of death – a strong romantic sub-plot.

Getting the facts, though, was like extracting winkles from their shells with a pin. "How did you react when the doctor told you the worst, that you'd have to start battling for your life?" I asked him.

"It's the name of the game," he said. "You have to take the rough with the smooth. Like, see, you win some and you're gonna lose some, eh?"

"Just like that," I mused.

Gary Platt felt he was giving an interview on *Hockey Night in Canada* in which, you'll notice, sweat-soaked guests speak in little eight-second bursts.

"See," he reiterated, "you win some, then you lose some."

"So you shrugged it off," I said, then added: "I bet you didn't. I bet, if you think back, a helluva lot went through your mind. You were dying, weren't you?"

"Yes."

"Okay then. Let's hear what you *really* did."

That, I think, jolted Platt into realizing that he wasn't being interviewed on television – that how he expressed himself wasn't important so long as he imparted information. There was no need for bravado. No one was going to argue with him or ask him questions he couldn't answer. All that was wanted was his fullest recollections, as best he could give them.

"It's kinda hard to talk about it," he said.

"Let's try," I said. "I'm not going to embarrass you. Tell me the story and we'll sort out the bits that you think are too personal later. We can leave them out, perhaps."

What transpired was pure gold. Platt remembered the shiver in his spine as the doctor delivered the news. He recalled dining that night with a team mate who gave him a little plaque inscribed, "God is With You," then hurriedly leaving for Montreal – and chemotherapy. In places, he drove 100 miles an hour, wondering if he would ever live to see his wedding. Not far from Detroit, Michigan, he pulled to the side of a main turnpike, and wept.

From that moment in our first meeting, the facts flowed a little more quickly. Weeks later, after several short conversations that neither taxed Platt's mind nor blurred his memory, I was ready to write. A lot, however, was due to his wife, Brenda, whom I asked to sit in on interviews. Sometimes, a person the subject knows can effectively help ease tension in an interview by taking an active role.

The Canadian tenor Jon Vickers posed a different problem: how to deal with the unpredictable. He was insightful and genial enough – until I touched on a wart. Then he leapt from his seat and almost blew my head off. "I don't want that in!" he roared. "I'd much prefer if you didn't use it!"

What was the fuss about? I'd simply reminded him of his performance as Tristan in Wagner's *Tristan und Isolde* at the Dallas Civic Opera. The story went that, as he finished his final aria and lay down to die, the audience found it an opportune time to cough, even though a glorious English horn solo was beginning to rise up from the orchestra pit.

"Stop your hacking!" the dying Tristan was said to have grunted from the corner of his mouth as he lay prostrate in a darkened corner of the stage. It had instant effect.

I could visualize the scene well. Vickers, massively built, his barrel chest arched upwards, his oak-tree arms dangling, his bright, blue eyes burning with anger behind closed lids. Had he yielded to an impulse that must so often confront many artists like him? Was the story true?

"Yes," Vickers said, "the whole damn thing's true. But I've told you, I don't want it used!"

"Why?" I asked.

"Because it'll show me up in a bad light. People'll think I'm some kind of . . ."

"Wait, Mr. Vickers," I said. "Properly told, that anecdote can show the reader what a selfless singer you are – that having done your bit in the opera, you were feeling for the hornist."

Vickers softened. "That poor man," he went on, "was playing his heart out – oh, such a beautiful solo! Typically fine Wagner. I felt the audience should've heard him out. And all they could do was hack!"

"Fine," I said. "Why don't I say that? Why don't I tell the anecdote and explain why it was that you shouted?"

"All right," he said, mellowing.

Vickers had inadvertently raised the point that some anecdotes can often be bent to show either facet of a person's character, the good or the bad. His fears were not totally unfounded. I was able to convince him through some gentle persuasion, however, that in its context and nicely fleshed out, the story of his dying Tristan would draw a picture of Saskatchewan's Jonathan Stewart Vickers – one of the best Wagnerian tenors of all time – bringing to the stage an innate sense of dedication, a feeling that an opera doesn't merely rest on rousing overtures, stirring preludes, soaring arias, and full-blooded choruses, but on pastoral English horn solos, too.

When well-known people relive for freelance writers such vivid moments in their lives, it inspires another often-asked question: Why would celebrities willingly give so much of their time? A politician running for office, of course, needs the media to state his case. The up-and-coming starlet wants to be better known. The local businessman hopes publicity will sell his product. But the world's biggest superstars? What would they want from a man like me? Most get all the publicity they need from reviews of their work, record jackets, film credits, or appearances on television talk shows where they can say all they consider necessary to promote themselves in just a few minutes. Yet literally dozens of celebrities have fitted me, a writer they had never known or met, into their hectic schedules.

Pavarotti answered all my questions in a five-hour interview spread over two days – even though, on the evening of one of them, he was performing in Verdi's *Rigoletto* at the Lyric Opera of Chicago. Someone doubtless convinced the busy Claude Taylor he should cancel a meeting to meet me. (Our conversation went on for so long that he missed lunch, too.) Why would Paul Anka cut short a recording session to fly me from Los Angeles to his Las Vegas home, take me to dinner, and talk until three in the morning? And why, beyond recognizing an obvious platform for his philosophy, did Chief Dan George agree to a strenuous three-day interview in that Vancouver hospital room?

The simple explanation is that there exists a little vanity in all of us: that despite what they may say, most people feel honoured to be a part of a serious article or book that will cover their lives accurately and in good taste. "Great artists," says conductor Alexander Brott, "are astutely aware of the public's frailty for souvenir and they willingly supply the demand. They often don't need publicity any more than Coca Cola does, but just as Coca Cola wants to maintain its corporate image, so do they. They also like knowing their public, and the media are giving them what they've worked so hard for over many years – that wonderful thing called 'appreciation'."

Wilf Carter, I remember fondly, was sitting under his car port waiting for me to arrive. He uncoiled himself from a patio chair and shook my hand warmly. "I've been waiting about twenty years to meet you," he said. "You ask the wife!" To celebrate the occasion, he had bought the unlikely combination of doughnuts and champagne. What Carter really meant, of course, was not that he had been waiting for me, Adrian Waller, but for a chance to talk at last about *everything* that had happened to him, more particularly, the way he had carved success out of adversity. If you asked Luciano Pavarotti or Jon Vickers, they would doubtless admit to the same.

Almost without exception, people who are profiled for their achievements shake their heads disbelievingly. "I still can't believe it's all true," Paul Anka told me when I reminded him that he earned $10 million annually, depending on how hard he wanted to work. "When I look back, it's been one fascinating incident after another. There's been a lot of luck, too. I'll admit to that. But in the main, it's been a series of stories about an ordinary Ottawa kid riding the heartbreaks and the disappointments, all the while hoping that something better was around the corner. Something nearly always was, and that's the bit I like telling writers about, because in its way, it's a sort of philosophy for others. I like to talk about the hard bits first so the easy bits fall into truer perspective later."

Does Anka's observation tell us something? Does it suggest that, having done our homework to find out where the hard bits were, we're equipped to pitch into an interview that is almost certain to incite the subject to talk? I believe so. Where we begin, and with what questions, is not so important. What is, of course, is how, through good interviewing, we get all the facts we will need – fully fleshed out.

That means listening, guiding, prodding, and unlocking information in the subject's head. It can also entail helping people who appear self-conscious, who have never before been interviewed, to articulate their ideas. Some may be so intimidated by a notebook or tape recorder and stumble aimlessly over the swamp of grammar, that they can't say what they mean. There's always another day, you can tell them. By then, with the ice broken, you may both start to enjoy the interview – proof that you won't be forcing someone into something they never wanted to do.

8. People and Places

Building characters through dialogue / dialect / describing people / describing places / the travelogue / using people and places together

"People and places are the twin pillars on which most non-fiction is built."

WILLIAM ZINSSER

ON WRITING WELL

Almost all the stories you'll ever write, it's safe to say, will be about people in their own territory: at home, at play, or at work. People give life to stories, which is why writers seldom, if ever, write solely about locations or "things." A sports field without players is as dead as a concert hall without an orchestra. Every stretch of road, every meter of sewer, has behind it a politician far more interesting than the tarmac or pipe itself. And in a back office of that gloomy institution you may one day have to profile, it's reasonable to assume, there's almost certain to be a proud, contented man or woman just aching to tell you how they formed it or helped it grow.

The interview, then, should be much more than merely a chance to milk a willing mind for stories. Meeting people face to face and getting to know them enables the writer to capture what they say and in their own special environment – the very things, in fact, that the tape recorder misses and that help readers visualize the scene, like Luciano Pavarotti watching his guests eat steaks with red wine while he pecked woefully at a plate of zucchini and rice in a futile attempt to shed weight.

Even more important is the opportunity the interview should provide to capture the way people express themselves. You could be the most elegant literary stylist on earth, and for some of your stories you might have to be, but always remember that your well-chosen words will never out-perform the subject's. His will bring to your pages an enthusiasm, a special language inextricably hooked to his trade, or charming expressions that will root him in a certain era and in a particular part of the country. By capturing his dialogue, you will make him credible, authentic, and interesting. It will be your most effective way of revealing him to readers.

Without concrete evidence of a person's nature or love for what he does, they are expected to take the writer's word for it, which is not good enough. Strong dialogue will enable your characters to speak to your audience for themselves.

People are rarely interesting if they utter the predictable. When a gas main explodes, displacing an apartment building's tenants in the night, one of them is nearly always quoted as saying, "I was frightened. I thought the whole world was caving in!" Readers subconsciously reply, "Who wouldn't be?" Then they dismiss the all-too-simple observation as something the reporter simply got the poor victim to say. Under many circumstances, particularly when they've been caught off-guard, people can be made to say almost anything. The challenge for the good writer is to talk to as many as possible to uncover the kind of quotes that transport readers into the very heart of the drama.

An elderly woman recalling the tornado that tore through Woodstock, Ontario, in 1979, did just that. "The fridge came at me across the kitchen floor," she told me, "and I saw my hubby out of the corner of my eye ducking the television, some chairs, and this horrendous shower of glass. Then I prayed to God. I said, 'Dear God, if I *must* die, make it quick and painless. Don't make me suffer no more. But spare me, *please* God!' Next thing I knew I'd been blown down the basement steps and had hit my head on the furnace. I was bleeding like crazy, but happy, because all of a sudden I heard my daughter-in-law's baby cry. The kid was still alive, and so was I!"

Sketching people can be a writer's woe, and often a needless one at that. To describe every doctor, social worker, or parent who may appear in a story about the phenomenon of "latch-key" children would be as silly as wasting words to depict their offices and homes. In this kind of piece, descriptions aren't necessary, because experts are pulled into a story to lend weight to an argument, not to intrude upon it. The children, however, are an entirely different matter. They need to be very carefully depicted, which brings us to one of the basic fundamentals of all writing: when a story is built around characters, readers must "see" how they look, and "hear" how they speak.

For a profile, this is paramount. The success of a profile, after all, depends entirely on how well the writer can introduce to his audience someone they might not ordinarily care to know. Here, the necessity for grabbing not only tiptop dialogue but a sprinkling of physical description applies more than ever – if only to ensure that the subject neither looks nor speaks like the person you profiled in the magazine's last issue. None of your characters should appear the same as any other.

Does Luciano Pavarotti resemble Wilf Carter? I hope not. An opera tenor would be just as ridiculous belting out "There's a Love Knot in My Lariat" in a stetson at the CNE, as a Country and Western star appearing in a black cloak in *I Puritani* at the Met! Somehow, and he'd be the first to admit it, Carter *belongs* among mementos in a Florida mobile home. And a salubrious efficiency apartment on Chicago's Lakeside Drive seems just right for the globe-trotting Pavarotti. The two men enjoy contrasting lifestyles, see the world through dissimilar eyes, and have vastly different artistic goals. As characters, they are no more alike than are the corpulent tenor Jon Vickers and Gary Platt, the shy, chunky ex-Chicago Black Hawk. And where they work is as different as Flin Flon and Bangkok. All this must be brought to the readers to help them visualize characters in their own setting.

A useful device for character-sketching is dialect. But this can be precarious territory. You must always decide at the outset what purpose you want dialect to serve, and remember that it immediately puts readers into an outsider's position and prompts them to say, "Look at the way this guy speaks! Is this going to be important?" You may, of course, want to achieve just that effect. Be constantly aware, though, that dialect is inherently comic and can detract when your character needs to be serious.

Sometimes, it may transform the subject from a real-life person with a lot of important observations to make into a stereotype with only a repertoire of one-liners that do nothing to enhance his or her nature – or your story. I've seen dialect purposely used to ridicule, and when it has inadvertently smacked of racism. I've also noticed how hard it can be to read, in which case it's been pointless.

Above all, dialect gives readers extra work, and this must be made as pleasant as possible. One sure-fire way of ensuring that it is, is to abandon ideas of trying to reproduce heavy accents or speech pathologies phonetically and take a much simpler route. If dialect *is* important to the piece and *must* be used, it's far better done sparingly or by suggestion:

- "Where y'all expect me to put this heah theng?" asked Hank Snow when he found no safe place for his guitar in a cluttered Grand Ole Opry dressing room. "Y'all thenk I'm a magician?"

- "Listen, guv'nor," a Cockney porter at London's Covent Garden market told me while I was writing a London *Daily Mail* feature on the old institution. "If this 'ere place ever shifts or goes dahn the tube, *I* won't be 'ere to see it. You can betcha bleedin' boots on that. I'll be six-foot under, guv'nor, and you'll 'ave a longer bleedin' beard than I got!"

These two examples raise another point. As a character, the Covent Garden porter was irresistible, providing a neat, final quote with which I could sew up my piece – just the ending I needed, in fact. But was his accent lost on my readers? The chances are that had they been Americans, it would have been. And maybe, just maybe, Hank Snow's Southern drawl, the trait of nearly all Country singers, would have been wasted on the English. More certain is this: inexperienced writers are usually better off circumventing accents and dialects. They would be wiser to stress other speech peculiarities instead – idiosyncrasies in phrasing or in the cadence of sentences as their subject draws on whatever words he can to express himself, however incorrectly these are used.

This is highly individualistic, too, and a very useful device for drawing characters. Take, for example, the hero in *The Gamblers*. His real name was Harry, but to Gamblers Anonymous members he was "Baby Bull" or "The Mouse." Which did Harry prefer?

"I don't give no hoot what the fellas call me," he said. His voice, though loud, was flat with fatigue and a permanent cold; words came slowly as if he were learning to speak all over again. "But if it comes to the crunch of the matter, I actually prefer 'The Mouse.' If you wanna know the truth, they called me 'Baby Bull' because I used t'be one helluva size, all of about three-hundred pounds, and was full of bull most of the time, anyways. Now I've straightened myself out quite a bit and lost weight, 'The Mouse' seems to fit me better. It's got more dignity, and stuff like that. But, as I say, I don't give no hoot either way."

With Harry's permission, I sat in his living room one night specifically to note how he looked. He was a wide man, I remember, not so much from obesity as from immobility, carrying with him an abundance of loose flesh mostly at his middle and where his neck once was. This area had now been taken over by heavy jowls hanging low at the front, and bulging over his jacket collar at the side. Except for wispy, gingerish sideburns, which gave the general impression of having been permanently stained by nicotine, his huge, round head was hairless. His drooping eyes and sagging, twisted mouth with its well-fleshed, protruding bottom lip, spoke with guilt and remorse of the long, dead years that had inflicted a shine upon his grey and only suit.

I also recall Harry saying, "You're writing this book about me because you know I still got a lot of straightening out to do and that I should've went into personal bankruptcy over gambling long before I did, as the missus says. Well, it's okay by me. If it can help some other poor guy, I don't mind telling you my rotten, sad story, if you really wanna hear about it."

He was one of several ex-gamblers I was interviewing for a book that made excessive demands on my descriptive powers. That project taught me more than anything else that writers – non-fiction and fiction – really need to study the people they write about, always and everywhere. Sometimes they have to ask what lies behind a smile, a tear, or a burst of nervous laughter. When a tender look turns stolid, they must find the reason for that, too, then form words to describe the face itself.

But how? Perhaps there's special insight in the *wrong* way of doing it. For many years it was customary to tell readers that our women were either "long-legged, willowy blondes" or "pert, pretty brunettes" or a combination of both – "pert, willowy, long-legged brunettes with blonde streaks." (Men invariably seemed to escape such triteness.) Older women were inevitably "bleach blondes in their mid-forties" or "frail, grey-haired grandmothers" leaning on their canes. Regrettably, some of this still spills into stories today, even in our magazines. What rubbish it is! Such threadbare devices recklessly applied to make dull copy bright aren't useful pieces of description at all, but value-judgements. In literary terms, they're discriminatory, sexist, worthless, shallow, and inane. No one wants to read, either, that Donald Sutherland is tall ("Taller than what?" asks the editor) or that Dustin Hoffman is short ("Shorter than Groucho Marx or a fire hydrant?") because they know both men from the movies.

Readers expect writers to portray people well, which is not always an easy task. Description brings together two powerful forces: your visual perception and your words. To some people, even among those who have never written, description is somehow second nature. To most of us, though, it's something that comes only with practice. During interviews, professionals list those features that distinguish a particular physique, astutely omitting those that are common to all physiques. In essence, this is how I sketched artist Maude Lewis – in her own place – in a profile for which description was absolutely indispensible:

> She was frail and barely five feet tall. Polio in adolescence, and arthritis later, had left her horribly deformed – hunchbacked and shoulderless, with thin arms that folded across her chest like a bird's damaged wings. For all this, she smiled a lot but shyly from beneath a thatch of grey-brown hair. Her pale blue eyes shone like candles. "If nothing else," a friend said, "you'd remember Maudie for the way she looked."
>
> Others knew her for her God-given talent. For more than 30 years, she'd been a fixture in the little village of Marshalltown, five kilometers from Digby, N.S. – painting. Usually, she sat at the window or the open door of a little roadside house many people dismissed as a tool shed. It measured a mere 10 feet by 12 feet and was never fitted out with electricity, running water, or a telephone. It wasn't even insulated to hold in heat from the big, iron stove or keep out cruel winds that swept mercilessly across neighboring farms in winter.
>
> But neither Maude's terrible handicaps nor the dimensions of her tiny, one-roomed shack confined a spirit dedicated to art. She shared a long, successful marriage to an illiterate, kind ex-farmhand named Everett Lewis, and with his help – and with hands so badly twisted and gnarled they could barely hold a brush – she created a wonderful artistic legacy.

Admittedly, Maude Lewis' physique differed greatly from others, which made my job relatively easy. But this sketch was drawn from many pages of notes taken while speaking to people who saw her daily over several years before her death in 1970. It was a lot of work, much more than is usual for me. Most magazine articles require only a few sentences of description – early, as *Equinox* reminds us – so readers get to "know" important characters at the outset:

- Nearly 200 years after his death we are still wondering what kind of man Beethoven really was. His contemporaries described him as being five-foot-two or -three inches tall, with a round nose, an inflamed pock-marked complexion and unruly black hair swept up into a lion's mane. Those same sources say he was clumsy, vain, paranoid and downright unhealthy. Yet the romantic legend persists: Beethoven was a shaggy Titan with a defiant jaw, scowling brow and an indomitable will, who battled fate – alone.

- Ted Tarkka is a stout, silver-haired man with large hands roughened by long years of mending broken cars in the Geraldton body shop where he now keeps the books. At 70, age is catching up to his work routine; nothing, though, has diminished his love for animals and desire to help them. As the town's amateur "vet," Ted is a familiar, bespectacled sight in a baseball hat and windbreaker – his ointments, swabs and bandages in a fishing tackle box – striding off determinedly to rehabilitate an owl struck by a car on the Trans-Canada Highway or a fox left bleeding by indiscriminate hunters in the woods. He's been doing this for half his life.

- He's a star now – a lean six-feet-two-inches tall and weighing 185 pounds, who has taken 40 major movie roles in a long, loping stride. That walk has been likened to a giraffe's on the one hand, and a clumsy slouch on the other. It's part of his character – like his face, long, gaunt and angular, topped by a mop of blond-grey hair that never knew a curl. His sullen eyes are grey-blue, his eyebrows oddly arched. His mouth droops and crinkles at its corners. "Mine," says actor Donald Sutherland, impishly, "is a face that only a mother could love!"

Description is absolutely imperative when showing readers how people and places enhance one another. A good example of this can be found in a *Chatelaine* piece on Montreal's Ritz-Carlton Hotel, which opened on December 31, 1912. From old photographs and newspaper clippings, the writer, Barbara Moon, caught the flavour of both the era and the hotel by introducing us to staffers and patrons alike. These characters *were* the Ritz. They made it what it was. They included Sir Frederick Williams Taylor, president of the Bank of Montreal, with his "rake's beard, black roll-brim hat and matching cape," being greeted by immaculate "brown-uniformed doormen" who doffed "bearskin hats" to all who entered either to stay, or merely to sip "le five o'clock tea" among tall, potted trees in the Palm Court. She unearthed pictures of "the rotund, English-born manager, Frank Quick," whom guests called "Humpty Dumpty." Her article contained brief descriptions, too, of Quick's successor, "a fearsome-looking Swiss" named Emile Charles des Baillets, who stood a thin, six-foot-three-inches and was suitably nicknamed "Rasputin" because of his "spade-shaped beard."

Old minutes spoke of one of the hotel's directors, Elwood Hosmer, who lived nearby but who spent his days drinking gin, smoking expensive cigars, and doing crossword puzzles in a leather chair near the lobby. From her research, Barbara Moon was able to tell readers that he was "delicate," and that another interesting character named Sven Rasmussen was "highly strung" and "fastidious." This added weight, of course, when the article explained how Rasmussen felt his Swedish name was entirely inappropriate to his ambition to become a maître-d'hôtel, and changed it – to "Charles of the Ritz."

Lovely stuff so deftly sewn together! It put a lot of life and movement into what otherwise would have been just another story about just another building.

But what of places by themselves? A paragraph or two may be enough to introduce the location of a well-known event that will dominate a story. But evoking the mood of an entire district – the kind of trees, shops and houses it has, or its proximity to the sea, a mountain or an historic site – will require a great deal of descriptive writing.

In the late 1970s, while travelling through Greece on that bus, I decided after a lot of thought to pitch my story with the kind of action that is typical of any large Grecian centre, but known only to people who have seen it. I spent an entire day compiling a lead which created atmosphere, I hope, without telling readers what they were already likely to know:

Sipping an ouzo in Plaka, a quaint corner of old Athens, I was confronted by a series of heartening events. It was late on a warm October morning, and I sat in an outdoor taverna on narrow Lissikratous Street, where a curious mixture of shops sold watches, toys, clothes, fine silver and meat, all within a block of each other. Greengrocers had spread beans, pistachio nuts, eggplants and pomegranates in boxes on the crumbling sidewalk, leaving little room to pass. The air was heavy with spices and barbecued lamb, but light with the throbbing music of the bouzouki.

Behind me, not a warrior's cry away, the mighty fortress Acropolis, the 2,400-year-old marble-pillared temple to Athena (Goddess of the Spirit) proudly on its shoulders, towered in Greece's big, golden sun – a monument to both victory with honor and a glorious passage through the ages.

About to pay my bill, I saw a man. . . .

This brings us to that constantly troublesome journalistic entity known as the travelogue. Some magazines, and most newspapers, simply require travel writers to visit a destination and provide a mass of basic facts: what it looks like, how much it costs to get there, what sights are worth seeing, and whether or not restaurants and hotels take credit cards. This kind of story functions more as a service piece, helping readers decide on a suitable spot for their next vacation. Better magazines, however, expect considerably more. They still require a lot of basic information, but need it to be skillfully fed into a narrowly focused piece in which fresh descriptions and the writer's personal impressions predominate.

This leads the writer to ask, "Okay, but what part of my trip do I write about?" The answer is simple: just the interesting bits and certainly *not* all of it! To most of us, each day spent on that last holiday remains important for a long time afterwards because it was *our* trip. We reflect with wonder on what we saw, as though we were the first people ever to witness it. When talking to friends, that's fine; when addressing our readers, we need to bear in mind that although they might not have seen this wonderful place for themselves, they could already know something about it.

They might know quite a lot, in fact. Innumerable brochures have already told readers that San Francisco is built into the side of a mountain, that Tobago has a big, romantic moon and silky-white beaches, that London has pigeons, and that the Italian city of Pisa has a twelfth-century leaning tower. So why tell them again?

Readers now want to peep behind all this. Who are the people who live on Tobago? How much of a nuisance are those pigeons? What are Pisa's engineers doing to prevent the tower from eventually toppling to the ground? Readers expect all the new and interesting information you were able to find out about the place you visited, as well as the most exciting moments of your trip. But above all, they need to know what made your stay different from anyone else's. This means researching a place long before you see it so you can start assembling first-hand observations the moment you arrive.

But there's another useful ingredient for spicing-up the travelogue – adventure. That's not to suggest you must contrive to *create* adventure. Your intuition, however, should tell you when an interesting experience is about to loom, and you must want to let it guide you. Adventure need not mean being arrested in Moscow or being confronted by a man with a spear in Borneo. It can be a simple experience that will help you explain just a little more of what that visit meant to you, and provide something dramatic to share with others.

I remember two such instances, each deserving of stories of their own. In a sidewalk café in Avignon, during one of several trips through France, I met a taxi driver and a farmer who had dined together every Tuesday night for twenty years while their wives played bridge. Through them, I got to know a lot about how the so-called "ordinary people" understood their country, its history, politics, and direction.

Both men were proud of their hobbies. The taxi driver took me to his home to show me his paintings; the farmer insisted that I see scrapbooks which revealed him in the unlikely role of France's champion rodeo rider. The following day, both insisted that I join them for lunch on the sand at Nice, where their wives would barbecue a rabbit. When I arrived, the beach was teeming with nudists!

In 1974, I visited George Bernard Shaw's old homestead in the beautiful village of Ayot Saint Lawrence, Hertfordshire, England, only to discover that it was closed to the public for renovations.

"With a little bit of luck," said the caretaker, a friendly man in his late seventies, "we'll be open next week. But it all depends on the painters. The trouble is, nowadays, they don't like hard work no more. Things ain't what they were in my day."

"Probably not," I said. "But this time next week, I'll be back in Canada."

Detecting my disappointment, the caretaker invited me in, served tea and muffins, then gave me lucid, first-hand knowledge of what kind of man Shaw really was. ("I knew 'im, guv'nor. I knew 'im better than I ever knew any of my seven uncles. I knew 'im like the back of my 'and. He could be a difficult ol' blighter, he could. But I liked 'im. And he liked me! That's the best bit. Gawdknows what would've 'appened if he didn't!") He showed me Shaw's office and a shed, shaded by a mulberry bush at the edge of a meadow behind the house, where the master found the solitude he needed to craft his plays.

As I was leaving, the caretaker's face crinkled into a mischevous smile and he gave me a dozen pre-printed postcards like those Shaw had used to answer his critics, expound his views on such topics as Temperance and his Forty-Letter British Alphabet, and correspond – always in the third person – with admirers. "Mr. Shaw," one card read, "is frequently asked to read literary manuscripts or unperformed plays and pass judgement on them. As he is not and has never been employed by publishers or theatre managers to do this, his opinion could be of no service to authors, and, even if favourable, might prejudice their chances seriously. He is therefore obliged, in their interests no less than his own, to rule out such activities." My visit to Ayot Saint Lawrence was an adventure indeed.

These stories signify the luck of being in the right place at the right time, but also demonstrate travel writing's most important premise – never to see a place only through a tourist's eyes. When your turn comes to write a travelogue, let your spirit of adventure take over. Somehow you must beat any existing language barriers and crawl into the heart of a local community. In this, your instinct for a good story will again be your guide.

Wherever you go and however you choose to do it, whether it be driving across the Sahara Desert in a Jeep or traversing the backwaters of Malaysia in a canoe, remember the travel writer's goals. Make readers "see" the sights, "smell" the air, and "hear" the sounds. When you find respite from the unrelenting sun in a corner of a magnificent cathedral, take readers with you. Get them to "know" the place you visited, if not like it. Above all, ensure that your readers get to "meet" the people you met and "hear" what their city, town, or country has to offer – in their own words.

But here's one final caution. I don't mean that characters have to be quoted endlessly to appear interesting. On the contrary, paragraph after paragraph of uninterrupted dialogue from one person appears amateurish, to say the least. Quotes are most effectively used as a painter uses a dab of white paint here and there to highlight or accentuate a detail on a canvas. Carrying that analogy into writing, a dab or two of what someone says and how he says it effectively injects spark into sections in which narrative and description predominate. In other words, long quotes detract from good style; when used sparingly, dialogue is always considerably more powerful. And never quote the obvious. Quote only those fragments of your interview that cast new light or allow the subject to reinforce what is important to your story – "with a splash of passion," says an editor, "and as a way of showing readers how someone feels or felt."

9. Building the Story

The beginning / the middle / the ending / general statements vs. specifics / the profile / issue stories / human interest / the drama

"Writing, when properly managed (as you may be sure, I think mine is), is but a different name for conversation."

LAURENCE STERNE

(1713-1768)

When I began writing professionally, in England in the late 1950s, I was introduced to a curmudgeonly old editor who had penned twenty-seven books, most of them novels, edited an encyclopedia, written numerous articles for journals, newspapers, and magazines, and had read his poetry on the BBC. To me, just starting out, his output seemed formidable, and I was therefore surprised when he asked to see samples of my work.

During our first and only meeting, I remember, he asked what seemed then to be an anomalous question – "What do you know about architecture or construction?"

Since he had recently renovated his 200-year-old mansion nestled in the rolling hills of Sussex, where he drove a Rolls-Royce, took part in the local hunt, and reared sheepdogs, I deduced the editor wanted me to write about his lifestyle for any one of numerous magazines that delved into rich and famous lives. I responded accordingly. "Well," I told him, "I have a cousin who's studying to be an architect and my grandfather was a bricklayer. So I can soon find out."

At that, he grunted, then puffed and fidgeted with annoyance. "I'm not talking about tradespeople," he said. "I'm talking about how you organize your material after you've done your research – how you pull it all together to make it work for the reader."

Some months later, when I began writing feature stories for London's *Daily Mail* and *Daily Express*, both highly competitive, mass-circulation newspapers, his words fell neatly into place. A good piece of writing, no matter how long or short, must be built block by block and secured by good, strong mortar.

Editors, it seems, are forever searching for words to describe aptly the organization of ideas in writing. One, a former colleague, used to liken crafting a magazine article to making a suit: Everything must be planned according to a pattern, cut to size, carefully positioned, then stitched strongly together without displaying ugly seams. Another would talk about the foundations of a house with its joists, beams, and pillars nailed securely enough to support a heavy roof.

Though unquestionably hyperbolic, these are both reasonable analogies. With research well done and transcribed into notes and mental memos, the writer is confronted with the seemingly on-going dilemma of trying to decide what should go where and why. The goal, of course, is to ensure that the finished work reads logically, naturally, and smoothly, and holds the reader's attention paragraph by paragraph and block by block, right to the very end, without falling apart or collapsing.

What a challenge it is! Yet it must be accomplished with precision. Here, at the very core of writing, the amateur and the professional are clearly set apart, the latter by his ablility to make all arguments, observations or points of view clear from the outset, following a theme, a plot – or both – to a proper conclusion.

There are many right or "workable" ways to build an article. There are considerably more wrong ways. The newspaper reporter doesn't have to suffer the construction agonies too long, if at all, because most reporting conforms to what is known as "the inverted pyramid." That is to say, the most important or dramatic facts supporting that day's angle are put high up in the story, diminishing in importance or petering out thereafter. The reason for this is simple. If suddenly confronted with a space shortage, an editor can simply lop the piece off at any point, resting assured that essential material is not being lost.

If you study a good magazine article, however, you'll see that it has almost the opposite structure. Important facts and a good "grabby" introduction are always necessary to entice readers' attention, but the magazine writer is expected to shape or fashion work so that powerful or important facts, anecdotes and quotes are all distributed throughout the entire piece and not confined to only one part of it. Ideally, the result is a solid opening, a rich middle, and an appropriate ending which leaves readers feeling that they've just experienced something totally satisfying.

This shrewd apportioning of research into blocks of material, each honed to make their point without wandering off course, is what makes a piece of writing intelligent and compelling.

I wish I could offer a set of rules that would help you structure all your stories, but I can't. I can, however, give you some useful guidelines. First, you might want to outline your story, not for the editors this time, but for yourself, listing all the points you wish to make and in which order. Some of this order will already be in your story proposal, but with further research you may have found that the topic is far more complicated than you at first thought. In this case, more planning will be absolutely necessary to make the finished story hang together.

Most writers work this way. They recognize that a second outline makes it easier for them to stick to the point. I usually draw a diagram of the piece I'm working on and pin it on the wall above my typewriter. I can then plan my construction, develop it with blocks of information which follow each other logically, and then create sensible, practical bridging. The bridging is the seams or the mortar, remember, and it must always appear natural, not clumsy or clever.

From my diagram, I'm also able to see that the piece is never top heavy and can hone certain parts of it out of sequence as they occur to me or as particularly cumbersome pieces of research rear their heads. Above all, this method enables me to start thinking about an ending long before I start putting my work on paper. It may sound odd, but you can't write anything until – before you start – you know *exactly* where you will stop.

Other writers work solely and effectively from their transcribed notes. If this is your choice, you must take great pains to sort them into appropriate piles, even if it means cutting them into pieces – a sentence here, or a paragraph there – and pasting them onto larger sheets of paper so they won't get lost. This system can be efficient if you acknowledge that these piles must then be placed into a workable order according to how you want your story to be built.

Let's suppose you were writing about a race horse. You would put information about the animal's physique into one pile, its success on the track in another, its rigorous training into a third, its personality into a fourth, and so on. You'd also want separate piles of material on when the horse was bought and by whom, and how, when, and where it was sired. That done, you would then need to arrange them into some sort of sequence, always asking yourself: Which points are the most important and should appear early in the story or be saved to make a dramatic ending? What aspects of the animal should I present first so that those that follow will be better understood?

Again, this technique may sound too simplistic, because research so often overlaps from one area to another. It is, however, a useful, practical starting point. It's also a reasonably flexible system because, as you progress, you'll be able to switch the piles around, add to them or reduce them while watching the main body of the story grow. All you'll need then – and it should be in your research, if not in your story proposal – is a powerful conclusion and an interesting, arresting lead.

Ah, the lead! Many writing teachers will tell you that the opening sentences introducing the story's first anecdote or spilling its first facts, are crucial. It is the lead, after all, that will either draw readers in or turn them away. This explains why many writers, including myself, spend an inordinate amount of time on its creation, reshaping it endlessly until it is what we call "spot on" or "sharp" or "direct."

How long should an introduction be? There are no pat answers. Some leads hook the audience with just a few well-baited sentences while others, particularly those that launch long pieces, exert a slow but steady pull over several pages. Readers of intellectual or literary journals are quite happy if their writers start an article discursively. They simply stick around, patiently wondering, waiting, and speculating on the point the words will eventually make. For beginning writers, however, this course can be hazardous. Most readers are restless. They want to know, soon, what exactly is in the article they are reading, for *them*. They need to be yanked into it within the first three or four paragraphs at most. If they're not, they'll read something else.

With experience, you'll discover that each type of article poses a different set of problems. There will be times when having found a suitable jumping-off point, you'll cast it away in favour of something you think is better. On re-reading your piece, you may then decide that the original lead was more appropriate after all, and promptly reinstate it. Then a few days later you'll probably want to replace it with something entirely different, with more impact.

Faced with this confusion, as you often will be, you must always ask yourself one simple question: "Does this lead work?" If it does, even though it may not be the best you've ever written, be eternally grateful, and plough ahead.

There are numerous ways of starting a piece of magazine writing. The most effective may harness facts to conjure intrigue – like Silver Donald Cameron's opening to "A Gift of Imagination" in *Homemaker's*:

> I like to visualize Albert Einstein sitting on the tip of an advancing beam of light, his mane of white hair streaming in the solar wind as he roars through the curved universe at 186,000 miles per second, exulting in the difference between what we see, as he passes, and what he sees from his unique vantage point.
>
> A writer's fantasy? Not at all: The idea is Einstein's, not mine. It occurred to him in 1895, when he was 16 years old, and it was one of the speculations that allowed him to think about the nature of light and movement, time and space, more boldly than any other man since Isaac Newton. Ten years later, Einstein published five papers that shook physics to its roots, made it possible for other scientists to imagine photovoltaics and nuclear fission, and changed forever both the world we live in and the way we understand it.

Another, different type of lead may be carved out of an unusual idea, a surprise, an interesting question, anecdotal action, or a unique combination of facts laid out in such a way that they nudge audience curiosity and hold it. Notice how Thomas R. Brooks combined fact, anecdote, viewpoint, and emotion in his deft, straightforward introduction to "Auto Theft Turns Pro" in the American edition of the *Reader's Digest*:

> Every 28 seconds, somewhere in the United States, a car is stolen. That's 1.1 million vehicles a year. If your turn is next, chances are you will never get your car back. If you do, it possibly will have been stripped for parts. When Connecticut police showed a West Hartford owner his new Buick Riviera – minus fenders, hood, doors and wheels – he wept.

These two examples show us, uncompromisingly, the role of the lead. Beside being "grabby" or clever, it should show readers *what the story is going to be about*. That is to say, it must sit naturally at the top of the story as a signpost, giving very clear directions as to where the story is headed.

Articles that require the most carefully focused leads are those which, to survey a topic, round up material scattered across a wide geographic area. Everything within them must ultimately come together as one meaningful entity. An effective device for accomplishing this is "the bullets" lead. Sometimes, one single, powerful case history contains enough elements on its own with which to pitch a national piece. More often than not, though, the bullets will serve you better:

- In Vancouver, Charlie Harrison went straight from elementary school into a vocational school, where he was training to be an auto mechanic. But two years ago, aged 17, he dropped out and has since become one of the 500 functionally illiterate youths seeking work through Vancouver's Youth Employment Service. "Life's pretty grim," he says.

- When he finished among the top four students at Toronto's George Brown College of Applied Arts and Technology last fall, Joe Smith, 22, approached 71 firms for a job as a commercial artist – with a portfolio his teachers said was impressive. "But people just aren't hiring," he says. He is still looking.

- Mary Jones, 21, spent four years getting her BA in history from Dalhousie University, Halifax, hoping to teach school. On graduation, she distributed applications to 42 schools in four provinces but was unable to secure one single interview. "A degree is useless," she said despondently. She is still without a job.

There should be no doubt from these three improvised case histories that they are introducing a story about unemployed youth. Similar techniques can be used to pitch stories about trends, or the widespread consequences of virtually anything. I moulded a similar lead to show, with powerful case histories, that suicide among young people was a national problem rather than one confined only to

Toronto or Vancouver. I also used one to begin an article on the numerous ways Canadians in different parts of the country were making money from handicrafts. The "bullets" lead doesn't always provide the most compelling introduction to a sprawling story – just a practical one that is bright, informative, and on-target.

In their search for those "grabby" leads, many writers confuse clever writing with glibness, which briskly compounds any other problems they may have had. Glibness not only connotes laziness, but suggests to readers that the writer has found the subject too big or important to handle and is trying to disguise ineptitude behind wit or cockiness. For instance, I once read a newspaper profile of actor Sir Laurence Olivier that began: "He opened his hotel room door in a flame-red dressing gown and furry carpet slippers. 'Come in, dear boy,' he said. Sir Laurence Olivier is in town to . . . ."

Surely Sir Laurence is worth more than this. Surely his wearing a flame-red dressing gown and furry carpet slippers was far too trite an observation to build into *any* section of the piece, let alone the one that started it. Surely the feature writer could have found a better reason for imposing himself on a profile. Because the main body of the story was about Sir Laurence's work, I would have much preferred a lead showing him in action – playing in *Hamlet* on one of the world's most celebrated stages, or swinging on a chandelier, his sword outstretched, in the film *Coriolanus*. This, after all, is how we, as *his* audience, have come to know him; in magazine terms, it is how we might best introduce him to *our* audience.

One of the secrets to launching profiles is to catch people in the act of being themselves as we know them – that for which they are acclaimed. The same applies when profiling an institution. The first question the writer should ask is, "What is this thing really known for?" The writer must address this by building the answer into the introduction. Hence my story on the War Amputations of Canada, so widely reputed for helping the physically handicapped, began with a war amputee knocking on the door of a New Brunswick home to help a seven-year-old boy who had lost an arm when he fell under a train. A piece I wrote on the Royal Canadian Legion, the war Vet's best friend, started with a case history showing the organization helping a former World War II infantryman get a government disability pension.

The word "show" is extremely important here. Newspapers can get away with simply telling the news, but magazines must *show* the full force of their topics. To do it, they need the odd general statement, yes, but they must always strive to illustrate major elements with an example – an anecdote or a case history. Given this, it seemed obvious that Luciano Pavarotti needed to be introduced to readers in a way that would immediately prime them for a profile while setting the nature and tone of the entire article. Newspapers could start pieces about the great tenor by saying how badly he plays tennis or rides a horse, but a magazine would need to illustrate from the outset how, and with what kind of panache, he has taken on the world of music. Readers want to see Pavarotti as they know him, in action, in the act of being himself, capturing public attention – and winning hearts doing it.

I chose to do this by starting with an anecdote about Pavarotti starring in an unmitigated operatic triumph. In so doing, I was also considering the market. This piece, remember, was to be condensed in the *Reader's Digest*, whose editors show more than a slight preference for leads that embrace examples or anecdotes unless alternatives can assert the topic better, which is usually not the case. Deep inside me, though, I honestly felt that an example of Pavarotti's prowess would be the most effective way to start a profile of him for virtually *any* good magazine:

> It was February 12, 1972. At New York's Metropolitan Opera, tenor Luciano Pavarotti burst on stage in a dark-blue, gold-braided suit and black leather boots as Antonio in Donizetti's *The Daughter of the Regiment*, to tackle one of opera's most awesome tests: the aria "Quel destin," with its spectacular chain of nine high Cs. Nearly 4,000 people jamming the theatre that night wondered if, like many tenors before him, he would crumble under the strain.
>
> Pavarotti wondered, too. But spurred by "a power from beyond," he reached up and up, his voice soaring above the orchestra in splashes of brilliant sound. On his final, lingering high C, the audience erupted into an ecstatic ovation and overnight, a ticket for the opera – and not a New York Rangers hockey game – became the hottest in town.

Though important, the lead is relatively minor when we look at the structure of the magazine piece as a whole. The opening, which needs to be catchy, is always followed by a few healthy paragraphs of information of greater significance. In essence, these spell out the writer's goals – how he or she views the topic and plans to deal with it.

If you were to study well-written profiles in magazines like *Saturday Night*, *Chatelaine*, *Reader's Digest*, or *Equinox*, you would conclude that this second section, which news magazines aptly call the "billboard," provides a pillar – and one of the sturdiest in the entire article-building process. If the lead establishes the topic and theme, then this second section indicates, through a few hard details, exactly why the story is being written and why readers should bother continuing with it. A flippant "billboard" would suggest a lightweight piece; a strong, informative one denotes that the writer is about to make a serious attempt to explain his subject fully.

In my Pavarotti piece, then, the "billboard" showed why he was eminently worth profiling. Instinct tells the writer that the kind of anecdote that introduced Pavarotti now primes the reader to ask, "What exactly has consolidated his place among the best, and to what extent has he endeared himself to millions?" After the lead, the writer must inform readers, yes, but coax them deeper into the article by keeping them inquisitive.

Here, the "billboard" begins with a general statement soon to be supported by specifics:

> At six-feet-two-inches tall and an estimated 320 pounds, Luciano Pavarotti is larger than life in more ways than one. He has an irrepressible zest for food and fun and a glorious honeyed voice which *Time* once described as being "as perfectly focussed as a laser beam." Uniquely, it explores the highest reaches of the tenor range, encompassing rich, thrilling Bs, Cs, even Ds – "money notes," Pavarotti calls them – which earn him more than $40,000 a night and $1 million a year.

From then on, the "billboard" must continue its take-off with each paragraph amplifying the one that precedes it. More emphasis needs now to be placed on pertinent information and thought rather than on entertaining details. The readers have been hooked, we hope; the task now is to transport them and still keep them intrigued while, at every chance, telling them something more we think they ought to know.

To ensure that the flight is easy, we must devote special attention to the last sentence in each paragraph. It is the springboard to the next, so we must install within it a little spark of humour, or an element of surprise, or another piece of bait.

Some of this is contained in the Pavarotti story's next section – another general statement, with the specifics to support it closely on its heels:

> Hordes of faithful fans trail him across oceans, mob him at stage doors, fill his performances to capacity and send him gifts. When he sang the death-doomed artist Cavaradossi in Puccini's *La Tosca* in San Francisco in 1982, a devotee delivered a set of oil paints to his hotel room. Another lent him a Rolls-Royce Silver Cloud for his entire two-week stay, knowing that he likes . . . .

And so the piece moved on. Soon, I knew, readers would want to know where Pavarotti was born, how he grew up to love opera, and what events led to his fame. All this was built into several blocks comprising the most important part of any article – the middle section where, in all magazine pieces, the central, most integral ideas are fully developed.

In an issue story, this mid-section is called "the body," the place where the writer takes pains to background the problem in detail, always addressing the broad questions: How did this thing happen? How did it get that way? In a profile of an institution, the question is similar: How did this place become the way it is? In the profile of a person, the middle is also suitably known as the "bio section," where the writer compiles a chronology of the subject's life from birth to the present, touching on all pulse points on the way. Now the main questions to be addressed are, Where does this person come from? What makes him different or talented? How did he get where he is? In other words, How did this man called Luciano Pavarotti turn out this way?

With plenty of adventure and action, this section – "the guts of the piece," editors often call it – could be stretched to several pages. If the subject's life is unusually quiet, merely a clear, unhindered line to fortune without peaks and valleys, it should be trimmed back to make space for more intriguing material later. "All writing is good," Voltaire reminds us, "save that which bores."

The construction of the one-person human-interest story, however, should never be confused with that of the profile. Profiles are made of wrinkles and warts and the struggles, triumphs, and disappointments that engendered them. Human-interest pieces, on the other hand, are generally confined to people involved in only one specific cause: suffering, perhaps, or a successful scrap with authority. Of course, readers will still want to know a lot about the central character involved, but in a completely different way. Rather than be fed a full account of where the person was born and what kind of childhood he had, readers ask for the mid-section to contain a comprehensive overview of how his plight arose, what he did to live through it and how he finally conquered. Again, the question is similar: How did this *dilemma* get this way?

You could say that, whereas profiles are small things about big people, human-interest stories are the opposite: big things about small people – forces or events over which they have absolutely no control. It's essential to remember this because it lies at the crux of virtually *all* human-interest stories.

These kinds of pieces need to be pitched so that they immediately catch the central figure at the predicament's very pinnacle or at a moment when he or she is trying to do something about it. Thus I started a story about a man named Claude Brunet, who launched a class action suit against the union of non-professional workers at the Montreal hospital where he had been a patient for twenty-two years, by showing him steering himself up a ramp at Montreal's Palais de Justice on an electrically powered stretcher to start proceedings in Quebec's Superior Court. The opening also described him being trailed by two men in wheelchairs, among the 276 chronically ill "brothers," as he called them, on whose behalf he was seeking compensation for the "inhumanity, indignity, and suffering" each claimed he had endured during a twenty-four-hour illegal strike nearly a year before.

Having established this, it was then time to explain, in the "billboard," previous labour unrest at the hospital and its effect on patients, most of them bedridden – like forty-one-year-old Brunet, who had been a paraplegic since spinal meningitis struck him down when he was eight. Another block explained, anecdotally, Brunet's fighting spirit and how he had worked feverishly for many hours over several months to recruit patients' support. The article's mid-section dealt, in chronology, with a series of court appearances and adjournments – those highs and lows – until he won a $142,000 settlement. A closing quote from Madame Pauline Vanier sewed up the story neatly. "In the divine scheme of things," she said. "it may well be that Claude Brunet is one of the most effective people alive."

In the down-to-earth, journalistic scheme of things, the ending of a story is much more important than many writers realize. Having endured a roller-coaster ride through Pavarotti's career, or patiently rolled up and down the Palais de Justice ramp with Claude Brunet, readers don't want to be left high and dry. Subconsciously, they expect a conclusion that suits the lead – one that will take them a little by surprise, perhaps, but which nonetheless seems absolutely right.

If Pavarotti is introduced to them on a "high," it would be anticlimactic for him to bow out on a "low." (He didn't. A critic said that his was "a voice kissed by God," which made a good title for the article, too.) Since Claude Brunet is first seen embarking on a court fight, purportedly for the good of his fellows, readers expect him to win. If he doesn't, they want to be fed some redeeming factors instead – optimism, or good stemming from bad – which will linger long after they've put the magazine down. We don't want to know that mankind has no saving graces, do we?

The Brunet piece had a natural, victorious, built-in ending, and there are other stories like it – the cops who get their man, for example, and revel in the results of their efforts when they see him sentenced to prison. Other stories may well have obvious conclusions, too, but these may need explaining and bolstering. Suffice it to say that many writers, again including myself, put almost as much effort into a story's ending as they do its lead. So much so, that they often write it first.

What happens when a topic contains two main forces: all the makings of a good profile made infinitely better for having a strong human-interest ingredient? How is *that* built and focused?

A good example, and one carrying a structure that may be applied to several different kinds of pieces, is my article about a woman named Alice Winant, who channelled shocking suffering in Auschwitz into a career as a successful sculptor. Since her concentration camp experiences were integral to the piece, they needed to be built into the lead. The most effective introduction, I knew, would be a scene-setting capsule that actually showed how art transformed her terrible anguish into profound optimism for her future. I found it, I think:

> On a bleak winter's day in 1946, doctors at Stockholm's St. Görans Hospital ordered 17-year-old Alice Winant encased in plaster from her toes to her armpits. A year before, as Auschwitz prisoner A11,685, she'd been brutally flogged by a guard who then kicked her repeatedly in the face, stomach, and back, leaving her for dead.
>
> Now Alice suffered from TB of the bones, which would keep her in the cast for two years. *Yes, I'm alive*, she told herself repeatedly, lying helplessly on her back with only her arms and head free, *but at what cost?* By the following summer, and still not knowing if her recovery would ever be complete, she was grateful for life, vowing to start it all over again by putting Auschwitz's horrors behind her.
>
> "Is there anything we can get you?" a nurse asked her. The sun streamed in through the window and Alice was smiling against her pain. "Yes," she replied, "some art books."
>
> The nurse got these from the hospital library. Then, recognizing Alice's need for occupational therapy, persuaded her sculptor friend, Carl Helbig, to visit her. In only days, in fact, Helbig was at Alice's bedside clutching a shoe box containing a kilo and a half of wet clay. "This is for you," he announced.
>
> "Me?" Alice asked, puzzled. "What do I do with it?"
>
> "Make me something," Helbig told her, "to celebrate your joy for life."

Predictably, the reader now asks, "Did she? If so, what? And how important was it, anyway?" The piece continues:

> From Auschwitz's shocking remnants, something good was about to emerge. No sooner had the nurse put the clay into a bowl on Alice's chest than she began moulding a little foot – "probably symbolic of my yearning for freedom," she says. Then she made other limbs, "as if she wanted to speed the protracted process of her own ravaged body," one critic later observed.
>
> Soon, she was shaping the clay into candlesticks, ashtrays, and buttons. Helbig glazed and fired them in his oven so Alice could sell what she'd made to patients, visitors and staff. When she finally left the hospital in May 1948, she went into business as a self-taught artisan, selling handcrafted jewellery and ceramic sculptures.

Now begins the "billboard" section, the reason for the piece:

> Today, Alice Winant is a serene, soft-spoken woman of 57, with large brown eyes, a shining smile, and a mass of raven hair – "a stunning artist," observes *The Christian Science Monitor*, "who strikingly resembles Elizabeth Taylor." Thanks to Helbig's encouragement and her own tenacity, she has transmuted her Auschwitz experiences. Once threatening to destroy her, they now fuel creative powers so great that Alice enjoys a busy career as an internationally revered sculptor.

In the reader's mind, this last general statement needs substantiating, to be fleshed out – not by me, the author, but by art experts. And if her career *is* international, it must be apparent in assessments from across oceans. Here they come:

> "Your works breathe tenderness, joy, affection, and enormous pride," Dr. Cécile Goldscheider, curator of Paris' Musée Rodin once told Alice. "After all you've been through, it's a miracle you can still see the world through such optimistic eyes."
>
> Indeed, critics and art experts from London to Rome and Madrid to San Francisco have hailed her prodigious output of 3,000 sculptures for mirroring gratitude for survival instead of anguishing over physical and mental suffering. Her family of characters shows what she calls "a spirit of unconquerable, unrelenting love."

Okay, fine, the reader now says, but what does this family of characters look like and how do they depict Winant's spirit? Here they come, too:

> Wide-eyed, good-looking children tug at mothers' skirts. Jaunty fathers embrace saucy sons. When portraying teenagers, Alice engages them totally in worthwhile pursuits – playing happily, sharing secrets, and nearly always holding hands. One of her latest works is a two-metre bronze statue – which sold for $24,000 – of a teenage boy practicing his violin.
>
> "Alice Winant creates the children she never had but always wanted," declares art historian Dr. Max Stern, director of Montreal's Dominion Gallery, "and makes them revel in her

> own love for humanity." Israel's *Nachrichter* says that Alice's sculptures express her courage and "unwavering belief in the dominance of good over evil and how love must *always* triumph over hate."

After more blocks of anecdotal information about who owns Alice Winant's sculptures and how her husband encouraged her, the reader is ready – in the mid-section – to know when and where she was born, what kind of parents she had, who they were, and how and when the entire family was taken to Auschwitz. Her concentration camp experiences have been told in several blocks in the story's middle, culminating with her release and her being admitted to that Stockholm hospital.

What happened there has been explained in the opening paragraphs, so this part of the story can be simply touched upon lightly, then left. Now, though, the reader demands to be told about the events that caused Winant's career to take flight. So in more anecdotes, I explained how, with the continued encouragement of her husband and friends, she saw her work accepted by a top gallery:

> Overnight she was thrust into world-class company. One of her little statues was flanked in the gallery window by those of Auguste Rodin and Britain's Henry Moore. "Alice is between two good men," Moore quipped with a wink. "No, no, no!" retorted the noble Italian painter-sculptor Marino Marini. "She appears among *three*. The picture behind her is mine!"
>
> From the early 1970s, Alice Winant never looked back. Winnipeg's John A. Macauley, a noted art collector and member of the National Gallery's buying committee, acquired two of her smaller sculptures when they were $300 each. Those same pieces would later fetch $3,000. A Japanese art dealer. . . .

This story, nearly five thousand words long, addressed yet another question that applies to profiles: How does this person *stay* that way? It ended with tributes to Alice Winant's indomitable spirit and how it has enabled her to resist letting her sculptures speak of such a distressing past.

Dramatic stories are another matter. They need to be built completely differently, usually so they immediately hook the reader with a powerful incident, a turning point, or a natural climax in the drama. That's definitely not to say you could begin with the outcome, as a newspaper would, because this would divulge the ending and give the writing absolutely nowhere to go. The reader must always anticipate *something*, after all. As Charles Reade says in his *Recipe for a Successful Novel*, "Make 'em laugh; make 'em cry; make 'em wait."

No one's likely to laugh while reading a properly told story of a dramatic rescue, though the opportunity for ironic humor should never be lost. The job here is to simply tell a strong story with the best possible narrative, always peppering it with what the victims thought and felt as they contemplated their escape or rescue.

Sometimes the logical introduction to a drama is at its beginning, with the events leading up to it fed in later. I did this in my story of a plane crash:

> Their ordeal was over. Or so they thought. And pilot Gerald Kruschenske sighed with relief, mopped his brow and muttered: "Thank God." For 33 hair-raising minutes he'd gripped the steering column of his twin-propeller flying ambulance, trying frantically to land it against fast-diminishing odds – failing engines, and a blinding blizzard. While searching urgently for a landing spot, a doctor and nurse were tending a young woman dying of encephalitis.
>
> Now, on that bleak afternoon of March 28, 1979, he'd skillfully and miraculously belly-flopped the aircraft, a little Piper Aztec, onto frozen Devil's Gap, separating Treaty Island from the mainland near Kenora, Ont. All on board escaped injury, but no sooner had the aircraft come to a sickening, skidding halt in a shower of snow and slush, than another drama was unfolding.
>
> "We've landed on the ice, okay," Kruschenske, a muscular six-footer of 30 radioed in a taut voice. "But we're sinking!" The seconds were ticking away.

They were, indeed. The plane sank, the patient drowned, and the three survivors swam to shore. Close to death from exposure, they were picked up nearly an hour later by a helicopter, thanks to the pilot's cry for help only seconds before his radio gave out.

Real-life detective stories usually work best when they're begun at the beginning. This gives the writer an ample time span in which to develop the very thing that holds these pieces together – plot.

There would be nothing wrong, for example, if you chose to show a bank being robbed, then worked through a straight, chronological account of all the police work entailed in bringing the culprits to justice. Agatha Christie did this all the time. The victim was mysteriously found dead in the library and from then on, the author had both suspects and policemen bobbing in and out of her story until the case was ingeniously solved. Agatha Christie wrote fiction, of course, but if ever you tackle a real-life detective piece, you'll often find yourself employing a novelist's techniques: exploiting the action, developing important characters, making sure they say interesting, pertinent things, and weaving them in and out of a strong narrative as mouthpieces or "spokespeople" in the sub-plots.

Yes, techniques for building non-fiction are often closely related to those used in fiction. Some of the world's best novels, after all, are based almost entirely on fact, with the names of real-life characters changed to hide identities, and sub-plots of romance and conflict introduced to make the story fuller. Some factual stories I've written – the two women RCMP officers who posed as drug couriers, for instance – contained so much daring, by so many interesting people in action set in numerous intriguing places, that they could easily have become novels or movies with a minimum of embellishment.

Personal stories can be built with a lot of flexibility. The thing to remember here is that you must establish yourself early so that readers will know instantly that this is you speaking directly to them, that it's *your* story. That being the case, you must appear frequently thereafter. You become the spine of the piece, the theme, the reason for its being. If you suddenly disappear, readers will ask where you've gone. They'll start speculating on the reasons and, in so doing, lose interest.

The second and most crucial point to keep in mind is that the subject must lend itself to first-person treatment in the first place. It must be a story which would not work without you in it. Don't try to handle an issue story this way, just one in which you truly are the legitimate central figure with something special to say and share.

Whatever story you may be building, after you've sorted your research into piles, drawn a diagram, or made notes of the high points around which you will plan it, you'll at last begin to write. These words will not be your best, however. They'll merely suffice as you create strong blocks in the long construction process.

Since your primary concerns are, for the moment, mechanical

rather than literary, typographical errors, sloppy grammar, and poor spelling should also be of lesser concern. You are now making your start: positioning the bulk of your material as you aim for a creative use of anecdotes, quotes, and hard facts.

To do it, you will move blocks of writing literally from one page to another with such respectable writers' tools as a stapler, scissors, and glue – work made infinitely more simple by the word processor – fixing them where you think they belong in this very rough draft. Like all writers, you'll change your mind a dozen times, and as you do, your draft will resemble a map of the world rather than something you'd want anyone to see. Don't worry. Remember that while building, a dirty manuscript containing notes to yourself in the margins, crossings-out and arrows pointing to new directions, denotes the honest, hard work writing has always been.

Inevitably, you'll decide to pluck a strong anecdote from the body of the story, where you may already have sufficient bright material anyway, and use it to strengthen the opening. Slightly re-angled, you'll decide, a case history you thought at first would usefully illustrate the predicament in the lead of an issue piece might more aptly document the solutions at the end.

Statistics will worry you, too: How to use them in context to make the point for which they were originally compiled, without letting them litter the text and turn your story into dry, dull reading. Statistics usually stand up on their own, though they sometimes need to be interpreted. Through all this, you must produce the very thing that will give your audience a smooth ride – a strong, intelligent narrative running in a logical, uncluttered line.

10. Building the Book

The work / the chapter as an entity / the diagram / staying on track / suggested construction techniques / "clothes-line" system / the writer and the word processor

"I have not made my book any more than my book has made me."
MICHEL EYQUEM DE MONTAIGNE
(1533-1592)

Make no mistake about it, writing a book is a mixture of pain and pleasure. It can have you wondering whether all the effort is going to be worth it at one moment, then, at the next, enthusiastically visualizing the publisher eagerly awaiting your sweat-stained masterpiece.

Purely in terms of volume, a non-fiction book like this one of 80,000 words, equals one polished 2,500-word article assigned by a magazine with high standards – roughly thirty-two times. I say roughly because any book of this length is certainly not thirty-two articles. That's far too simple. It is more akin to a topic much too big for a magazine article to handle adequately and really *needing* 80,000 words to explain it properly. The work is then divided into as many sections – or chapters – the writer feels is necessary to make it appetizing and give readers plenty of breathing space.

Not even chapters can be compared to articles. The chapter is really only part of a much larger story, whereas the article is a story unto itself. If there *is* common ground, however, it is this: Just as articles need a theme, a core, or a spine to pull the material within them together, so do chapters. The difference is that in chapters, these elements must always represent part of the overall theme, core, or spine of the text, and contribute something totally individualistic in the process.

Nor can the work involved in writing an 80,000-word book be remotely equated with that needed to produce thirty-two 2,500-word articles. Although the proposal and research techniques are akin, the overall effort is apportioned much differently. Thirty-two articles means as many separate research projects on as many different subjects, while a book generally entails one concerted effort in one direction. This might be construed as time-saving, because facts gathered to support chapter three, say, could also contain material that will fit into chapters seven or nine. Researching the opening might also unearth material for the ending, and so on. But any time saved here will more often than not be spent on actually putting the book together. It is laborious work, indeed.

If constructing a magazine article is putting up a house, building a book is certainly more like erecting a skyscraper. And if a house needs a detailed plan, the skyscraper requires a blueprint unequivocally calling for bigger, heavier blocks, cast-iron rivets instead of nails, girders not beams – and heavy-duty concrete in place of mortar to hold the building perpendicular on a solid foundation. By that definition, if the Leaning Tower of Pisa were a book about oranges, its author would conclude it with a chapter on tangerines.

The longer you write, you'll discover, the greater are the chances of veering off track. This is why many writers, yet again including myself, invariably develop later chapters first, then write toward them to achieve organizational unity. In fact, we often produce key chapters well out of sequence – a sort of ping-pong effect – bridging them to their neighbors later. Above all else, writers want to ensure that 80,000 laborious words after first setting out, they have always argued the same points and have made their characters consistent.

A well-built book with strong bridges and a natural, logical sequence, prevents writers from exposing their ineptitude by resorting to phrases like, "Let's back-track for the moment," or "As I mentioned earlier." If properly thought out at the blueprint stage, the book should impart a lot of information clearly and brightly with each block of information holding readers' interest, and chapter after chapter taking them further and further into the heart of the subject.

Here again, magazine-writing techniques prove invaluable to non-fiction book authors, even some novelists. But while the magazine piece is expected to handle only a couple of sub-plots at most, a book rich in information and ideas – a complex biography, maybe, or an action-packed adventure, can have many. All must be put into the diagram so they won't be forgotten and can be slotted into their proper places in the manuscript. Also, while the magazine article generally has space enough for only a handful of characters, a book can be stretched to accommodate many.

Obviously then, biographies or adventures are considerably harder to construct than, say, gardening books or hobby guides, which are not so much concerned with plots, themes, and people as with giving readers help or advice in an attractive way. Usually, subjects for how-to books have "departments," each of which can be made to serve as an independent chapter. But biographers aren't nearly so lucky. Nor are adventure writers. Apart from having to carve characters and build action, they must work incessantly hard to find ways of breaking their story into chapters. They must also put equal effort into devising workable openings and closings for their books.

After a lot of forethought, you might decide that the best way to tell your story is by starting at the beginning and, providing the subject contains enough events, working through it in an uninterrupted passage save, perhaps, for a couple of flash-backs. On the other hand, the topic may be so complex it requires a general opening chapter on what the book is about, with others following in a logical sequence. By logical, I mean that like the two- or three-paragraph blocks in a magazine piece, each chapter must serve to make the next better understood.

Ideally, your sense for the dramatic will tell you that each chapter needs to end in a way that will make readers want to go on to the next. Again, this is all too simple, too. The variables and possibilities available to book authors are boundless, and there are no hard and fast rules they can follow that will guarantee success. All they can hope to do is produce manuscripts so well built that they cover the topic fully – much more comprehensively than a magazine piece – and leave no questions unanswered or loose ends untied.

If there's a lesson in how to *not* construct a book, it comes from the woman who phoned saying, "I have seen the devil, sir."

"You what?" I said, a little taken aback.

"I have seen the devil, sir. With my own eyes. And I've written about it."

"Marvellous idea," I said. "You may have a best-seller. Lots of people would like to know what that sunovagun looks like. I know quite a few in the publishing business who'll get to meet him one day!"

"Well, sir," the woman went on. "I saw him, I swear to God, *twice*! He came to the front door when I was ironing. I nearly died! Please will you read about my story for me and let me know what you think?"

One of the silliest things I've ever done was to agree, and the following day, the woman poked a 400-page manuscript at me as if it were hot, and said, "There, sir. I typed it with my own fingers."

I began leafing through the text with interest. The first four chapters comprised an exquisitely written exposé on sorcery, which I immediately suspected had been written by a theologian and not by the woman herself. Chapter five was about witchcraft, also the work of someone else, I surmised. The opening words of chapter six, however, will always remain indelible. "Now," they began, "I come to the point you have all been waiting for. One day while I was sitting . . . ."

When I speak of exerting a slow pull to open a piece of writing, I certainly don't mean one spanning five chapters! You can't put the reason for your book that far down. Applying basic non-fiction rules – and despite the bizarre nature of the topic this really purported to be a non-fiction book – the woman should have opened the door to the devil in her first or second chapter, at least. Then she ought to have spent some time backgrounding the events leading up to it. By about chapter four, she should have invited the devil in, and devoted the rest of her narrative to what happened during both that first visit and the subsequent one. Throughout all this, the reader would expect an enormous amount of description, conversation, and a lot of personal impressions and feelings – all embraced in high peaks and deep valleys serving to make the story revealing, chilling, and tense.

"Why waste time," you might ask, "assessing a book based on what would seem on the surface to be nothing but an aberration?" The question would indeed be valid, except that in writing, we can't afford to dismiss ideas so quickly. If, for instance, we start challenging credibility gaps in literature, Alice would never have run down the rabbit hole to her Wonderland and the big, white pig wouldn't have called that meeting in the barn in George Orwell's *Animal Farm*. Admittedly, these books are fiction and the woman's wasn't. But it alters nothing. An aberration explained well and made interesting, if not totally plausible, can provide an excellent subject for a non-fiction personal story. Huge sections of *The Bible*, the best-selling non-fiction book of all time, remember, were *founded* on aberrations.

So the unlikelihood of anyone meeting the devil is irrelevant. So is the woman's later confession that she had in fact "borrowed" the first part of her work from two other authors. The simple point remains that what she showed me was improperly built. (There were many other things wrong with it, too: loose, bland writing, trite description, a lack of tension, poor character development, few original thoughts, no fear and, believe it or not, no conversations with the devil himself!) Accordingly, it stood no chance whatsoever of being published until she had considerably reworked it.

"That's what *you* think," the woman said.

"That's what I *think*," I replied carefully.

"Then I'll get another, better opinion. I put a lot of effort into all this!"

She had, indeed. But it was all in the wrong direction. I got the impression that on those chapters she could genuinely claim as her own, she had laboured without a plan. She had typed them out in an orgy of enthusiasm hoping they would turn out well. Had she come to me first, I would have helped her draw a diagram of how I thought the book should have been constructed.

Your diagram needs to be as full as you can make it, touching upon all the pulse points in your topic and showing how you have rationed them out so readers will always find something to latch on to, chapter by chapter. If your subject doesn't have a sufficient number of pulse points, at least one per chapter, then you might discover the hard way that you're trying to build a book out of what merits only a magazine article. Not only should your sub-plots each be slotted into the diagram, but also the names of those people and locations that will be part of them.

On standing back and examining this diagram, as you will on numerous occasions as you work, it should be instantly apparent if the book is likely to be top heavy or if the reader will be constantly asking what the theme is. By now you will also have begun sorting your research into piles. There will be lots of these, with innumerable lists of points you want to include, plus notes reminding you of where information has overlapped and suggesting those spots into which you might want to fit it.

I usually start a book by typing out complete blocks of information, some several pages long, others of lesser importance consisting only of a few paragraphs. I then label each with the number of the chapter into which I initially think it belongs. About half of this material ends up where I originally intended it to go. The other half is used to bolster sections elsewhere.

Some pieces of research to which I can't immediately assign a spot are slipped into one of the two files always at my side. One marked "oddments" contains material I *may* need later. The other, which I call "inserts," will accumulate all manner of notes, some as long as ten pages, others as brief as one single word, that I *will* use when I find the correct place. Tucked into the manuscript after it has been better formed, each will help put an important aspect into better focus, brighten the odd paragraph, or strengthen an entire scene. The important point here is that I throw absolutely nothing away until the job has been done, and neither should you.

As this work continues over several weeks, I find that my notes soon form a pile thicker than I expect the finished manuscript to be. That's fine. I then know that I've more than likely done my research reasonably well. As I write, however, literary finesse is still unimportant to me, though I make a special effort to get such fine details as names, distances, and statistics correct, to save having to check them later when they will be hard to locate without reading through the entire manuscript.

Do this preliminary work well, and you'll be ready to start using those hefty blocks of notes to form actual chapters. From then on, as you feed in the sub-plots, scenes, and characters contained in other blocks, your book will grow more quickly than you ever thought it would. This, in turn, will give you a psychological lift, and the impetus to keep moving forward. You'll think of new elements to add, and a more precise concept of the book's final construction will form inside you.

For me, this is the most exciting part of book writing. Soon, however, I resort to a technique I've developed over the years to help me refine the organization I've done so far. I call this my "clothes-line" system. Developing chapters are strung together with Scotch tape and left dangling side by side like washing from a piece of cord which stretches from one side of my office to the other. At a quick glance I can see how the work is *really* shaping. If I find I have two "dryish" or heavily statistical chapters back to back, for instance, I'll immediately want to separate them with one that includes people and movement. If the book is top heavy, I'll spot that from the "clothes-line," too, and correct it.

The greatest value of this method is that it encourages me to apportion my writing time more resourcefully – according to my mood. On some days I might feel like re-organizing a chapter that is particularly complex, statistical, even technical; on others, I may feel the urge to tackle more lyrical, romantic, or descriptive passages. Before each bout of writing, I simply sit back, survey my "washing" and ask myself, "What best fits my mood?" I've been known to spend many a day flitting among odd spots throughout the entire book, administering a "general clean-up." There have also been days when I've concentrated solely on only a few paragraphs in a difficult section.

As chapters grow, I work on dove-tailing the blocks within them. I then lay each on the floor so I can examine it more closely – on my hands and knees. Friends smile. On occasion, when seeing my work strewn from the kitchen to the front door, they've been known to ask if I'm being paid by the word or by the yard! Indeed, to anyone who has never written, all this might seem strange, if not downright idiosyncratic. It may well be, but it's nonetheless an effective way of ascertaining whether my organization still adheres to my diagram and that the theme and sub-plots are still intact. It is *my* way of doing it – a system, admittedly eccentric, which works well for *me*.

More than anything, it provides me with something else I feel authors should develop: a *visual* concept of writing. I like to know that what I've so far written bulges where it should and doesn't bulge where it should not. That is to say, I want to *see* that the high points really are just that – nicely expanded and detailed, and that sections of lesser importance or interest in between are pruned as far back as possible. I also hope to know from this that all my characters have good entrances and exits and have been given relevant, incisive dialogue.

Once again, the stapler, scissors, and paste pot re-emerge as I begin moving entire blocks of information, and sometimes only paragraphs or sentences, either within chapters or from one to another. It's all trial and error because, later, I've been known to shift it all back to where it originally started out. When my chapters are episodes in a long story, as opposed to being separate topics in a how-to book, I seek to ensure that they have spring-board endings that will propel readers forward. It is seemingly endless work, but properly administered it proves invaluable later when I turn my attention more fully to what I have been doing all along – setting down those words I want to see in print. Or some of them.

When writing books, of course, the word processor is invaluable.

One of its shortcomings, though, is that it conceals virtually all of a long text, allowing only a few paragraphs to be visible on the screen at one given time. And for many years, this is precisely what kept me from investing in one. Not being able to see a large piece of writing in its entirety when I wanted to seemed to be a serious flaw. Thus virtually all my work – including this book – has been done with two fingers on a manual typewriter, then has been sent to secretaries for clean-typing on an electric typewriter. More recently, as one of them fed my articles and books into her word processor, I began to see the values of this remarkable invention.

The word processor removes the drudgery from retyping and makes cutting and replacing all those blocks of information considerably easier. I mention this in the context of building books because I believe this is where the word processor's real virtues lies. Entire sections of text can be switched from one chapter – or file – to another in a matter of seconds with just a few strokes of a few keys. By pressing a couple of others, I discovered by watching various manuscript typists, it's also possible to correct the names of people or places mentioned throughout an entire text.

I eventually became so convinced that the word processor was indispensable to the professional, long-distance writer, that I finally bought one of my own, though far too late to have any profound effect on the work I'm doing here. I have used it enough on letters and story proposals, however, to be able to attest more avidly than ever to its worth. Contrary to common belief, it does not stifle creativity. I don't let it. I attack its keyboard as I have always attacked keyboards – with reckless abandon, and with the same two fingers. And to check for shape in all future books, I will simply string the printouts from my "clothes-line."

With practice, I'll soon be able to correct spelling and typographical errors simply by inserting a diskette "speller" and scrolling the text. As time goes on, I will find a diskette thesaurus useful, too.

When I'm finally satisfied that the direction of my book is clear and that it has been properly tailored, either in the belly of a computer or on paper hung up as "washing" or laid on the carpet, I will turn my attention to refining the absolute essence of all good written expression – prose.

11. Attractive Words on Paper

Clarity / simplicity / avoiding clutter, long words, and jargon / familiar word combinations / elements of style / the sentence / the paragraph / first-person writing

"We like that a sentence should read as if its author, had he held a plough instead of a pen, could have drawn a furrow deep and straight to the end."

HENRY DAVID THOREAU

Broadly speaking, non-fiction is a craft calling for thought, imagination, and precision. One corner of it, however, is very definitely an art – writing. Your ideas and direction, of course, are already clear, and thanks to that early work – the story proposal, outline, or diagram – you will have been spared a lot more work. The points you want to make stand firmly in ABC order: A makes B understandable, B makes C understandable, and so on. Now you'll be using syntax, grammar, punctuation, and words as effectively as you can to put it all down, to tell the reader what you know, think, or have found out.

It goes without saying that this needs to be done in the most attractive way possible. Language should be crisp and imaginative. At times it can be clever and colourful. Always, though, it must be intelligent and clear. Anecdotes help us show our readers what we want; statistics enable us to document it or give it force. But unless the writer can develop the skill for setting it out so that it's understandable and enjoyable, the world's most well-meaning research will prove useless.

According to Jonathan Swift, to whom prose came with such uncanny ease, writing was not a complicated matter. In 1720, while Dean of St. Patrick's Cathedral, Dublin, he told a junior clergyman that it was simply "putting proper words in proper places." Nothing, I can assure you, has altered since. The principles of good writing – or composition – remain much the same. Words used ineptly pile up on the page and stand between the reader and what is being conveyed. The ultimate aim is to use them so adroitly that ideas, information, emotions, thoughts, and feelings are transmitted without loss of intensity or clarity.

Probably no art, however, is more underestimated – as we are so poignantly reminded in *Alice's Adventures in Wonderland*:

> "Do you mean that you think you can find out the answer to it?" said the March Hare.
>
> "Exactly so," said Alice.
>
> "Then you should say what you mean," the March Hare went on.
>
> "I do," Alice hastily replied, "at least – at least I mean what I say – that's the same thing you know."
>
> "Not the same thing a bit!" said the Hatter. "Why, you might just as well say that 'I see what I eat' is the same thing as 'I eat what I see'!"

It's excellent logic indeed. And even if it *is* a little hard to follow on the first reading, it serves to illustrate the essential difficulty in all writing, one that plagues most people, let alone many writers. That is, selecting words to communicate effortlessly with precision and simplicity. "A word is not a crystal, transparent and unchanging," said Oliver Wendell Holmes, "it is the skin of a living thought and may vary in color and content according to the circumstances and time it is used." This is all the more reason, then, why the power and texture of every single one of them needs to be weighed as fastidiously as the professional musician considers the significance and value of every note, however long or short.

None of this is intended to imply that writing is so excruciatingly difficult it is beyond your reach. Writing well isn't easy – but it can be easier than you think. First, you must really *want* to write well. Second, you must acknowledge that being able to assign proper words to proper places depends entirely on how well you grasp a slew of fundamental points covering a multitude of common problems. I'm not sure that all these can be taught. (No book or professor has ever laid claim to transforming a foggy writer singlehandedly into a brilliant, graceful wordsmith.) I know with much more certainty that, through zealous practice, many of the rules of good writing *can* be learned.

If you think, however, you must string together big, fancy words and high-flying phrases to make your writing interesting, you're definitely wrong. Unless you aspire to be a professional poet or novelist, you need only put across what you want to say simply and clearly – ideally in the *shortest* number of proper words that most people will best understand. Composing good prose sentence by sentence and paragraph by paragraph is a tremendous challenge in itself. If writing is to fly along swiftly and uninterrupted, it must be spared the engine problems and excess baggage that big, cumbersome words and high-flown expressions create.

Take a tip from Shakespeare. He used almost childlike words to relate ideas so profound that they swept around the globe never to be forgotten. On the brink of desperation as he seeks to revenge his father's murder, for instance, poor Hamlet doesn't ask himself, "Should I act upon the urgings that I feel within me and thus cease to exist, to become extinct, to expire?" Thank God he doesn't. That kind of language is far too flowery and dull to have any dramatic impact whatsoever. What Shakespeare does make his hero say as he stands at the edge of a cliff contemplating suicide, is a powerful, six-word sentence any average high school student could have composed – "To be, or not to be."

Admittedly, not all of Shakespeare's writings are that easily understood because he lived in a different time and culture. The fact remains, though, that his plays and sonnets are littered with phrases that continue to have enormous impact long after his death because they muster power through utter simplicity.

George Orwell is one of numerous twentieth-century writers who have been similarly admired for clarity. "The great enemy of clear language," he said in his famous essay, *Politics and the English Language*, "is insincerity. When there is a gap between one's real self and one's declared aims, one turns as it were to long words and exhausted idioms like a cuttlefish squirting out ink." He was then quick to show us what he meant in the crystal-clear opening to his novel *Animal Farm*:

> Mr. Jones, of the Manor Farm, had locked the hen-houses for the night, but was too drunk to remember to shut the pop-holes.

> With the ring of light from his lantern dancing from side to side, he lurched across the yard, kicking off his boots at the back door, drew himself a glass of beer from the barrel in the scullery, and made his way up to bed, where Mrs. Jones was already snoring.

Linguistic economy is not only reputable, but sacred. "In the beginning God created the heaven and the earth," *The Bible* tells us at its opening. Is there a better, more direct lead? While a cub reporter on the *Sheerness Times-Guardian* in my grandmother's home town, I reported a court scene in which a woman "threw herself to the floor sobbing uncontrollably" when her son was imprisoned for breaking into a bicycle shop. With excellent reason, the editor wanted to see me.

"Did Jesus throw himself all over the place bawling his eyes out?" he asked. "Of course he didn't. Don't you know the two most powerful words in all the Scriptures? One simple sentence – 'Jesus wept.' Remember it!"

I always have. All it really takes to put a lump in readers' throats or break their hearts, is two familiar words – proper ones, in proper places.

Part of the lesson here is that if, while writing, some lovely, inspired, or dramatic phrases come to you, by all means include them. But then, with cold, objective eyes you must ask yourself, Do they confuse? Do they detract from clarity? Do they relate to a point in the story? Or are they merely decorations? If they are any of these, pare them away immediately without giving them a second thought. You must then proceed confidently, full steam ahead on the main line, with more pressing matters – telling your story so it is meaningful to a lot of readers.

Remember as you go, though, that whatever you write, be it a biography, issue piece, or travelogue, you must always start where those readers are. Long before writing you should already have wondered just how much they know about the topic. Chances are that other than what they've heard on radio or read in their newspapers, they may not be familiar with it at all, so they'll need plenty of explanatory detail.

Don't forget, either, that the quickest way to bore and lose readers is by writing above their heads. And if you follow that old – and wrong – advice about catering to the mentality of a fourteen-year-old, you will surely insult them, which is worse. Your prime purpose is to *explain* something, not try to convince readers you're more intelligent than they are.

Obvious barriers to communication, and there are dozens of them, must always be avoided. One of these is jargon – phrases and expressions known only to people with specific knowledge or interests. Using these is a common fault among writers attempting the transition from trade and technical journals to consumer magazines. First, jargon impedes communication. Second, it removes the human quality from writing, adds unwanted words, and makes for a style that is turgid and hard to read. Example: A scientist using tedious scientific jargon wrote, "The biota exhibited a one hundred percent mortality response." He could, of course, have written, "All the fish died."

Inflated words don't really impress anyone – least of all, readers. In Ottawa, a highly-paid civil servant relying on government jargon, or "governmentalese," produced a costly study on "High Speed Vertical Transportation Units." Believe it or not, he was really talking about elevators. This makes us wonder if Julius Caesar's wonderful line would have survived so long had he said, "I arrived, I surveyed the situation, and proceeded to attain the maximum strategic advantage." What Caesar said, in fact, in a letter to Amantius in 47 B.C. announcing his victory on Pontus, was "*Veni, Vidi, Vici*" – "I came, I saw, I conquered."

Bureaucratic jargon, used mostly by governments and industry, has three overriding characteristics. One is the tendency to use euphemisms to avoid saying what may otherwise sound unpleasant – "inner city" for "slums," or "urban renewal" for "slum clearance," or "correctional institution" for "prison." Suddenly, our slow-learning children have become "underachievers," and our garbage collectors are "waste-disposal personnel." (When I was in the British army they were "sanitary technicians.") No one ever seems to die these days; they "pass away." They rarely have accidents, only "mishaps," and no longer buy anything but "purchase" it. And what's wrong with finding something instead of "locating" it?

The second main feature of "governmentalese" is the awkward piling up of nouns used as adjectives. When the United States government first considered gasoline rationing, a bill aimed at effecting it referred rather clumsily to "end-use allocation." Hardly anyone could figure out how this would work.

Nouns in government circles also are distorted to become verbs – "optimize," "maximize," "prioritize," "privatize," "concretize," "potentialize," "hospitalize," "concertize." There are dozens more which have invaded our language with so much regularity and force that they no longer confuse so much as appear stodgy and ugly.

This can't, however, be said of a public notice issued by the United States Environmental Protection Agency (a mouthful in itself), which spoke of the "Ocean Disposal Permit Program." What? The Americans are about to dispose of our oceans? How dare they! What the program seeks, of course, are ways of preventing the wanton disposal of chemicals and sewage into oceans. Naturally, if this continues long enough it may indeed dispose of oceans, but that's another matter for another book or magazine piece.

How governments choose to communicate among themselves and address their workers is entirely up to them. It's a free country, after all. Sadly, though, a lot of their growing arsenal of horrible jargon is demolishing every-day communications between ordinary people. An honourable defence is that *we* make a language to suit our needs; a language does not by any stretch of the imagination make *us*. But it falls to writers seeking to produce high-quality work to respect words and use them as precisely as they can.

Thus I can't help but shudder when American television reporters – people who should know better – tell us that the United States government has "mandated" a decision, or that a Senate plan has been "mothballed." On airplanes I chuckle as the flight attendant announces that passengers are to "extinguish all smoking materials." I know she's telling us we mustn't smoke, but why can't she say so? Just the same, I look around me to see what "smoking materials" really are or could be. One day, perhaps, I'll see an unfortunate pipe smoker smouldering from a hole he's burned in his jacket pocket, then I'll know.

Barriers always arise when writers set out to impress readers rather than inform them. Specialized fields are literally jam-packed with communicators who have a compulsion to deliver complex sentences, thinking these will make them sound more credible. The subconscious feeling passed on to readers is that the writer hasn't cared enough to express himself in a warmer, more attractive way.

Try telling that to a Vancouver sociologist. In a paper he handed out at a conference he said, "One of the primary reasons for marital disharmony is, without doubt, economic." Why didn't he say this so people would understand it without having to work it out? Surely, with consideration for us all and a bit of extra effort, he could have written, "Many husbands and wives fight over money," a perfectly acceptable sentence with its feet firmly on the ground.

The overuse of clichés is another sin. The noun *cliché*, now well entrenched in the English language, is derived from the French verb *clicher*, meaning to make a printer's stereotype. That is, to produce a plate from a matrix or mould taken from set type. So *cliché* connotes something solid and unbendable; as a linguistic device it has no place whatsoever in good writing.

The problem with clichés is that they've appeared in text so many times that they no longer give it flavour. Once ingenious – hence their overuse – they deaden writing. They make it senile, if you like, detracting once again from personal style. Most tend to be wordy, anyway. "Each and every one" makes any self-respecting writer wince. It's a redundant cliché using far too many words in a hackneyed way to say something extremely simple – "each."

Here are more to avoid: "In the nick of time," "bits and pieces," "you and you alone," "part and parcel," "betwixt and between," "kith and kin," "lo and behold," "leaps and bounds."

Use *any* of them and I promise that the editor of a good magazine will immediately sense your poor style results directly from laziness – saying the first, most obvious thing that enters your head without searching out something better. We are confronted with hackneyed words and phrases every day of our lives, in newspapers and on radio and television. But as writers, we must recognize them, make a note of them, laugh at them – but leave them alone.

Another common writing fault is the unwitting garnishing of prose so that it becomes windy or cluttered, again to sound impressive. Too many journalists prefer "at the present time" or "at this point in time" or "currently" or "at the moment" – all instead of choosing the simple, shortest word available: "now." Sometimes, they substitute "now" for "presently," which is grammatically incorrect. "Presently" means soon.

Other windy phrases include "in the event that" (if), "in the majority of instances" (usually or mostly), "with the possible exception of" (except), "in back of" (behind), "until such time as" (until), "she totally lacked the ability to" (she couldn't), "in a position to" (can), "in view of the fact that" (because or since), "despite the fact that" (although), "by the same token" (similarly).

Just imagine the cumbersome effect when clutter and clichés are put to work side by side:

> By a majority of 35 to five, City Council last night voted to give the green light to find a solution for one of the biggest political hot potatoes in recent times and one that is, at the present time, taking the public by storm. It will be allocating $5 million to the erection of new traffic lights where there are presently none because the intersections are too recent.

God forbid that you or I should ever write a paragraph like that! Yet you'll spot an almost identical one from time to time in every second-rate newspaper in the country. I much prefer the following because it makes for brighter, clearer, and far less pretentious reading:

> City Council ended a public controversy last night by voting 35 to five to spend $5 million to equip new intersections with traffic lights.

May we be spared those "political footballs," "political hot potatoes," "pork-barrel politics," and "political storms." And will someone talk quietly to that run-of-the-mill radio announcer? He has a *genius* for clutter. "Hey, take a load of this folks!" he says. "At this point in time we are experiencing quite a bit of precipitation. That's the good news. The bad news is that when those big black clouds get to free themselves up by morning, it's gonna get even worse!"

What he seems to mean is that it's raining hard now, but will do so harder tomorrow.

To keep a reading audience interested it's imperative to always use familiar *combinations* of words. One of Franklin D. Roosevelt's speech writers wrote, "We are endeavoring to construct a more inclusive society." Roosevelt, a shrewd communicator, immediately changed it. "We are going to make a country," he said, "in which no one is left out." Surely that's far more precise and appealing. But here's a caution. By familiar word combinations I don't mean incorrect grammar that is unclear. Example: Sally's mother says she can't go out on Sunday." Who can't go out? Sally or her mother?

With every good intention, writers can so easily string words into sentences that may be instantly misinterpreted:

- "Truck drivers always make good time, loaded or unloaded." (That's useful to know.)

- "The car my father was following stopped suddenly, and he was struck in the rear." (Really?)
- "The prisoner appealed to the judge." (Does this mean the judge took a liking to the prisoner, or that the defendant made an impassioned appeal while being sentenced?)
- "At the age of two, my father died." (I don't believe it.)
- "We had friends for dinner and toasted the Queen."

Replace where you can second- or third-degree words with those that are first-degree. First-degree words immediately bring an image to mind while the others need to be "translated," which is yet more work for readers. Write "live" rather than "abide," "reside," or remain"; "face" instead of "countenance" or "visage"; "book" not "volume" or "tome."

Always avoid foreign words. English is versatile enough without our needing to borrow from other languages. It's better, for example, to write "mistake" instead of *faux pas*; "already done" or "something irreversible" is more immediately understood than *fait accompli.* I knew a *Montreal Star* book reviewer who had majored in Latin. He reminded his audience of it every time he wrote by littering his text with Latin mottos. Since most of us don't speak Latin, it's safe to assume he lost nearly all his readers as he tried to impress them with his knowledge.

Other words best left alone are those groaning platitudes that sound absolutely ridiculous in conversation yet never fail to find their way into manuscripts – "roseate," "fabled," "wondrous," "phenominal," and "tantalizing." They're not so much *bad* words, just frivolous and exaggerated. Similarly, other oft-used words that gush are best omitted because they immediately ask readers to interpret them – "attractive," "charming," "romantic." What one person considers charm and romance, after all, might well be exceedingly unattractive to someone else.

Slipping informal or colloquial speech into a passage whose predominant tone is formal or general, creates a barrier, too. Sometimes this is done for shock value or humour. But sudden shifts in style that have no apparent motive distract readers and suggest the writer has lost control or is trying to be clever. A good writer knows what he or she is doing, and why. By calling attention to what is being said by the way it's being done, style changes are asked to perform double duty:

> President Ronald Reagan appeared on national television last night and issued a stern warning to terrorists. "We will see you don't benefit from your cowardly acts," he said.
>
> This cute, sugar-daddy of a man, went on to praise Israel in its fight against . . . .

Informal English, which is all too often grammatically incorrect anyway, is more safely used only when quoting someone as in this assessment of the Montreal Canadiens' star defenceman Bob Gainey, by former New York Rangers right winger, Anders Hedberg:

> "He's the kinda player that never gives up. He's always gonna come at you. But when he does, he'll do it right. Bob's got class, see. He's a class guy on the ice and he's a class guy off."

There are, however, always exceptions to this rule. A colleague once ghost-wrote a first-person story for a baseball player, electing to do it as the man spoke – in colourful, Black English. In so doing, he disregarded so-called Standard English for language that would give his piece the colour, tone, and authenticity it needed. But his is a very rare talent. And can we ever forget J.D. Salinger's exquisite novel *The Catcher in the Rye*, written in the idiom of his sixteen-year-old hero, Holden Caulfield?

So far we've dealt mainly with how simplicity and clarity are impaired by verbosity and the banal. But there's more to consider in developing a good writing style – that troublesome, self-contained unit we know as the sentence. I say troublesome because to fit properly within that larger organism, the paragraph, it must be fine-tuned and balanced. When it is, it complements the sentences that precede or follow it to make words roll along instead of drag.

This leads naturally to the age-old discussion: When is a sentence too short or too long? That I can't answer. Neither, probably, could Dr. Samuel Johnson who was known frequently to carry his to a quarter of a page! What I *can* tell you is that when sentences are too long by current standards, they make heavy demands on modern-day spans of attention and create for the writer the extra risk of running off-track with wrong tenses, perhaps, verbs that don't agree with nouns, and misplaced adverbs and adjectives.

Long sentences – like Samuel Johnson's – are really several joined together by semi-colons. When semi-colons are plucked out and replaced with periods, sentences are automatically shortened and become brighter for it. They will, however, often need to start with "and" or "but," grammatical imperfections that have won some stylistic acceptance over the decades. The reason for this is simple. While "and" or "but" may offend literary purists, they do enable readers to stop at logical places to catch breath before carrying on. Similarly, a chain of sentences that are much too short lacks weight and dignity. It not only makes for jerky reading but suggests that the writer has lost control – that his or her work is so brittle, it will crumble to pieces at any given moment. So there is room in composition for short *and* long sentences, each acting as a foil to the other.

Mixing sentence lengths gives writing the interesting rhythms it needs to keep readers involved. So shrink your sentences, if necessary. Make them poignant. Make them sad. Let them occasionally surprise or delight your readers. See that they live and breathe and, to purposely use a horrible cliché, "leap off the page" with clear, concise, bright, simple words. Give each sentence a special character – a little world of its own. Always remember, though, that like a musical phrase, it should help mould a thought and lead somewhere. And however long or short you make the sentence, it must be part of a larger universe – your manuscript.

A useful technique for maintaining rhythm within a paragraph is to invert the odd sentence. A lot of English teachers today are quick to condemn inverted sentences, claiming that they make writing "indirect." Their point is well taken. But, these teachers should really explain the *use* for inverted sentences and demonstrate how they may be used to change focus – not always to the best advantage. "The town was completely flattened by a terrible twister" does not have the same impact as, "A terrible twister completely flattened the town." Just as serious is an inverted sentence that compels the writer to use a passive verb instead of an active one, thus producing more words than are necessary: "The cherry tree was chopped down by George Washington." (Passive verb and nine words.) "George Washington chopped down the cherry tree." (Active verb and seven words.)

Sometimes, especially when the writer is striving for a refreshing note of lyricism or a mood change in a passage packed with hard facts, inverting can be useful:

> Over the past 20 years, Statistics Canada reports, our youth suicide rate has quadrupled. It has nearly tripled in the last

> decade alone. In 1976, for example, 616 people aged between ten and 24 ended lives barely begun; by 1986, that figure had soared to 1,702. And by 1989, Statistics Canada predicts, it will have topped 3,000.
>
> Before it is too late there is much to be done, not only by psychologists, schools and hospitals, but by you and me – ordinary people who care.

Inverted sentences need to be used sparingly and, for the sake of rhythm, rarely two together. Too many can slow the pace of the text; none at all will have the writer churning out phrase after phrase with the same metre.

Rhythms are also created by the number of words each sentence contains. One of the simplest sentences I ever wrote was the lead to a story called "A Day in the Life of a Hospital," condensed in the *Reader's Digest*: "Midnight fell, and high above the hill the great hospital was hushed, its blinds drawn against the moon." Unfortunately, an editor preferred his own rhythm and made my sentence conform to it simply by changing "moon" to "moonlight" – "Midnight fell, and high above the hill the great hospital was hushed, its blinds drawn against the moonlight." I prefer my own version, but then, as that editor pointed out, "Perhaps rhythms are personal things."

The sentence, of course, falls within the larger unit, the paragraph. This is all too often construed as yet another complex part of writing, yet it need not be at all. The one guiding rule to follow is to make each paragraph develop a single idea, or topic, rather than several that will end up being scrambled together. This should be made clear in a sentence introduced as early as possible, first so the reader is not kept waiting too long to find out what the paragraph is about and, second, to give you, the writer, the time you may need to develop what you want to say.

As you write, you'll find that you can expand a single topic within a paragraph with five sentences or fifty. Just how many isn't that important. Make sure, though, that you don't let your paragraph become too long and uninviting to read, that all your sentences contained within it are organized so they never stop moving forward, and that they introduce new pieces of information as they go. Above all, all sentences must link smoothly to the ones that follow.

Neat, self-contained paragraphs are so integral to explicit writing that it's worth re-examining those you have written and, purely as an exercise, try re-working them one by one to see if you can make them better. Satisfy yourself that each is informative and fluid, that it talks about the same thing throughout, and that it concludes with a simple, final sentence – "the clincher," writers call it – which reinforces what you have been saying and primes your reader to want immediately to start the paragraph that follows.

A good prose style tells readers a lot about the writer. Hence you must always find words and expressions which enable you to sound like yourself – as you really are. Newspaper reporters and technical writers are trained to reveal almost nothing about themselves, and this is one reason why most of them write so blandly. Magazine writers and book authors, however, need to divulge something of their nature and frame of mind in their work. From the outset, readers will need to decide if the writer is being serious, cynical, cunning, or funny. They'll also detect through the writer's style if he or she is sincere, authoritative, knowledgeable, and earnestly trying to share.

This brings us to the use of the first person, long a controversy in writing circles. Newspapers and many magazines don't want it, preferring their writers to preserve their anonymity. Colleges discourage it. Universities shun it, particularly in term papers. The reasons are simple. Writing in the first person can too often be "an easy way out." When I was teaching written English at the University of Montreal, students would put "I" into almost everything they handed in, whether it deserved to be there or not.

- "I think that venereal disease is a terrible problem," wrote one.
- "I guess travelling is fine if you like it," another said.
- "If you ask me," one student opened her essay, "*Romeo and Juliet* actually stinks quite a bit these days for me. Maybe it's because I'm tired of it."

Obviously, if we're expressing our views or writing opinion essays, the "I" is acceptable, though not always necessary. If writing about a personal experience, the "I" and "me" and "we" and "us" are imperative. If we've convinced the editor that any other story will be warmer or make for better reading via the first person technique, that's fine, too. I could hardly travel Canada on that freight train without telling readers what I saw, heard, and thought. Nor could I take them into computer dating without showing them whom I met and how I felt about them. Sometimes, the best way of explaining a topic is to experience it first. (That sense of adventure again!) If you were writing about people's difficulties in discovering second careers, you could legitimately set out to find one for yourself, then tell readers what happened to you. It would be an effective way of giving the article a theme.

Most stories you will ever write, however, will require you to be an outsider. (In thirty years of writing, I've found a reason to use the first person fewer than a dozen times.) You will usually be surveying a problem, showing readers how something works, or how a person lives. Generally speaking, articles or books like these do *not* lend themselves to the first person. Nor does that student's view of venereal disease. As for the trite observation about travelling, the second student could have written "It is fine if you like it," and left it at that. She had found the wrong essay in which to insert herself, and this leads us to the main point: We must always make an honourable entry into a text and never foist ourselves upon it egotistically.

A well-known music critic did that. Assigned to interview the pianist Artur Rubinstein, he wrote, "When I asked Rubinstein if he was happy with his career, he said, 'Oh, yes.'" This self-indulgent piece of journalism exposed other flaws. It was unnecessarily verbose. And Rubinstein's short response hardly set the world on fire, either. The critic would have been far wiser to have persevered with his questioning, hoping for a more enlightening response, or contented himself with, "Rubinstein said he was happy with his career."

Here again, there are exceptions to the rule. I once read an essay based entirely on a writer's conversations with Sir Laurence Olivier while both he and the actor were on board a ship. It worked because the writing was clever and the author was able to make himself part of the story subtly, without sounding as if he had pompously intruded upon it. Pomposity in writing is the biggest barrier of all, which brings us full circle. The surest way of sounding such is to use language that belongs to bureaucrats and not yourself. Strip your sentences down to their barest components. Add adverbs and adjectives sparingly. Avoid clutter; leave only that which is organic and strong. And remember, a clear, well-balanced sentence and a strong paragraph are never an accident. They are hard work.

Enjoy writing, though. Enjoy the challenge of saying not what you *think* you mean, or what you intended to mean, but what you *do* mean.

12. Writer's Block

The symptoms / the effects / the causes / the solutions / gaining distance / changing pace / working to put words down

"I have cultivated my hysteria and joy for writing with terror."
CHARLES BAUDELAIRE

At a seminar I gave at Montreal's McGill University in 1983, I said in passing that writing comprised a series of crises and our success as writers depended on how well we coped with them. I referred to the obvious obstacles: searching out ideas and refining them, ferreting out obscure research, organizing appointments with busy people, structuring, and fighting words. The last thing I wanted was to spark a debate on any of these because I was there to speak about interviewing.

As is often the case at seminars, however, someone invariably latches onto only a part of what I've said and thrusts it to the fore, and this one was no exception. "I don't agree with you at all," said an elderly man who collared me in a hallway afterwards.

"About what?" I asked.

"About the crisis of putting stuff down. I get home from the office, have a martini and dinner, then sit down at my typewriter to rid myself of all my pent-up feelings. Writing's wonderful therapy, and the words always flow like mad. They really do!"

"Yes," said a woman overhearing him. "But you only ever write what enters your mind. Writing's a hobby to you. You don't have to produce articles within the bounds of research, accuracy, and deadlines. You only write head-pieces."

"No excuses, madam," the man said. "The words should still flow. If they don't, you're not a writer!"

"And you, sir," the woman replied in a shrill voice, "are lying. If you've never had writer's block, may you go fry in heaven!"

To diffuse a potentially explosive discussion, I told both participants they were referring to entirely different things – the man to writing's legitimate value as therapy, the woman to meeting day-to-day challenges of crafting saleable words when she didn't feel like doing it. Suddenly, she turned on me. And how do *you* deal with it?" she asked. "Don't tell me *you* don't suffer from writer's block, either."

Of course I do. We all do. I've never met a writer who doesn't. Even the most experienced professionals fight writer's block. Their preliminary work well done, they suddenly and irrationally dry up. Putting down words becomes menacing to them, terrifying, intimidating. So they succumb to the powerful urge to postpone it, finding other, non-writing activities instead, anything from washing the car or mowing the lawn to feeding the squirrels or browsing through a bookstore.

Sometimes they might leaf through their research or read their published stories hoping to come across something that will perk up their spirits, ignite a spark, and propel them back to work. But all too often nothing does. This is *real* writer's block. It is that moment of self-exposure to what writing can be – a shocking struggle to summon the enthusiasm that makes finding any words, let alone the proper ones, as painless as we'd like it to be. "It happens every time I sit down at the typewriter," says a busy *Sélection* writer. "That's nearly every day."

I can't go that far, though in varying degrees writer's block has impeded progress on every story I've ever written. And it hasn't necessarily been a worry over words. Any emerging ideas, as I sought to shape sentences, seemed clouded or dead. My language was prosaic. The rhythms were wrong. So I sat staring into space, wondering what to do, and hoping that tomorrow's work would be more productive. It has nothing to do with laziness or a lack of discipline, but more with finding myself inexplicably uninterested in working on the piece. When that happens it shows in the writing; knowing this all too well, I've been left with no choice but to stop writing for several days.

Even newspaper reporters who produce shorter pieces suffer from "the block." Go into any newsroom anywhere and watch them nibbling at their pencils. Usually, of course, they're thinking out their stories, but not when they reach for the phone to call home or stroll over to tell a colleague a joke. Stop by at any large magazine and you're almost sure to see the odd editor or staff writer flipping through the newspaper, and, every few minutes, traipsing off to the water fountain. They are not necessarily reading for ideas. Nor are they thirsty. Their problems are in their typewriters: pieces of paper only a quarter-filled with words because those they really want – the bright, interesting ones – are locked away in a corner of their minds and they've lost the key.

I've seen freelancers so debilitated by writer's block and concerned that it was affecting their production rate – and their incomes – that they have cried, threatening never to produce another story. They do, of course, because the problem is usually only temporary. It's been known, though, to stay with some writers for several months, stopping them from finishing books their publishers were waiting anxiously to release.

"I've got five assignments on my plate," says a Toronto writer, "and they're all pieces I really want to do. But I can't find the way to do them. I've got lots of research done, but I can't bring myself to write. I feel washed-up, burned out, finished. I can't go on."

"But why?" I ask.

"The funny thing is," the writer replies, "I don't know. I never know what lurks behind writer's block. Do you?"

There are probably as many different forms of writer's block as there are writers themselves. Obviously, we write better when we're relaxed, though some of my best work was produced while I was tense and tired. Karsh the photographer adds weight to this. "I judge the success of each assignment," he has said, "by the amount of sleep I lose the night before."

Understandably, producing bright copy is easier when we are worry-free and happy, though examples to the contrary abound, particularly among poets. The genius Miguel de Cervantes was enormously prolific against odds so staggering no modern-day writer could ever cope. He lost the use of his left hand while in combat for the Spanish army. He was captured and sold as a slave in Algiers. On his release, he married, but the marriage failed because he couldn't make enough money from writing his plays to sustain it. He spent two terms in debtors' prisons only to return to a life outside of loneliness and utter desolation.

Around 1600, while in his early fifties, Cervantes was so poor that the only living quarters he could afford on his meagre income from poetry was a bed under a lantern on the landing of a Madrid brothel. Since the place was frequented mostly by sailors, it was seldom quiet. Often drunk, those men stomped on his manuscripts, kicked over his ink, stole his quills, swore at him, and occasionally even knocked him around. Undaunted, however, he continued to work because he had something to say – a towering masterpiece called *Don Quixote de la Mancha*.

Today, conditions are significantly different. We don't have debtors' prisons and writers are rarely so impoverished that they need live in a brothel. Yet when writer's block descends, we can be driven to despondency. It happened to me in 1969, while writing my first book, *Theatre on a Shoestring*, in a Hamilton rooming house. I put the manuscript away, then spent a lot of time trying to find out why my zest for something I truly loved had waned so drastically virtually overnight. Maybe there's help and consolation in what I discovered.

First, I concluded, it was not related to my disposition or whether I could afford my rent. I had become dispirited through my own inadequacies. The book had mechanical faults which I was astute enough to spot but too inexperienced to fix. Was my first chapter really the right one to begin with? I wasn't sure it was. Would it fit more comfortably into the end of the book? I felt it might, but wasn't certain. Would chapter two provide the logical place to start? I didn't know. Was the writing rich enough? I knew it wasn't. How could I right all of these? God knows.

I was afflicted, of course, with the kind of block that paralyses one particular project, and certainly not all, which explains how, while writing that book, I was able to complete other work with relative ease. Sometimes, I told myself, writer's block can signal when a book or article is so dreadfully wrong it should be abandoned in favour of something else. Conversely, I was also aware that when writers become so emotionally tied to a book or an article, their vision is fogged and they are unable to see their ideas clearly. Mistakenly, they too often interpret this as waning interest. Fortunately, I didn't. I chose simply to set the manuscript aside for a while and, as events transpired, it was the best thing I could have done.

Nine months later, when I resumed writing, the solutions were as glaring as the faults, and I set about repairs with abandon. Now, whenever writer's block affects me, as it surely does once a week, I ask myself if I'm being handcuffed by poor construction or if I've become a prisoner of the topic. Am I too close to it? Am I having difficulty sorting out my research? Often, this is also the case. But when we recognize a problem, we are well and truly poised to solve it.

Another reason for "block" is a natural pursuit of perfection. Writers marshal their facts, thoughts, feelings, and emotions, wondering ceaselessly how the big world beyond their office walls will react to them. Will readers laugh in the wrong places? Will they dismiss the work as bunkum? Will the editor reject it even though it *is* an assignment. Writers are also supposed to shape words to dazzle, inspire, help, and carry the solid weight of authority. This haunts them, too, as they wonder if they'll ever see their words printed.

In writers' minds, the responsibility seems awesome. They tighten. If they haven't started to write, they don't. If they have, they find plenty of excuses for stopping. Writer's block becomes an amalgam of self-protection, timidity, and insecurity, and to fight it off we must constantly remind ourselves that chasing perfection is ludicrous. All we can do is our honest best with what ability we've developed, and trust the rest to Signor Pavarotti's "power from beyond."

Freelancers have been known to advocate all manner of solutions for writer's block. Many think they can remedy the problem by opening small offices away from home, others by renting cottages near lakes so, when they're suddenly unmotivated, they can dive into other waters. But do these address the problem? Some writers swear by behaviour modification – small rewards for work well done. (They say nothing, by the way, about punishment for work that isn't.) All this suggests that writer's block stems purely from procrastination, which is a symptom, and ignores such obvious causes as anxiety and apprehension.

A New York writer with a PH.D. in psychology feels strongly that rewards really do work – "a nap," he says, "watching television, jogging, a drink, even a cookie." These might well create useful opportunities for a rest, but that's about all. (Not since I was four and in love with a rhinoceros have my sagging spirits been lifted by a cookie.) He and others who claim to have done research in this field, maintain that writers can reduce procrastination by "getting into the habit of producing a determined number of words every day during a set number of writing hours that suit their temperament. And what they miss one day, they must compensate for on the next."

Those same writer-researchers talk of increasing the rewards – from one cookie to two, or thirty minutes of television to one hour – and using an alarm to signal when it's time to stop working. For me, an alarm would be annoying, especially if it sounded when I'd finally got going.

But are these the solutions, either? There's a lot of sense, of course, in writing between 8:00 a.m. and 1:00 p.m., perhaps, or from 5:00 p.m. until 10:00 p.m., then saving strength for tomorrow. But I don't subscribe to rigid patterns at all. Since we can't wait for inspiration to set us in motion, we should accomplish as much as we can when we are feeling enthusiastic. In other words, there are times when we really *want* to churn out words; we should seize upon these opportunities, and do as much as we can in case writer's block rears up later.

I follow this route. To help me, I begin each day by reading what I wrote yesterday. It puts me into the mood – particularly when I see how rough it is – and elevates me psychologically. I might then start editing this work and, without realizing it, begin to rewrite it. Soon I find myself creating *new* sections in the manuscript and am heartened when I see it growing. With more work in this direction, I tell myself repeatedly, I'll be onto something special.

Often, when I don't feel like writing, I warm up by switching to other working chores like jotting down story ideas, phoning an editor, or answering a letter. At least my time is not being wasted. If the words still won't come, I take myself off to where I don't have to worry about them unless I want to. In so doing I'm "distancing" myself from my piece to distil it objectively in a different environment. This doesn't necessitate a trip to Barbados (though a holiday in the sun, good food, and romance never hurt anyone), it simply means a few hours' break that will change the pace of my day, and my mood with it.

There are countless ways of doing this without spending a fortune: swimming, cycling, or even sitting on a park bench thinking. Twice a week I visit a shopping centre for coffee and a bran muffin, mainly to watch people and ponder my piece through, because I believe that we don't have to sit before a typewriter to write. While there, I plan the balance of my week's schedule, always setting goals to complete sections of an article or an entire chapter by a certain date.

Ironically, I began suffering badly from writer's block during this very chapter. It had nothing to do with my enthusiasm or the work I had done on it the previous day. I was cornered and, as is so often the case, I didn't know by what. So I went to the library to read up on Cervantes. That done, I returned to my car only to find I had locked myself out. You might think that a serious predicament, but for me it wasn't. The experience proved extremely useful. Instead of calling a taxi, I decided to walk home. Three kilometres later, the troublesome chapter had been formed clearly in my mind.

"Treat it like an issue piece," I was telling myself. "Document writer's block, then explain the symptoms, effects, and causes. And be sure to finish it with a section covering the solutions."

For the most part, my worries were over. I cycled back to the library with a second set of keys, put my bicycle in the rear of the car, then went home to write. I couldn't get there fast enough. The tempo of my day had been unpredictably altered and this had given me extra thinking time. As a result, the words tumbled one upon the other. The ideas seemed fresh. They weren't, of course, because I'd already jotted them into my diagram. What *was* fresh? The way I felt about expressing myself.

There have been times, though, when nothing has worked. Not a walk. Not an ice cream cone. Not an hour on a park bench. Nothing. I have then told myself firmly that I *must* write. We can't merely "think" about writing or waste time "making plans" to write, or devising excuses to "start writing tomorrow." No matter what, when all else has failed, we must make a start. I force myself to put down words because this is my job, after all, my income, the means by which I afford to own a house and travel the Caribbean. I remind myself that writing the story or chapter can't be postponed any longer. So I roll blank paper into my typewriter and begin.

Long ago I learned that writer's block will only ever be beaten by at least writing *something*. It need not be sparkling and won't be. It need not even be good or passable. But while the story is confined to my head, there is absolutely nothing I can do with it. When it's on paper, however, I can look at it, feel it, chuckle at it, swear at it, even show it to a colleague for advice. As dissatisfied as I always am with my first attempt to write a story, I know, too, that I can change it a thousand times over. I want to see words concretely on the page – and the sooner the better. Dozens of writers I know are forever talking, planning, and worrying about an idea, but it never gets written. I remember them and remind myself of that old newspaper adage, well-worn perhaps, but always so applicable – "Don't tell me! Write it!"

Once again, it's seldom necessary to start at a story's beginning and continue to its end, so I don't, especially on difficult days. And neither should you. Remember my "clothes-line" technique for building books? It can also be applied to articles. Pick out those sections that seem to be easiest or fit that day's mood, and tackle them first. Working out of sequence for the moment won't be important. You'll be making the first strides toward seeing your piece take shape. On occasions I've preferred to craft the ending first; on others I've managed a tenuous assault on the story's middle. Starting by crafting the lead, however, would seem somehow like firing a rocket without knowing where it will land.

Knowing that I have more than enough information for the reader, I surge ahead, concentrating entirely on structuring sentences. If they don't emerge as I want them to, I start working in note form. Here, momentum is paramount. So I write without stopping to check spelling, style, logic, even some facts. I know I have them, so they can wait their turn. I want organization now, block by block, paragraph by paragraph, and to get it I move on, inserting questions to myself which can be answered when I feel like resting:

> It was a fine day last spring (month?) and Joe Cummings was strolling (how?) along (what?) road trying to find the arena. He was tired, despondent, weak, and angry. His wife (name?) had asked him not to take time off from his job as a (how much per hour?) plumber at Smith & Company because they needed all the money they could get. But in a show of (what exactly?) Joe had decided to do things (better words needed here) *his* way. All he wanted now was that arena, and . . . .

This is an improvised example, of course, and exaggerated. But it serves, I hope, to show that waiting for *all* the details while forming a paragraph will definitely hold you back on occasions when moving forward is of utmost priority.

Another way of overcoming writer's block is to try writing as completely as you can, but starting slowly and with determination. I use this method most of all. I simply begin to transfer facts onto paper phrase by phrase, sentence by sentence. It's laborious and for a while it shows. But at least I'm writing and not wasting time. The first paragraph is always a disaster – full of typos, wimpy, passive sentences, ponderous generalities, and sloppy English. This isn't me working, but my typewriter. Paragraph two is just as bad. The quotes are flat. Now, sentences twist around and bite their own tails. My tenses don't agree. Nor do my clauses. Who cares? Paragraph three, however, begins to reveal the imprint of the human soul – mine! By paragraph four, I'm starting at last to sound more like myself. I'm establishing a rhythm. My brain is warming, if not to white heat, at least to a comfortable working temperature. I'm beginning to enjoy this.

By paragraph five, and still not even stopping to adjust grammar, correct facts, or change the typewriter ribbon, I've passed from reluctance to an eagerness – to reach paragraph six. I'm in motion now. Full flight. Nothing can stop me. I'm only sorry when the paper runs out and I must insert a new sheet. The words are pouring out. So are the typos. If Jehovah's Witnesses ring the doorbell I won't answer. Whoooops! I've just typed "pissibility" for "possibility." That'll make the editor grimace. (I wonder who she'll be?) I'm writing now. I haven't written like this for days. Oh, no! I've written "now" for "not". But I'm loving every moment of it. The words, I mean. Why can't I do this *all* the time?

Because we are human beings and not machines, we can't hope to be productive each day. Writer's block is an affliction that will strike you over and over again, not even dissipating with experience or success. In fact, the more you sell to the best magazines, the more you may dry up because of the high standards for which you must constantly strive. All you can do is cultivate ways of preventing it from dragging your creative life into a pit of inertia. Believe in yourself, your ability and opinions, or seek the support of those who do.

Our best animators are our friends. That's why we have *them*, and why they remain close to *us*. When I begin to struggle, I sometimes resort to a trick I taught myself back in my newspaper days. I imagine a friend, then pretend that I'm telling her my story. Because she really *is* my friend I know she can't wait to hear what I have to say. She's intelligent, though, and won't tolerate anything inconsequential or trite. And of all the people I know, no one dislikes language that is overly dramatic, artificial or "fashionable" quite as much as she does. My challenge is to keep her interested, understating rather than overstating as I proceed. My friend wants my story to be clear – and unmistakably mine.

Quite often I share writing worries with friends. They don't always understand, and I can't expect them to. ("What the hell's writer's block, for godsakes? Sounds like something you put a typewriter on when it's being repaired.") But they listen, which is helpful. "I'm wiped out," I once told my developer friend, hoping the optimism which lifted him from nowhere by the bootstraps would rub off on me. "I can't find energy, inspiration – or words."

"You think you've got problems?" he mused. "I'm afraid to go into the office. I never know what I'm going to find there. I've got to sign a six-million-dollar deal before lunch tomorrow and a twelve-million-dollar one after supper! On top of this, I'm beginning to hate the whole goddam business! I don't feel like working anymore. I don't have to, but if I retire, I'll drive my wife crazier than she already is and be bored as hell! Maybe I'll try writing. That's what I'd really like to do."

Such conversations do not provide practical answers, but they can be encouraging. When a friend consistently reminds me of his inner hunger for writing, it somehow reinforces the notion that the craft *is* an act of ego after all, and that we might just as well admit it. I do – every day. But I also try to feed off writing's natural energy to keep myself afloat, as Cervantes must have done in that brothel. And when I'm about to sink, I tell myself that nothing is forever, that many worries are dispelled by distance and time.

Sleep is the most efficient "distancer" of all. I believe that when we think deeply enough about a problem it impregnates our subconscious so that during the deepest slumber we are still mulling it over in our minds. This may partly explain why a dilemma can seem insurmountable late at night, yet be easily resolved the next morning. More certain is that sleep provides another element so integral to the writer's craft – a fresh eye. You'll need this.

13. Polishing

Revising / self-criticism /
trimming out "freeloaders" and other excess words /
honing the sentence / condensing

"I have only made this letter rather long because I have not had time to make it shorter."

BLAISE PASCAL

At last, you're on the home stretch. Despite several bouts of writer's block, your story – once an idea – now indeed has flesh, and lots of it. All your facts, arguments, and anecdotes have been stitched or cemented together in logical sequence. The blocks are solid, the transitions smooth. Now you have a manuscript ready for the editor.

But wait once again. That's wrong. If you're wise, you won't send it yet. Remember all those fabricated yarns about authors reciting publishable words into tape recorders? Well, stories about good writers impetuously firing off their first drafts aren't true, either – not if they want to impress the best magazines and publishing houses. Their first draft is really only the beginning of the final onslaught, and so is yours. It will almost certainly have a lot of rough edges, and smoothing them out is likely to be more work than you previously imagined.

Experienced writers always produce a *rough* first draft, which is as bright, tight, concise, and interesting as they could make it while they wrestled to put research into palatable words. With cold, objective eyes that have been refreshed by time and sleep, they then scrutinize their text, finding numerous passages they dislike. What seemed so right as they wrote, is now plainly wrong or unclear, they discover. So they take up pencils and start ruthless self-editing to make the draft more readable and more professional.

This process is called polishing, and after research and structuring, it is by far the most widely misunderstood and underemphasized aspect of the entire writing craft. Its importance cannot be stressed more strongly. Polishing finds the writer sharpening the first draft so that the narrative is active, well integrated, and moves the story along smoothly. It's the end of the production line, so to speak, the writer's equivalent to what corporate people call "quality control." It's also the last chance to spruce up structure and prose before you pass the story on for an editor's scrutiny.

Polishing well entails examining closely everything you've written, not as the writer now, but as the reader. It invariably involves a lot more than crossing out superfluous words, however, because you'll surely find passages that will need to be completely reworked. A lot of writing and rewriting was done as you transcribed research notes and built your text, of course, but did you do it well enough? Chances are you didn't. You had other worries to contend with. During this final clean-up, you'll find out where those faults are, and put them right.

Ideally, you'll view your work as if you were your own worst enemy and make friends once again with the scissors, paste pot, and stapler, even the wastepaper basket. You won't be alone. Nearly all professionals work this way. They detach themselves from their manuscripts first, then return to them with vigour. What was once a first, clean manuscript soon becomes a morass of heavy markings and major surgery.

Ernest Hemingway – a master of simplicity, too, by the way – was noted for this. On finishing each book he quickly shut it away and started another. Three months later, he set aside his present assignment, retrieved the completed manuscript and began altering it brutally, work he contended that was the difference between a rejection slip and a sale. To most freelancers, of course, so much time to polish is a luxury. Having lavished love and attention on one piece for so long, they need to be paid for it as soon as possible so they can enjoy the security of cash in the bank as they tackle the next. Waiting months before re-evaluating a story is not always necessary. You'll be surprised what misgivings will leap from your manuscript after you've rested it for only a couple of days.

Rewriting to polish need not be the drudgery many people consider it to be. On the contrary, it has its own excitement. If the first draft is like giving birth, then the second has the satisfaction of rebirth. To do it properly, you must – above all else – develop the habit of self-criticism. For this, it's always useful to have around you an objective critic of your work, preferably someone who knows writing and who can point out places where you've been unclear or clumsy, either with language or with the organization of your ideas. Much more important is that you eventually learn to do this for yourself. "If a man means his writing seriously," says John Ciardi, the American poet and critic, "he must mean to write well. But how can he write well until he learns to see what he has written badly?"

One way to develop a capacity for self-criticism is to spend a lot of time closely examining other writers' work. In your daily and personal reading – newspapers, magazines, short stories, and novels – stop from time to time to ask: What idea is the writer conveying in this or that paragraph? Has he made it clear? How? Why did he choose this verb or adjective over several others? Could I have said essentially the same thing more powerfully or succinctly? What makes his writing appealing or what makes it drab? Occasionally you'll come upon a paragraph that strikes you because of its vividness and clarity; you instinctively recognize it as being good. When you do, stop and examine it with particular care – as the writer now in the role of reader – to see how the author has managed to have this effect upon you.

Such analysis will tell you that the most successful writers are the most scrupulous. First of all, they're sure of their facts and you can tell it from the way they communicate without gimmicks or verbosity. Second, they have a fine sense of structure. Their ideas follow a logical and consistent pattern from beginning to end, and they use well-chosen words with a sense of authority. They know exactly what words will be the most effective for the purpose they had in mind. What you *won't* know, however, is how rigorously they polished and just how many words they struck out. You will have read only the good bits because the rest was thrown away.

As you polish, you'll detect innumerable instances where your first choices of words were inadequate. Initially, as you struggled to transcribe your research notes, they were all you could think of. Now, though, they fall far short of saying what you mean with excitement or conviction. The writing lacks compelling qualities, metaphor, simile, good rhetoric. It may be colourless in places, without insight or enthusiasm. In spots, it may be over readers' heads. Even the most accomplished writers discover all this. They notice, too, that "first-draft fever" caused them to use more words than they need. As the fever subsides and their vision clears, they find many opportunities to pare away superfluous material. And so will you.

You can begin by tossing out "freeloaders." These are words that impose themselves on sentences and give absolutely nothing in return. By removing the first and last words in this following example, we're left with exactly the same meaning expressed in less space: "All the trains were halted because of terrible weather conditions." Minus "freeloaders" it becomes, "Trains were halted because of terrible weather."

More examples? Easy. Although we all try to write well, carefully avoiding clichés, windy phrases, and jargon, "freeloaders" inevitably creep in. They are insidious, and by far the average amateur writer's strongest trait:

- The audit cost the company the sum of $300,000. (We can do without "the sum of.")
- Needless to say, he will suffer the consequences. (We don't need "needless to say.")
- It was his determination that made him great. (We will lose no sleep whatsoever if we strike out "it was" and "that." The sentence will then say simply, "His determination made him great.")

Look, too, for redundancies like these:

the Province of Newfoundland	=	Newfoundland
the whole world	=	world
consensus of opinion	=	consensus

Many words have both a noun and a verb form. If you've leaned on the noun form, you'll notice your writing is still weak and wordy – "hold a meeting" (meet), "give consideration to" (consider), "made a landing" (landed). Again, having spent so much time on other areas of bright writing, we might have let these extra words slip past us, too. Now is the time to scratch them out:

effect an improvement	=	improve
make provisions for	=	provide
take action	=	act
give a speech	=	speak
have a conference	=	confer, meet
hold an examination	=	examine, test
be successful in	=	succeed
make a choice	=	choose

Writing is automatically polished and trimmed back when we cut out prepositions. As long as prepositions perform their proper function – to introduce phrases and help relate them – that's fine, leave them in. But when they monopolize a sentence so that their presence becomes painfully apparent, they're cluttering your text. Change them.

pile of wood	=	wood pile
reports from overseas	=	overseas reports
money for spending	=	spending money
deductions for taxes	=	tax deductions
carpet in the living room	=	living room carpet
write a letter to the editor	=	write the editor a letter

Polishing allows us to rid the manuscript of all those words or expressions we like using even though they don't belong. Nearly everyone is guilty of this. Sometimes we go so far as to contrive to slip in the odd expression we like. Cynically but shrewdly, Samuel Johnson pointed this out. "Read over your compositions," he advised, "and when you meet a passage you think is particularly fine, strike it out."

No one need go that far, though we should be careful not to use words only because we have warmed to their tone or sound. If a piece of writing is forced to fit around something that isn't integral to it, that part sticks out and calls attention to itself. If cutting out a favorite word makes us feel ruthless, then we must be just that – ruthless.

For many years I was enchanted with the words "ubiquitous" and "undaunted," and used both at every opportunity. One day, while reading through old manuscripts, I discovered to my horror that I'd included each twice in one piece! I've rarely used them since. A friend admitted he, too, liked using certain phrases. Proud of his

Scottish ancestry, he would describe young women as "comely lasses" from one story to the next. He was unaware of this until a reader pointed it out.

Polish thoroughly, and you'll find similar faults in your work. More often, though, you'll discover many instances where the *same* word appears in the *same* sentence more than once. Sometimes when writing for absolute clarity, this is unavoidable. But if you spend time in thoughtful editing, you'll almost certainly be able to circumvent it. Look what I did here:

> You'll discover many instances where the same word recurs in one sentence. When writing for clarity this is sometimes unavoidable, but with thoughtful editing you can eliminate repetitiveness.

Polishing should expose those places where you may have used too many verbs or adjectives. I often include several of both when writing my first draft then, during revisions, choose which ones I want to retain. In your quest for colour, you may have done the same without noticing that all are still there, some even contradicting each other. I've seen in a manuscript, "She skipped and trudged all the way to the bank giggling and laughing." I was never quite sure what exactly it was she did.

This is, of course, another common sin among amateurs – overwriting. Just as the worst amateur painters tend to overwork their canvases by adding too much or irrelevant detail, so aspiring writers clutter their manuscripts with excess description. The result? Triteness. This problem occurs when the writer is unable to recognize the difference between colourful prose and fancy prose. Colourful writing earns its place by illuminating a person, place, or incident; fancy writing draws attention to itself by being either cumbersome or artificially slick. It quickly becomes apparent to the reader that, by using the wrong words extravagantly, the writer has interrupted the story's movement.

Employing the novelist's techniques in order to garnish nonfiction will have the same effect. There are many of these, of course, and when we come upon them in novels, plays, or films, we're quick to recognize them as devices for heightening drama or deepening sentiment. But when used in magazine articles or non-fiction books, they become forced and appear silly and contrived.

In 1974 I was a guest panellist at a discussion on polishing during a writers' conference at Toronto's King Edward Hotel. Most of the questions dealt with the need for writers to acquire self-editing skills by taking editing courses. Some participants felt they might be able to learn it by working on each others' manuscripts. Completely out of context, however, a woman asked me if I ever thought of using what she called "symbolism techniques."

"Not if I can help it," I said. "Why?"

At that point, the panellist on my left grabbed the microphone. "Oh, yes," he said. "I use symbolism all the time. You sort of need something like that to send your message."

That prompted another discussion. Did I ever think of employing alliteration? Or onomatopeia? Or stream of consciousness? "No," I admitted, "I try to tell a story without any of these because I'm a non-fiction writer, and we like to leave these things for those who try to be more creative."

"Oh, yes," said that colleague. "I find alliteration and stream of consciousness give a story a special feeling, a sort of clearer definition. I always put them in my first draft and there they stay."

Finally, we returned to polishing. That same panellist was asked if he rewrote or revised his work. "Oh, no," he said. "The moment you start tampering with art you sort of . . . well . . . damage it. You spoil its spontaneity. I send the first draft off and start something fresh. If the editor doesn't like it, that's too bad."

As you can imagine, I gave a different answer. Polishing, I maintained, was that part of writing I enjoyed most of all. I found I could generally do it leisurely, often with a pen, a drink, and a couple of dictionaries. I enjoyed the challenge of compressing words, seeing just how many I could cut from a manuscript without weakening it. I was grateful, in fact, for everything I could safely cross out because it reinforced the feeling that I really *was* being left with only the good, strong stuff.

On average, I said, I revised each magazine article three times, measuring my work's success by how dirty with markings each draft was. The one the editors bought was usually the fourth. My books generally underwent four revisions and were polished twice afterwards. (Some chapters in this book were overhauled six times, and later underwent four intensive bouts of polishing, two on hard copy and two on the word processor screen.) Each revision, I hoped, produced tighter, more precise work. Finally, I needed to tell myself that any more changes were purely arbitrary, and at that point I had considered my job done at last. Before printing the clean final manuscript, however, I read my work aloud to test it for rhythms and meaning, and to find any clutter I may have overlooked. "Some more complicated stories," I added, "obviously need considerably more revisions."

After the session, the man on my left told me he'd found my answers "extraordinarily interesting and revealing." He had no idea, he said, that profuse polishing didn't spoil writing. I was quick to point out that I'd found *his* answers revealing, too. I'd never thought that it did! Nor did I think it fair, I told him, to make readers sitting down to enjoy a magazine article go belly-down through a maze of alliteration, stream of consciousness, or onomatopeia for some hidden meaning that couldn't be explained by simple words and sentences.

"I suppose you're right," he said. "I suppose polishing is sort of brushing-up."

It is – and much more. Polishing also provides the last chance to correct important details like spelling, dates, and names. You will probably have pencilled these into your first rough draft or ensured they were intact when you typed your research notes. But when information is repeatedly transferred from one page to another, a lot of mistakes can occur. As you re-work or smooth your piece, you'll be amazed to find how remiss you've been.

Just as important, you may discover through polishing that your characters aren't well enough etched or that their dialogue needs smartening-up. Perhaps you'll also find spots where you've drifted from the theme. You may need to recast the lead to make it sharper, or bolster the ending with a few extra sentences to strengthen its emotional impact.

Polishing should show you where you can make some sentences more emphatic by turning them around or by changing tenses. To help the logic of your thoughts become more apparent, entire paragraphs may need to be revised and moved. Poor punctuation can be at the root of some problems. Too many commas, for instance, makes reading especially hard going. These can very often be usefully replaced by dashes or brackets, which isolate parts of a sentence with a lot more simplicity and impact. Sometimes you may want to use colons to reinforce a point, or a semi-colon to separate two main clauses. Be careful of semi-colons, though. They're rarely used correctly. Most often, it's better to replace them with a period. And watch your punctuation in general. Manuscripts unusually littered with dots, dashes, brackets, quotation marks, question marks, exclamation points, hyphens, oblique signs – or any other intriguing figure you may find on your typewriter keyboard – immediately smack of amateurism.

It's perfectly all right, by the way, to edit and compress quoted words in dialogue as long as you don't lose either the sense or the flavour of what was said. (It is not, however, acceptable to compress quoted words that have appeared in print. Any phrases or words you edit out *must* be indicated with ellipses.) While you're at it, take out exclamation points that make otherwise intelligent characters gushy and phony – "Mommy said I didn't ride the horse very well at all, which is why I fell off!" or "Really, darling! I didn't expect you to come all this way to meet me!" Remove exclamation points and underlining that you may have used to accentuate a joke or an irony. I can assure you that readers generally like to discover and interpret moments like these for themselves.

Above all, polishing nearly always involves condensing on a larger scale – chopping away parts of a story and building new bridges across the gaps this will leave. Broadly speaking, this is an art: the work of experienced editors. But condensing involves techniques that almost anyone can learn. If you want to polish well, you must learn them, too.

You may come across two paragraphs that, on re-reading, should really be one, so you'll have to edit each down in such a way that they fit together snugly as one unit. Unnecessary anecdotes will need to be cut. Writers starting out too often collect as many as they can, then make the error of feeding them all into their first drafts. Anecdotes *are* important, but they should always be used sparingly and for one of two reasons: if the subject is "dry" and needs "humanity" to liven it up, or if the topic is hard for most people to grasp and requires anecdotal help to make it understood. Usually, one fact, anecdote, or example – at most, two – suffices to support a point. More just belabour it. If while polishing, you're reminded of a good story, ask yourself, "Will it really help to tell it, or will it slow the manuscript down?" If it isn't needed, leave it out and continue to compress your writing like you've never done before.

Finding those negative portions in your story and turning them around so they become positive will save you a lot of words. You'll be shrinking sentences, even entire paragraphs – pencil work which, for the most part, I always find fun to do. Example:

> It's not a question of whether or not we can do the job to the editor's entire satisfaction. That bit we know. But it all depends on what kind of research help or back-up we get and whether or not there are enough typists around to do the job.

That, if you haven't counted, is fifty words. It becomes more economical and direct when it's recast and trimmed back to twenty-five words:

> We know we can do this job and make the editor happy, but it will depend on the number of researchers and typists we have.

Cutting during this final stage also means recognizing when you've wasted words to remind readers of something they already know:

> Have you ever wondered how banks rate you as a credit risk? You are aware, of course, that it is a combination of facts about your income, your job and so on. But actually, many banks have a scoring system.

Those forty words have greater impact when stripped back to these twenty-eight:

> Have you wondered how banks rate you as a credit risk? Many have a scoring system and will give you extra points if you earn a good salary.

Polishing is very often experimenting with syntax – trying to find similar ways of saying the same thing, but better. As assignments pile up and you polish more and more, you'll do it with increasing facility. At the University of Montreal, I based entire lectures on polishing. By struggling to turn sentences around and squeeze paragraphs together, I felt, students would develop a lean writing style and increase their awareness of what sentences and paragraphs really were. After I had pencilled out the "weeds," their five-page essays often ran to only three. This gave me the opportunity to explain that writers don't pad with excess words, but with facts.

Remember that. If, after polishing, your assigned 3,000-word piece is now only 1,500 words, you will need to return to your research for more information. At so late a stage, this can be a nuisance, which is why most writers, like myself, produce a little too much in a text, then polish it down to size. Trimming, even condensing, throughout an entire manuscript and not just in parts of it, will almost always make it stronger, richer, and more compelling. A lot of writers type out a second draft only to find their story is still lacking. Then they start polishing all over again. You may need to do this. As you proceed with each revision, however, you must constantly ask yourself:

- Is what I have written interesting?
- Does it read smoothly with proper words in proper places?
- Does it contain all the basic information plus more? That is to say, have I covered the topic well enough, touching *all* bases?
- Are all the facts correct?
- Are all names spelled properly?
- Does the piece have an early and precise fix on place and time?
- Are all important characters described?
- Is the piece well structured?
- Does the subject advance steadily?
- Is it always on track, or does it wander away at points with superfluous information?
- Are all my arguments supported?
- Is all dialogue important and vivid enough to appear between quotation marks?
- Does the writing have a tone that suits the topic?
- If the story has action, is it clear?
- Can I shorten the text and still retain everything I so far have? (If the answer is "yes," you must begin pruning the piece back.)
- Have I been pretentious? (If you have, edit it out immediately or, at least, tone it down.)
- Do I have characters in my story who add little to the action and who say nothing important?
- Have I been honest and fair in presenting all the arguments?

From questions like these you must decide whether you still have more work to do – extra research or crisper, more lucid writing. But never fret. All of us who write books or magazine articles have suffered through stories that at first appeared easy, but so often seemed formidable when it came to putting them on paper.

There comes a time, however, when your assignment must end. When you're absolutely satisfied that you've explained your topic in as few words as possible, stop. You will have worked hard enough and earned your fee. All you need now is to send the editor a cleanly typed manuscript, with a margin down the left-hand side of each page for any comments she or her colleagues may need to make as they go through it before ordering your payment.

Don't ask which top corner you drive a staple through or where you number each page. It doesn't matter. I've never known any editor to reject a good piece of writing because the manuscript format was slightly unorthodox. Just make sure that your text looks inviting – no footnotes nibbling away at the bottom of the pages like pesky mice – just clean, straight, double-spaced type with properly indented paragraphs. "A professional manuscript has a kind of feel to it," a former *Reader's Digest* editor used to say. "You somehow know it promises something good before you even start reading it."

All you can do now is wait patiently for the editor's response.

14. Meet the Editors

Their "conflict" with writers / their workload and skills / what editors expect from freelancers / what freelancers can expect from editors / what can be learned from editors / fact-checkers

"An editor should tell the author that his writing is better than it is. Not a lot better, a little better."

T.S. ELIOT

In Tower Woods, Halifax, in 1828, two men marched sixteen paces apart to begin a duel. One was John Croke Haliburton, clerk of Nova Scotia's Legislative Council and a would-be judge. The other: Joseph Howe, later to become a Nova Scotia premier, but who for now was the crusading, twenty-four-year-old proprietor-editor of *The Novascotian*.

Angered by one of Howe's scathing editorials, Haliburton took aim – but missed. Howe was all set to shoot the politician dead when, in a sudden flash of goodwill, he decided the altercation could best be settled bloodlessly. "Let the creature live!" he shouted as he fired his pistol skyward. When challenged to a second duel a few months later, Howe refused, saying, "A live editor is far more useful than a dead hero!"

A lot of writers, however, might vehemently disagree with this. Literary legend has it that editors are hired by publishers to cheapen or distort authors' work and fight with them while doing it. They describe editors as disgruntled souls who inflict unnecessarily heavy pencils on manuscripts, merely to satisfy their egos and salaries. When they aren't doing this, we've been told, editors lead charmed existences, eating in good restaurants and vacationing at the publisher's expense.

Even today, some freelancers tend to perpetuate these myths. They think the best editors are dead editors, and resent those who are very much alive for enjoying the security of staff jobs while being blithely unaware of all the writer's struggles. If that's not enough, editors are accused of having too much power and inconsequential journalistic knowledge to support it. Writers are quick to dismiss them as green-behind-the-ears folk who bring to the enormous responsibility of handling literary masterpieces a splash of academia or some meagre newspaper experience, but an acute lack of worldliness. "They're not even writers," says one brittle freelancer who is constantly having his work rejected. "Yet they act like they are." Adds another, with gentle humour: "Imagine having an editor for an in-law! You'd have the worst of both worlds, wouldn't you? There'd be a mess in your personal life and one at work, too. And you'd never get anything printed!"

All this is worthy of mention only because writer-editor relationships continue to be the root of fascination and the butt of jokes. Those same legends talk of editors construing writers as spoiled beings because they *aren't* on staff and can therefore work or vacation at will. They consider writers, we're led to believe, as temperamental, sulky, and downright vain people who think – quite wrongly – that all their words are sacred. Editors are cornered at parties and asked if their fights with authors are ever resolved. Writers, meanwhile, are known to talk freely about how which editor has broken their latest string of pearls.

Unfortunately, unless put into proper perspective, these rash fables may establish the atmosphere in which the keen writer starting out meets his first editor – and the new editor full of wonderful intentions is assigned to her first writer. Neither should fear the other. Editors *can* be bad just as writers *can* be naughty. Usually, neither is the case. In the best editorial circles, writers enjoy the security of knowing that however well they might have polished, the editor's eyes – the keenest and freshest of all – will still spot ways to improve their work. And while editors may not indeed be writers in the strictest sense of the word, most write well enough to exercise their own special skill: finding literary defects and putting them right. "An editor," said the philosopher Robert Zend, "is blessed with the talents of others."

A striking paradox is that the more successful and experienced the author, the more he or she is likely to listen to what the editor suggests. In so doing, writers quickly discover that editors can be remarkably understanding. Of course editors know that freelancers must toil hard to write articles and books while doing other jobs. They're aware, too, that an author's work is made of his bones, heart, and liver, and that anything altered without good reason is almost certain to question his ability or hurt his pride. The good writer knows that an editor's changes to a manuscript represent her legitimate sharing in its creative process, making the story better than it already is. As long as both understand this and view their relationship as one in which the article or book wins and no one loses, the chances of altercation – especially a duel in Tower Woods – are slim indeed.

Like writers, editors come in all shapes and sizes, with an assortment of personalities and various degrees of proficiency. Generally, they fit into three categories. First, there's the sleekly dressed figurehead editor of the mass-circulation women's magazine. She leads a somewhat honeyed existence, lunching with celebrities, attending garden parties, and travelling the country speaking to service clubs. Before leaving, however, she delegates editorial work to juniors. It's just as well. She was not originally hired as a journalist, anyway, but more as a public relations person who might improve her magazine's image.

Some men's magazines in New York City have friendly, hard-drinking equivalents who make contacts rather than edit. The news magazines, in fact, have Diplomatic Editors whose job it is to butter up politicians and visiting dignitaries, thus paving access for writers and photographers to produce cover stories about them later.

The second category contains editors who attend luncheons and press receptions yet still find time to handle copy and assign pieces. On small magazines, they have no alternative. They put their publication together almost singlehandedly, writing some of the stories and positioning copy, art work, and advertising. On larger magazines, however, life is considerably different. Senior editors could be discussing editorial policy with the publisher in the morning, lunching with a person they want a writer to profile at noon, then hurrying back to their offices in the early afternoon to work on a manuscript. They serve both functions because, although they plan and administer well, they're journalists at heart and enjoy their contact with the freelance writing world, of which they once may have been part. On most magazines, those on the editorial ladder's highest rungs know enough about each other's jobs to be able to step in and do them during times of illness or vacations.

Most writers deal exclusively with editors who belong in the third category. These are men and women who don't know a honeyed existence at all, and who spend their entire working days, and quite often some of their leisure time, honing manuscripts and planning issues. Their workplace is a sweat-tank of endless copy. The moment one manuscript has been edited, another is waiting. And whatever work it needs must inevitably be done against a deadline.

Deadlines go with the territory in journalism. Wire services have them every minute, radio stations every hour, newspapers every day or week. Magazines must cope with them ten or twelve times yearly, depending on how often they publish. For them, deadlines build with steadily growing pressure from one issue to the next and are usually slow and agonizing, with several mini-deadlines along the road. Thus, the relative quiet of a magazine's editorial department is often deceptive. Editors bathe constantly in tension and frustration behind closed doors, wondering if stories they've slotted into a particular issue will arrive on time and without requiring an inordinate amount of in-house work. All too often they're disappointed. A piece, which at first promised to be good, falls apart at the last minute. There are also times when there's nothing in the editorial "bank" to take its place.

Against all this, editors strive to muster for each issue an assortment of articles – something for all readers. If the magazine is national, they must see that it retains regional balance and contains broad coverage. And no two articles, they are painfully aware, should be remotely connected. Their cries for help, then, are all too familiar.

"I've got a hole in August," says one editor. "Anyone using that piece on acid rain?"

"Yes, me," a colleague responds. "I've marked it down for September."

"Can't you let me have it? You can use that salmon story instead. I need a strong issue piece!"

"I don't want salmon. I've already got animals in my line-up. I'm running the Siberian horses story. We can't have fish and horses in one magazine!"

I once discovered a *Time* editor sockless in his office, his white shirt dripping with perspiration, his face ashen, cutting a manuscript into pieces and methodically laying them out on the floor. He was using his shoes, stapler, calculator, and a jar of pencils as paperweights so that no part of the story would blow into the hallway when the air conditioning came on.

"What on earth are you doing?" I asked him. "That looks like a writer's job."

"I'm trying to make a bloody silk purse out of a goddam sow's ear," the editor grunted without looking up. "And I've got until the end of the afternoon to do it – or the magazine goes to bed with five blank pages! The irony is, the guy who wrote all this junk thinks he can write and no one's been able to convince him otherwise."

Book editors have deadlines, too – one per book. And whereas a magazine article might spend a few weeks in production, a book will often stretch into many months. Since each book is part of a publishing house's program of several and has been allotted a certain amount of money for editing, printing, and promotion, its deadline is crucial. I've known editors to try to speed up the production flow by taking manuscripts home in a suitcase so they can assess them quickly over a weekend and write to the authors first thing on Monday morning. One managing editor actually went off to her country home to completely restructure a poor novel. Seven weeks later she had done her job so well that on its release, it became an instant best-seller.

"The best part of that author's work," she recalls, "was his dedication to his baby daughter. The rest was so far out of whack it had me in a dizzy spin wondering if we'd have to release that fall's list without it!"

Stories like this are further proof of most editors' fervent desire to try to mend a broken story before rejecting it. But this one had an irony. No sooner had the book been acclaimed than the author was negotiating for the release of his next – with another publishing house.

Your relationship with the editor will begin the moment your clean, inviting manuscript arrives on her desk. If you've written a magazine article needing the minimum of in-house work, your association is likely to be short and businesslike, with any necessary discussions carried out by letter or on the telephone. (I've dealt with about two hundred different editors throughout my career and have met probably only thirty of them.) If, however, your work is a book, the relationship will almost certainly be longer and more intense, even if heavy editing isn't required. Get along well with the editor and each phase of the manuscript's production process will be pleasant, even friendly.

The editor's first job is to ensure that before accepting what you've written it conforms to what was originally commissioned, according to your proposal, in subject and length. If, for example, you'd been assigned to write a 3,500-word magazine piece on Inuit art, that's exactly what the editor wants and not 4,000 words on native people's art or 5,000 words on one artist you consider better than all others. Here, the book editor's task is more exacting. Imagine her reaction if an author were to barrel into her office and announce that since signing his contract to write on how to breed dogs he'd changed the rules – that his book was now partly a novel because he had allowed his imagination to run away with him. Imagine, too, the editor's reaction as the writer calmly explained that this now meant he was unable to contain the subject to 45,000 words as originally contracted, and was offering 90,000 instead! The editor – and, indeed, the publisher – would have seven heart attacks apiece, especially if the book was scheduled for launching as part of the coming season's list.

When a publisher calls for a book of a certain number of words on a specific subject, it's by no means a random calculation. It's based on market research which has predicted the kinds of people likely to buy the book and for what price. Any change in subject, therefore, automatically renders that research useless and the manuscript redundant. If, however, the editor's sole concern is a manuscript that's far too long, she'll most likely return it for cutting, which invariably means a lot of strenuous rewriting. Huge increases in a book's length inevitably translate into proportionately higher production costs; unless restored to its contracted wordage, the book may have to be cast aside as economically unfeasible.

Editors know they must anticipate problems like these and learn early how to cope with them. They also know there are times when they need to be helpful and understanding if the author of an eagerly awaited book falls sick, or if, through problems in his research or personal life, he's unlikely to meet his deadline. In this case, the onus is upon the writer to give the editor prior warning so she can make alternative arrangements. If she works for a publishing house, she'll want to amend her schedule and immediately start working to get another book into the pipeline. If she's a magazine editor, she must search for a replacement story for her issue line-up. Obviously, the writer's frankness at this stage will set the tone for a good relationship with the editor when the manuscript is finally ready.

The principles of editing articles and books are essentially the same, which tells us why editors often alternate between magazines and publishing houses. When the editor first sees the work, she does so in a different light from that of the writer, always with the readers in mind. Many of her suggested changes are made purely on this basis. Spelling errors and poor grammar are the least of her worries during the early stage, because they can be corrected with a pencil. On her first reading her eye will concentrate more on blatant factual errors or those parts of the text she considers racist, vulgar, obscene, sexist, or insulting – anything, in fact, which doesn't meet the standards of the publishing house or magazine.

None of us ever intends to write offensive words, but you would be surprised what, at the end of the long road, we overlook. When I wrote my *Guide to Music* I spoke about "the masses" and the editor changed it to "the people," explaining that "the masses" was pejorative, a put-down. On numerous occasions, for example, while innocently aiming for description, writers have mentioned that a person was black or Polish, facts that had no bearing whatsoever on context.

Simultaneously, the editor will assess the manuscript's clarity, tone, and construction, always asking herself if enough information has been explained as attractively as possible. Her notes to the author – either in a memo or in the manuscript's margin – could be a detailed explanation of where the work lacks in certain areas or an enumeration of its overall faults. These comments may translate into wholesale deletions of entire passages that are inappropriate or irrelevant, the addition of new material to cover missed points, or call for massive restructuring.

There may be times when the editor will also want certain parts of the text trimmed back and others more fully expanded to make for proper balance. Inevitably, she'll ask questions on certain points, requiring the writer to respond with either "yes" or "no." The replies will serve to satisfy her curiosity or help her better understand other points likely to crop up later. Sometimes, she might even decide that the manuscript is so good that it can undergo its first edit *without* the writer's help. In this case, she might fire off a note saying, "Thanks for a job well done!"

Whatever the nature or number of the editor's suggestions and queries, the author's responsibility is to address them all to show one professional's respect for another. If he doesn't, he's undermining the editor's role. He's more apt to respond willingly to requests for changes or clarifications, however, if they are made amiably. Instant tension invariably accrues when the writer feels his editor's aggressive questioning is based entirely on how she would have written the book or article had she been given the chance – or if she holds preconceived notions of how either could have been better done by someone else. If the writer suspects the editor wants to re-work his manuscript completely without good reason, this could lead to irreparable friction, too.

Similarly, a prickly author who resists all attempts to make his work better will find both his life and his future hard. An editor who believes the writer hasn't revised his work may suggest that it be refused. Such instances, however, are extremely rare. Normally when two conscientious professionals join forces in one common aim the results are fruitful. The editorial process then becomes what it should be: one of quiet negotiation, with the editor urging and the author thinking seriously about the logic behind her reasoning. Occasionally, since editing is a two-way thoroughfare, the roles may be reversed. The writer may urge and the editor ponder. But if both parties know what to expect of each other and agree on certain ground rules from the outset, the editor-writer relationship can be more than pleasant and friendly. It might even be fun.

As large and comprehensive as it may be, the initial edit is only part of the editorial process. Bigger magazines clean-type the manuscript, then – together with the source list the writer is expected to provide – send it to a research department whose staff will check every fact, line by line, word by word. By phone and by letter, researchers contact every source to check quotes, dates, and the correct spelling of names and places. They then verify other details in gazetteers and encyclopedias. This system was largely pioneered by the *Reader's Digest*, whose superb fact-checking setup has inspired others in the industry to emulate it. Like all magazine editors, those at the *Digest* demand accuracy to the minutest detail. According to its head office in the leafy town of Pleasantville, New York, nearly ninety researchers scattered throughout twenty major centres across the world scrutinize every typed line, checking every detail and examining every opinion the magazine prints. By the time the average issue reaches the newsstands, they will have verified about thirty-five hundred facts with more than fifteen hundred sources.

Other magazines, like *enRoute*, *Homemaker's*, and *Saturday Night* have similar systems – all part of an ongoing quest for editorial credibility. This inevitably means changes in the writer's text. The fact-checker assigned to a story is almost certain, for instance, to unearth the very latest statistics that will make it more accurate. Or she may find that in the time that invariably has elapsed since the magazine bought a profile, the subject has had a birthday, or his wife another child.

"You must never presume anything," says one *Digest* researcher. "Lots of people think Lewis Carroll wrote a book called *Alice in Wonderland.* He didn't. He wrote *Alice's Adventures in Wonderland.* And there's no reference at all in *Genesis* to Adam picking an apple, by the way – just a fruit. It could've been an apple, but then it might've been a lemon or a fig."

Editors and writers are always grateful to fact-checkers for catching errors and clarifying points. Usually if a source disputes an anecdote or denies an incident, the researcher or the editor will tell the writer it must be removed. Together they'll devise the right words to bridge the gap in the text created by this change. All final decisions, however, always rest with the editor, who is entirely responsible for what ultimately appears in print.

Book editors are responsible, too, but they don't have an army of fact-checkers behind them. All too often they must accept the author's word or question inaccuracies as they occur to them. Many editors, however, have such well-developed intuitions that on the slightest hint of an error or something that needs substantiating, they'll scurry for a reference book to check it out.

For the most part, they are their own fact-checkers, and good ones at that. But in larger publishing houses they usually have the benefit of yet another pair of eyes to help them – when the manuscript goes off for its finer copy edit. During this, which could last days, even weeks, the copy editor puts the manuscript under an editorial "microscope" as she combs more comprehensively for punctuation, spelling, and grammatical errors, and painstakingly strives for uniformity of style. She also checks some facts that may strike her as being wrong, and ensures that the names of ships, symphonies, books, and well-known works of art will appear in italics. She may then notice that a person has blue eyes in chapter two and green eyes in chapter ten – or that "color" on page one is spelled "colour" on page seventy-nine. She might discover that "centre" has become "center," and change it. At one point in the manuscript, however, she'll read "Lincoln Center," but decide to leave it because she knows that this is the way it is officially spelled.

Copy editors are also key people on bigger magazines. Like their publishing house counterparts, they make a fastidious sweep of the manuscript to prepare it for the printer, from which several sets of proofs will soon start flowing back and forth during a check for typographical errors. Some proofs will be sent to the author. By then, however, he'll be glad to see the last of his article or book until it appears in print. Thanks to his editor, it will have that ring of authenticity, clarity of expression, and deceptive simplicity which, as we now know, is the hallmark of all good prose.

Just as writers become "experts" when they research, so editors garner huge funds of knowledge as they refine manuscripts. One Toronto book editor says, "Even the worst piece of writing tells us *something* we didn't know before, even if it's only that a bunch of grade-one kids in Saskatchewan have been eating their school bus passes!" Editors also develop an appreciation for various writing styles, a profound insight into how their country is run, an unyielding desire to feed readers a lot of pertinent information, and a keen sense of humour. "When you do stories for *Badlife*, *Ontario Dying*, and *Equinoxious*," says the playful editor and general manager of an Ontario lifestyle magazine, "you never write the same way as you would for, say, *Catelaine*, *Homebreaker's* or *Toronto Strife*."

By consensus, writers agree that editors can teach them a lot, not only about the kinds of articles or books they usher into print, but about some of journalism's finer points. The best editors, in fact, have been likened to conductors of orchestras. Whereas the maestro's complete understanding of the rudiments of music and capabilities of every instrument makes him his organization's best musician, so the senior editor who has trained to be a critic, wordsmith, and administrator all rolled into one, is often the publisher's most accomplished all-round journalist.

My first editor was a cantankerous newspaperman who had written several novels, worked as a sports reporter, and was widely regarded as a political economist. He brought to his vocation as editor-publisher of the *Sheerness-Times Guardian* a passion for literature, a love for linguistic clarity, and a swashbuckling regard for editorial urgency. In the mid-1950s, he hired me off the street as a reporter on condition that I shaved off my beard and learned Pitman's shorthand within three months. As an apprenticeship it was second to none and remains living proof of newspapers being magnificent launching points for any writing career.

I wrote obituaries to learn accuracy and covered courts, councils, and inquests to exercise story structure and composition. I also made the tea on a gas-ring in a corner of the oily machine room behind a flat-bed printing press which, to the uninitiated, resembled the one Gutenberg might have used when he printed *The Bible* in 1450. On Thursday nights I earned extra money by counting the paper's entire circulation of 7,023 copies, wrapping them into parcels of two dozen each and loading them onto a truck to be distributed among local newsagents. It was work that continued well into the night. By 9:00 a.m. the following day, however, I was sitting with the two other reporters in the tiny, cluttered editorial office nervously reading those stories I'd written that week to see what, if anything, was wrong with them.

Something always was, errors both the editor and the senior reporter, who also processed copy, had missed – a misspelled name, the wrong street assigned to a fire or burglary, or a misquoted mayor. But recognizing faults, said the editor, was as much a part of learning the craft as writing itself.

What vexed him most was a story in which the obvious lead had been buried. He taught me that however insignificant an event might be to the reporter, it was nonetheless crucial to the people who had organized it. This being so, even the briefest news item needed to be carefully crafted so it was interesting and direct. "And you must always find an angle," the editor would insist. A sure-fire way to anger him was by writing:

> Sheerness Women's Guild held their weekly meeting on Tuesday last. Mrs. Harry Dobson served coffee and cakes and Mrs. Priscilla Grant donated the flowers. A motion was passed to organize an exchange visit with a sister group in Middelburg, Holland, next June.

That kind of reporting would have been returned with a terse note ordering an immediate rewrite – "Of course those blasted women held their meeting on Tuesday! They always do! Can't we find something new to tell readers?" I would then struggle to swap the words around. The more I looked at them, the more I felt they were in the only conceivable order to make any sense. Finally, when my head had cleared after an hour or so, I would muster the incentive to return to my notes and try an alternative structure. This time I would include an important quote, which brightened the little piece and gave it substance:

> Sheerness Women's Guild is to visit a sister group in Middelburg, Holland, next June, members decided at Tuesday's weekly meeting. Said Mrs. Priscilla Grant who donated the flowers: "We will welcome the Dutch women to visit us a few weeks later, and we hope this exchange will become an annual event."

It was elementary journalism to say the least. But it does demonstrate what the editor wanted – and got. A properly-angled piece, however long or short, would install a twinkle in his eye and he'd smile approvingly at the reporter's extra effort.

I recall that same editor wanting to see me because I'd used "lady" in a story. I entered his office with some trepidation to find him standing on his proof-strewn table dusting off a naked light bulb, his only source of light, with a handkerchief. "How many times have I got to tell you," he said staring down at me, "that the human race consists of men, women, and children who later become teens? That, believe it or not, is fact. Whether a woman is a lady or a man is a gentleman is a matter of considered opinion!"

One Friday morning while going through the paper with a fine-tooth comb for errors and a razor blade to cut out those stories he wanted followed up, the editor discovered I had misspelled the name of the new local magistrate with whom he had once gone to college. He roared into the reporters' room and fired me with a week's wages and promises of a reference that might, with luck, help me secure work with the opposition, the *North-East Kent Times.* At noon, however, he took the envelope of money back and re-hired me. On reaching the end of the paper, he explained with some remorse, he'd read my "Child of the Week" piece and it had made him chuckle.

Behind that editor's brusque exterior throbbed a warm, tender heart. He was kind, supportive, and forgiving so long as reporters were honest with their work, themselves, and him. One day he showed it. Another of my jobs was to write a social column called "The Showman," for which people came from several miles around to deliver contributions. One woman renowned for her vanity was forever arriving with accounts of her involvement in everything from library committees and the Red Cross to Meals on Wheels and the local drama league. When she fell ill, I naïvely wrote: "Mrs. William Hesseltine has been under her doctor now for six weeks and is feeling no better for it."

"I like it," the editor said crisply, with a knowing glint. "It's a very nice play on words so we'll leave it as it is, shall we? It'll serve the damn woman right."

In Toronto though the 1960s and early 1970s, editors entered my life with varying degrees of impact. The editor of *The United Church Observer*, who had a special knack for generating original ideas, persuaded me to dress as a hippy and mingle with those who had then made Toronto's Yorkville district their own, to write a story on how, as "misfits," they viewed religion. Another editor I dealt with, but never met, was the young woman at *Maclean's* who returned my computer dating article. It was usable as it was, she said in a covering letter, but it lacked "spark."

"We need anecdotes, anecdotes, and anecdotes," she added, "many more than you have so far included." I obliged and received a note from editor Peter Newman: "Thanks for a fine piece." I was happy to tell him that his colleague had "drawn it out of me."

Then there was the shrewd, enthusiastic woman in her mid-twenties who edited *The Gamblers*. I was her first writer, but it altered nothing. She read the manuscript twice then phoned to say that one of the characters did absolutely nothing to further the action or add anything to the theme. "He's an ornament," she said. "Let's get him out."

"Out?" I said. "But he's so colourful!"

"Colourful he may be," the editor replied firmly, "but all he does is sit there making odd comments, whereas all the other characters actually *do* something."

She got her way, and the book was better for it.

My most seasoned editor, however, was a brittle, lugubrious *Reader's Digest* staffer who had entered magazines via newspapers, television production, and book editing. He would be arguing with a colleague one minute and wiping his eyes over a tender story the next. Like most editors and writers, he savoured favourite topics, in his case, baseball and God. One imaginative freelancer suggested this editor deserved a tailor-made piece and invented a scenario in which mankind was pitching curveballs to God, who could only foul them off. The story never got written because writing is too much work for playing jokes. Nor would its motive have been appropriate, anyway. What this editor lacked in tact, he more than compensated for in integrity and goodwill.

Swept up by unpredictable jovial impulse, he would lumber to the coffee machine singing or quipping, "What a funny way to make a living! If I told ordinary people I spent all day changing words around they'd never understand. I mean, who deserves pay for changing words?"

What distinguished him most was his insatiable appetite for work. He gathered a plethora of ideas, which he submitted to monthly story meetings for opinion and approval, assigned them to writers, administered sections of the editorial team, and condensed manuscripts submitted by some of North America's finest freelancers. A story goes that he once persuaded a well-known writer to rework a story proposal three times until it was good enough to win an assignment. When the manuscript eventually arrived, he ordered her extra money for a job well done.

After one quick reading of a text he could say exactly where it foundered, then send the author a five-page letter saying how it could be fixed. Even those who resented the harshness of his pen recognized that by refusing to compromise his own standards he elevated those of others. "That's what editing really is," he'd say. "So long as writers rise to their tasks, I'll face up to mine. So would most editors, I should think."

15. The Writer and the Law

***The anatomy of libel and its defences* / sub judice /**
***contempt of court* / *privileged meetings* /**
trial by headlines* / *copyright* / *permissions* / *plagiarism

"There is no God-given right for somebody to propagate to thousands and thousands of people false facts which are damaging."

JULIAN PORTER, Q.C.

TORONTO LIBEL SPECIALIST

Nothing curls an editor's eyebrows quite so quickly as parts of a manuscript that hint that the writer might have broken the law. We're lucky. Our country lets us say what we think or know without fear of recrimination as long as we do not attack the defenceless or hurt minority groups. Just as the writer and the editor can have a turbulent relationship (unless they temper it with care, intelligence, honesty, and a sense of fair play), the author and the courts can have a *stormy* one.

In her satirical autobiographical novel *My Turn to Make the Tea*, about life on a fictitious weekly newspaper, British author Monica Dickens shows us journalistic incompetence with comic implications. The heroine, a willing, but haphazard court reporter so mis-writes the name of a Mrs. Nessie Parkinson, the plaintiff in an alimony suit, that it brings a woman named Mrs. Jessie Parkins to the paper's front office screaming, "You've made a libel of me!" The matter was corrected with a simple printed apology.

In the real world of newspapers, magazines, and book publishing, however, such incidents of mistaken identity aren't handled so easily. Nor are they funny. Sometimes regarded as a criminal offence and nearly always actionable for damages, libel can mean irreparable heartbreak for the victim, loss of integrity for the writer and his publisher, and cause all involved – regardless of who was right or wrong – lasting bitterness and anger. As Iago tells us in Shakespeare's *Othello*:

> "Good name in man and woman, dear my lord,
> Is the immediate jewel of our souls:
> Who steals my purse steals trash; 'tis something, nothing;
> 'Twas mine, 'tis his, and has been slave to thousands;
> But he that filches from me my good name
> Robs me of that which not enriches him,
> And makes me poor indeed."

Trying to understand the anatomy of libel is like walking through a maze backwards and blindfolded. Even busy lawyers admit to being confused by it. They know this law, of course, and understand it exists to protect. But its interpretations are a totally different matter, and usually for legal specialists. What makes libel particularly hard to grasp is that even though legal precedents provide useful examples on which courts may base decisions, each action has its own special character with a conflux of overlapping components. The briefest overview of libel in Canada reveals a spaghetti of variables that makes no two cases even remotely the same.

It's generally held, for example, that the dead can't be libelled. They have no rights, says the law, and can therefore suffer no wrongs. But successful actions have been brought when malicious criticisms have cast nasty aspersions upon a deceased person's family, who are definitely still alive. Usually, defamations against a group or a "class" of people aren't actionable, either. There have, however, been cases in which one member of an organization has claimed that although the libel was general, his reputation and integrity had definitely been damaged because of it.

Similarly, courts have drawn clear lines between premeditated statements designed to have prolonged effects and those that were impulsive incidents of abuse. A British court, for example, once ruled that calling a woman "a tramp" was indeed a despicable thing to say, but was unlikely to have been damaging because too many people regarded her as otherwise. Yet plaintiffs in Canada and Britain have successfully sued for less.

A lot of beginning writers are confused about the difference between libel and slander. The treatment is similar but the vehicle can be different. Libel constitutes written or visual defamation, while slander is oral. But if insults are written first then recited or read by an actor, orator, or broadcaster, they, too, become libel. In recent years, in fact, courts have interpreted the statute on libel to mean that all media defamations are libel, even those made extemporaneously. They've held, too, that libel can be contained in the literal meaning of words ("what an ordinary person without any special knowledge of the subject might conclude by them"), or in innuendo.

According to the Criminal Code, libel is "matter published, without lawful justification or excuse, that is likely to injure the reputation of any person by exposing him to hatred, contempt or ridicule, or that is designed to insult the person of or concerning whom it is published." To be actionable or indictable, such information or insult need only be made known to one other person who is not the victim. By this definition, a libellous statement contained in a magazine with 100,000 subscribers might constitute 100,000 different libels. More definite, though, is that anyone who *re*publishes defamatory remarks can be sued as if he were the person who published them originally.

No one can be judged guilty of libel if he or she is mentally ill, or if a damaging statement falls from a person's pocket. The law requires proof beyond all reasonable doubt that there was intent to publish it – as graffiti on a wall, maybe, as words scratched onto a lump of wood, or on the printed page – or that publication resulted from a lack of care. But just as language, with its cadence, inflection, and symbols, is far more than mere written or spoken words, so a defamatory statement can be made through images: a film, photograph, or drawing. Hence a few years ago, a British Columbia politician sued a Victoria newspaper claiming its cartoonist had depicted him as cruel and sadistic. The cartoon showed the politician pulling the wings off flies.

But what is "defamatory"? What does it *really* mean? Since 1275, when libel and slander were first adopted by the British Parliament to prevent newspapers from spreading insulting remarks about King Edward I and his late father, King Henry III, there have been several interpretations, which courts have applied at will. These range from "exposing a person to hatred, contempt or ridicule" to causing a victim to "be shunned and avoided." Today, judges most often add to these Lord Atkin's observation – that defamation "lowers a person in the estimation of right-thinking members of society." Thus a more complete legal definition of libel is that it "tends to lower a person in the estimation of right-thinking members of society generally, or to cause him to be shunned and avoided, or to expose him to hatred, contempt or ridicule, or to convey an imputation on him disparaging or injurious to him in his office, profession, calling, trade or business."

The implications can be titanic. When libel is both defamatory in character *and* false in fact, the criminal arm of our legal system swings into action, imposing heavy fines or prison terms of up to five years. Simply publishing defamatory remarks knowing them to be untrue is a criminal offence in itself; far worse is when untrue statements are considered seditious.

Fortunately, criminal libel in Canada is extremely rare. One of the most famous cases, in the late 1960s, was brought against a British Columbia weekly newspaper, which had already been convicted under the Criminal Code for counselling to commit an indictable offence with a feature story entitled "Cultivating and Growing Pot." The libel conviction was for awarding a judge "The Pontius Pilate Certificate of Justice" for "closing his mind to justice, his eyes to fairness . . . and for encouraging the belief that the law was not only blind, but also deaf, dumb, and stupid." Under another section of the Code the paper's publisher could alternatively have been tried for scandalizing the court.

Most libel actions against writers are without question the direct result of error or carelessness (misspelling a name and causing mistaken identity), utter incompetence (unearthing facts honestly thought to be true but discovering the hard way that they weren't), or a combination of both. In cases such as these it is highly unlikely that criminal charges would be laid. But if the writer justifies a defamatory statement simply by claiming it's "fair comment" or "in the public interest," that's contestable.

Was it in the public interest? Was it correct? Was it honest error? Has it really been damaging? These are questions for the law to decide. Libel victims eager to debate such issues launch suits in the civil branch of our legal system – the provincial courts – claiming to have suffered verbal attacks that were wrong, unwarranted, or unfair. They ask not for apologies or retractions, though these may be part of their settlements, but for money: compensation for damage to their health, reputation, family life, business, or general well-being.

Chances are, then, that when you hear that a newspaper, magazine, or publishing house has been ordered to pay libel damages, the writer or an editor has paid dearly for making a mistake or being sloppy. It could also mean that he or she published material sincerely believing it to be correct and in the public interest, but couldn't substantiate it in court. Ironically, and this should point up yet another facet in the myriad of libel, it does not necessarily mean that what was written was totally unfounded so much as that it could not be proved before a judge and jury.

In all libel actions, the onus is immediately placed upon the defendant to prove that what was written was justified – long before the plaintiff needs show that it was not. In essence, that's how it should be, but many investigative journalists feel the system puts them at a disadvantage. The law assumes, sometimes wrongly, that the plaintiff had a good reputation in the first place and allows him to bring dozens of witnesses into court to say so. The writer, on the other hand, may often have only a handful of people to corroborate his facts – in a time when more and more courts are being particularly harsh on the media.

A defence sometimes is that a plaintiff's reputation is already so low it has not been harmed any further by what was said. But this can be hard to prove. Judges and juries make decisions based entirely on the amount and quality of evidence they hear; investigative reporters, meanwhile, lament that even when they can prove the mayor is pilfering taxpayers' money, they dare not say so, even in the public interest, in case they are sued.

Most writers, particularly freelancers, don't have this worry because they're seldom expected to work on controversial stories in which the dangers of libel are so real. Nonetheless, as a protection, all large magazines send their articles to their lawyers, who scrutinize them with writing's obvious legal traps in mind.

There are many of these, and they can be hidden behind the most innocent facts written about common, every-day activity – references to people having "one too many," for example. These can be damaging indeed. To write that a man is single when he's married, for instance, is to imply that his wife is living with him out of wedlock. If she can prove this error caused her grief, suffering, or hardship, she may be able to sue. Several years ago, a Montreal photographer celebrated the first signs of spring by photographing the sun cutting through the budding trees on Mount Royal. While there, he also photographed a man and a woman embracing each other on a section of the mountain known to attract lovers. When the photograph was published in a local newspaper, the two people launched successful actions under Quebec law for breach of privacy. They were in love and married, it transpired – but not to each other!

What that photographer saw – in a public place, no less – was true. While the truth is a defence in a libel action, it must be weighed against motive. If, for example, a freelancer decided to tell readers for no good reason that a man who has led a blameless life for the past ten years was once jailed for embezzlement, he could be in serious trouble. If, however, the information was published while the citizen was running for public office, it might be construed in court as a matter of legitimate public concern. Or maybe the jury will have a different idea. Who knows?

Nor, contrary to what some young journalists will tell you, is the truth ever sustained by statements like "it is alleged that" or "police said." Wrong information is wrong information and when it's published it can have disastrous effects.

Let's look at a hypothetical story in which police say, "We're absolutely certain now that yesterday afternoon, Harry X pulled the trigger of that gun." Factually, that good quote, that revealing statement, is true because it can be assigned to a police officer. So the writer starts his story: "Police said last night that Harry X is being hunted for pulling he trigger of a gun that killed . . . ." He thinks he's covered himself. He may not have.

The facts *behind* that statement, however, could be entirely wrong. If it transpires that poor Harry X had spent the previous few weeks vacationing in Hawaii and couldn't therefore have been anywhere near the scene of the crime, he would have a watertight case for libel – against both the police officer and the newspaper that published the story.

Now let's suppose that Harry *had* pulled the trigger and was charged with murder. By using such an incriminating piece of information from the police in such detail, the reporter, who should have known better, would be finding Harry guilty before he had even gone to trial. In so doing, he would be violating the law in a different way – by spoiling Harry's chances of a fair trial.

One of our most treasured basic freedoms – and certainly one distinguishing ours from many other lands – is the presumption of innocence until it can be proven otherwise at a fair trial. The trial, then, is all important. It's the Crown's chance to make a strong case against the accused. In defence, the defendant is free to unglue the evidence against him. Writers know this of course, but in their spirited quest for anecdotes and facts, they can easily break the law again by inadvertently prejudicing a trial.

The rules on this are very simple. The moment a crime is discovered it may be described in the most intricate possible detail: a person found dead with fifty stab wounds, for instance, or a bank robbed by a man dressed as a woman. (Don't laugh, I once covered such a case at London's Old Bailey.) Once a person has been charged with an offence, however, it's what lawyers call *sub judice*, Latin for "under justice." In Canada this means you may not divulge details of a crime for which a young offender has been arrested. This is absolutely illegal. Nor may you report any details of a trial on which a judge has imposed a "gag" order.

In the United States, *sub judice* laws seem nonexistent. All too often we read that police are hunting down a man – and they name him – because, they unabashedly say, he held up a gas station and shot a cashier. Shortly after President John F. Kennedy was assassinated in Dallas in 1963, Lee Harvey Oswald was actually interviewed on television while under police escort, and asked if he fired the gun.

In Britain, a television reporter who dared to do this would have been arrested, charged with contempt of court, and sentenced to three months in prison. There, *sub judice* and libel laws are so strictly applied that reporters can only say, "Police want to interview a man they think may be able to help them find the person who shot a gas station cashier," or "a man is being questioned by police in connection with . . . ." At preliminary hearings, when a magistrate must decide if the Crown has enough evidence to send a defendant to trial before a higher court, reporters are forbidden to report any details that might remotely link the accused with the crime. At this point, of course, only one side of the case – the Crown's – is being heard. The defendant has a right to reserve his defence; he need not even speak. But if he does, to express remorse, sorrow, or guilt, it must not be published in case he decides to change his mind – and his plea – at his trial.

Defendants in Canada are not entitled to this degree of protection. Our best court reporters honour *sub judice* laws consistently, but others are not nearly so discerning. If ordered not to report details of a case by the judge at the request of either the Crown or the defence, reporters will always comply, or go to prison instead. But they'll construe from this that reporting all else in the courtroom is all right. So they happily tell readers how shifty the accused looked in a baggy suit and handcuffs, a bruise over one eye. Doesn't this imply guilt?

This journalistic abuse of our court system, *Saturday Night* once said, was "Trial by Headline." As an example, editor Robert Fulford cited the well-known case of a nurse accused of poisoning four babies at Toronto's Sick Children's Hospital – charges that were later dropped. While the story was "hot," however, one Toronto newspaper interviewed people who knew the young woman – neighbours who were "shaken and disbelieving," a graduate classmate who said she was so surprised to hear who the accused really was that she "didn't know what to say." The accused's boyfriend was contacted. He said "she was a very dedicated nurse"; a woman said she couldn't believe that her former roommate and best friend was "guilty of the murder of four babies." But "behind all of these statements," Fulford wrote, "was a clear subtext: how could a nice girl do such a thing!" He later added: "Every defence lawyer has handled cases in which almost everyone in the courtroom assumes, before the first witness is heard, that the accused is guilty and the trial is a kind of formality."

There is considerable confusion among freelancers starting out about another part of the law that affects them – copyright. One question I'm continually asked is, "What's wrong with sending the same article to, say, three magazines?" The short, quick reply is absolutely nothing, because writers own their work and can therefore do whatever they want with it. I usually respond more fully, however, by posing a return question: "What would happen if the first magazine to receive your piece decided to buy it and sent you a cheque? What then?"

At that, writers look bemused and ask what I mean.

"Well," I explain, "the moment they send you money, they've *bought* something, haven't they? It means they've bought the right to publish the piece because they didn't want anyone else to have it. It's sold. It's theirs. You no longer own the right to publish it. So how on earth would you be able to sell it to the other two magazines if they wanted it, too?"

Even this doesn't address the question fully, but serves only to explain that while writers usually own the copyright, they do not necessarily own publication rights, unless these are stipulated in a contract. What appears on the surface to be simple really is not. The proper answer lies in what rights the writer has sold or the publication has bought.

Generally speaking, the larger and more populated with readers a magazine's circulation area is, the more it pays its writers for the right to publish their work. The most valuable English-speaking rights are called United States rights – because the United States has the largest concentration of English readers. That's why freelancers from across the world like to break into the American market with books for big-city publishers and articles for magazines like *Playboy* and the *Reader's Digest*. The Canadian edition of the *Digest*, however, pays a little less to buy World rights, leaving itself legally free to send an article to any other edition except its American counterpart without paying the writer an extra fee. In other words it buys World (except U.S.) rights.

In much the same way, *Equinox* and *Chatelaine*, which both have readers in the United States, will buy North American rights. Most big Canadian magazines, however, pay less for Canadian rights, and this legally permits them to circulate an article nationally but not across international borders, which they never need to do, anyway.

Some magazines want what is called serial rights to an article so they can re-use it or re-sell it to another publication. For instance, *Equinox* buys North American serial rights to cover its American edition; *Chatelaine* needs to secure them so it can buy a story and then translate it for its sister French-language edition. Similarly, *Toronto Life* pays for Canadian serial rights so it may publish the same piece in *Epicure* or *Men's Fashion*.

The least expensive rights, however, are usually for one-time use. This means that after the article has been printed, publishing rights automatically revert to the author.

Copyright arrangements are further complicated when an author sells his article to a magazine on condition that he retains all rights to have it published in books. Example: the New York City writer Thomas R. Brooks sold "Auto Theft Turns Pro" to the American *Reader's Digest* but kept ownership of its book rights in case he wanted to re-sell it to a publisher for an anthology. So to reproduce part of his piece in an earlier chapter, I had to contact him for permission.

Here we enter that part of copyright concerned with the use of other people's material. There's a lot of misunderstanding about this, too. But there needn't be. The law is very clear. Once anecdotes, facts, opinions, and ideas have been published, they are in the public domain. If they weren't, research, folklore, writing, learning, even knowledge itself, would grind to a halt. All those wonderful stories about George Frideric Handel writing *Messiah* in twenty-three days, and what Pierre Elliott Trudeau thought and said about his vision for Canada belong to you and me. The only thing that isn't yours and mine are the words various writers have used over the years to set these stories and ideas down. These are protected like the Crown jewels, and anyone who steals them can be prosecuted for literary theft – plagiarism.

Published stories and facts that may help us illustrate part of a manuscript are available to us, then, so long as they are completely rewritten and don't contain anything of the original in either words, phrases, sequence, or echoes. We may slot published quotes from experts like professors, doctors, politicians or scientists into our stories, but these should be in context and attributed. Example:

> "Suicide among our young," says Dr. Diane Syer, head of the Crisis Intervention Unit at the Toronto East General and Orthopaedic Hospital, "is a shocking manifestation of despair from a group of people traditionally seen as having everything to live for."

Since Dr. Syer has said this in print so often, it's now in the public domain – a part of written history. Before quoting her or others like her, though, we should check that her words were reported accurately in the first instance and that she has not changed her views. (In this case, it is most unlikely.) She may also want to take the opportunity to refine the quote by making it broader or more succinct. This is probably the strongest case yet for a magazine's fact-checking system.

But be careful here, too. It's illegal to use too much of one piece of someone else's work. So if half the anecdotes and quotes in your article or book come from one source, you may be in trouble, however well you rewrote them. "When you steal from one author," the late Hollywood screen writer and humorist Wilson Mizner reminds us, "it's plagiarism; if you steal from many, it's research."

Actually, there's really no need to steal anything from anyone. If while writing you need to borrow a few lines or phrases, you may do so without permission so long as they're fairly brief and you say where they belong. You may safely write, for instance, that in his new book *How to Grow Geraniums*, author Joseph Blow says, "Thank God for flowers. Their blooms and scent are the greatest gifts to all people." If, however, you wanted to use anything substantially longer, it would be legally proper, as well as ethical, to check with Mr. Blow's publishers, who are most likely to be very helpful. Publishers exchange material all the time. Their only concern is that the use of anything they own under copyright – even when it's attributed – doesn't detract from the marketability of the original.

Quoting from private letters also requires permission. By law, letters belong to whoever received them and not the person who wrote or sent them. Again, if your intentions are honourable, that permission will usually be forthcoming. But here's another warning. Sometimes, letters, diaries and, indeed, authorships have been willed and thus have a new owner who might not be easy to find. Yes, copyrights *can* be included in a dead person's estate; it's therefore safe to assume that any fairly recent literary work is owned by someone, whether the author is dead or alive. The copyright of Orwell's *Animal Farm*, for instance, is in the estate of the late Sonia Brownell Orwell, the author's second wife.

None of this should imply that the law has made writing too risky. Nearly all jobs have some kind of risk and those that don't usually aren't worth doing. The permanence of words, however, guarantees that they'll always be around for all to take issue with. People may disagree with our arguments, even dispute our facts; all the more reason why we must remind ourselves, as we tackle each assignment, to take extra time to assure the absolute truth of every piece of research, as insignificant as it may at first appear to be. Each tip, lead, or idea needs a strong, responsible source – written in our manuscript in *our* words. When a writer uses false or damaging information or steals someone else's writing, the law may well be lenient, but an editor's trust will have been instantly destroyed. And that may take years to win back, if it can be done at all.

16. Recycling and Other Good Work Habits

Considering rights / instinct / cross-pollination of thoughts and ideas / simultaneous submissions / working routines / finances / interviewing habits / dealing with rejections

"I work every day – or at least force myself into office or room. I may get nothing done, but you don't earn bonuses without putting in time. Nothing may come for three months, but you don't earn the fourth without it."

MORDECAI RICHLER

Busy freelancers run businesses that, like almost all others, need to be lean and innovative to survive. They must be resourceful, too, and this – keeping busy and always free to select those subjects with which they feel most comfortable – is why writers try to mix writing magazine articles and books with assignments for radio and television.

Often, they have no choice. Almost without exception, freelancers wonder endlessly if they're adequately paid for the many hours of work each piece takes. The fee for a 4,000-word article for a top Canadian magazine is about $2,500. It sounds like a lot but, when you consider that to earn it the writer must spend numerous hours over several weeks researching and writing, it isn't. On computing their hourly pay rate, in fact, most freelancers ruefully conclude they'd earn more money driving school buses. To make their assignments more profitable, most of them re-sell their articles to other markets for whatever extra money this might bring in.

This is recycling, a process by which a writer uses the same idea and research to produce different articles for other magazines or resells one piece several times over to publications with different readerships.

To be successful, recycling must always be carefully orchestrated within the copyright law. If, for example, the writer has sold only one-time rights on an article, he or she is free to sell it many times over to those magazines prepared to use it in its original form – first, second, or third rights, and so on down the line. Not many magazines, however – and certainly not the good ones – will agree to buy only one-time rights on a piece of work because they want to print only those words that have not, or will not, appear elsewhere unaltered. Magazines working on smaller budgets are happier with the idea. One is *The Beaver*, another is *City & Country Home*. But the author should always question this arrangement. Very often a magazine is content to pay to use a piece once so long as it isn't resold to a competitor. Sometimes, an editor will stipulate that an article can't be recycled within a specific time from the date he uses it. This could be a matter of weeks, or it might be several months. And, take note, if a writer re-sells an original article on which he's sold world, United States, North American, or Canadian rights, he's stealing back something that is no longer his and, in effect, causing any new buyer to receive stolen goods.

For all this, many freelancers recycle their work effectively, and within the law, remembering that only the words themselves can be copyrighted and not the information or ideas they contain. This leaves them free to re-work and re-angle pieces and mail them to any number of magazines, sometimes on speculation, but usually as a follow-up to an introductory letter or phone call.

By this method, a bustling freelancer in Trenton, New Jersey, is reputed to have recycled an article on childcare 247 times. Not many of us can ever hope for that kind of success. We can, though, take comfort from knowing that there's probably a secondary market for virtually everything we'll ever write. The key is to find it, a job that is easier than you may think. Most writers ferret out little magazines they've never even heard of by buying *The Canadian Writer's Market*, published by McClelland and Stewart, or pamphlets listing all kinds of publications and journals, like the one sent out free by the Toronto-based Canadian Periodical Publishers' Association.

Recycling is yet another part of writing that relies heavily on instinct – to choose and write about durable, wide-appealing subjects in the first place, and to realize during research that with extra information and a different point of view, a secondary market is just around the corner.

The cross-pollination of thoughts and ideas plays its part here, too, as demonstrated by the writer assigned to cover an archeological dig. While talking to archeologists about what they had so far unearthed and what they hoped to find later, he noticed the brand name on one of several Caterpillar tractors used to excavate soil and rocks. He sold his article on the dig itself to a New York Sunday newspaper supplement, then garnered some interesting facts on the Caterpillar's role in the project and wrote a separate piece for a heavy equipment trade journal.

This, intelligent recycling at its best, is a system you can consistently apply to your own work as a writer. A solid general-interest article on how the government may be refurbishing an historic sight might have several possible markets all entirely different – in a city magazine, a heritage magazine, a popular history magazine, certainly in a local paper's feature pages, and possibly in any number of journals catering to the many trades involved in the project. The thing to remember is that for each customer, the piece needs to be slightly re-angled.

The newspaper and history and heritage magazines would mostly be interested in the site's fascinating past, what makes it unique, and why it's being restored. For the trade journals, however, this information would be somewhat incidental, but nonetheless deserving as background. Editors there (as we'll discuss later) would require more on how each trade or profession actually figures in the project, and doubtless some technical detail on the kind of equipment used. But with most of the basic research already done, this need not be an inordinate amount of extra work at all, just a few phone calls and some rewriting.

Stories on well-known personalities invariably appeal to several magazines. I once wrote a piece on bandleader Guy Lombardo for a newspaper's Saturday entertainment section, then recycled it into a story proposal that earned me a *Reader's Digest* assignment. I've resold profiles of such people as Paul Anka, Donald Sutherland, Oscar Peterson, Norman Jewison, Yousuf Karsh, Charles Dutoit and many others several times over, selling first to magazines that paid the most, then working down the line – rewriting and re-angling as I went – until I was left with a manuscript I was free to send out to any editor happy to buy one-time rights.

The secret with recycling profiles lies in writing only about durable people in the first place and not those, like nearly all sports figures and politicians, who are celebrities for a relatively short time. Some entertainers quickly become outdated copy, too. "Once a hot item," *People* magazine said of Michael Jackson, "he is now a faded bloom." His turn may come again one day; the lesson meanwhile is that it's far better spending time profiling people who are most likely to be "current" for some years ahead, rather than those who probably won't.

Profiles can often steer the astute writer toward other, completely different kinds of articles, as was aptly shown by the New York freelancer who visited actor Christopher Plummer to interview him for a men's magazine. She was so enamoured with Plummer's New England homestead that she arranged to write about that separately, for a house and garden journal. In Toronto not long ago, a newspaper feature writer dispatched to write about a star ballerina's career, noticed her fine collection of antique dolls and glassware. Zing! A second article! Like the man who covered the archeological dig, he got two pieces from one assignment and one visit.

In this business, we try not to waste anything – not a phone call, not a letter, not an anecdote. Parts of articles may end up in speeches; speeches may find their way into essays. Had my outline for this book been rejected, I would have chopped it up and used it as the basis for several lectures. Being resourceful is integral to professional writing, as are some of these other work habits that might be helpful:

• Never recycle the same article to two magazines vying for the same corner of the market – the exact same travel piece to two travel magazines in the same country, for instance, or the same medical piece to two competing medical journals. It will not only embarrass the editors, but finish you with two magazines that might otherwise have been good potential markets. Never use another magazine's idea. If, for example, *Chatelaine* asked you to profile a well-known woman and you later recycled the piece to *Homemaker's* or the *Reader's Digest* it would be unethical, no matter how much extra writing or reshaping was done.

• Never confuse simultaneous submissions with recycling something that you've already sold. The confusions caused by sending the same piece to several magazines have already been covered. But apart from who will get to own what rights, there are other ethical questions the writer must address – particularly where books are concerned. A publisher spends a lot of money to have a good proposal or unsolicited manuscript properly assessed by market research. Involving others in a similar expense for something they may not ultimately have the chance to buy, even if they want to, is a sure-fire way of antagonizing them. Don't deal with more than one publisher at a time. It's not professional.

• A reminder. While researching a story, you should know instinctively whether it will have a secondary market – whether you may eventually be able to recycle it. If you feel you can, collect lots of extra material. It will come in handy later.

• It's always better to gather a little extra research, anyway. It will obviously give you a better selection of facts from which you need only take the best. At some point, of course, you must stop researching and start writing. But it's safer to have too many anecdotes and pertinent facts than not enough. Good books and magazine pieces are invariably such because the writer had plenty of choice of what to build into his manuscript and what to leave out.

• There are a lot of good reasons for storing all research files. The most important is that several months after having sold a piece, it might at last be in an editorial pipeline and an editor may want you to recheck or divulge a source. Top magazines ask for the file to accompany the manuscript so that their fact-checkers may have a good start. Besides this, files will prove invaluable for you. If you decided to write another similar story there may already be some useful research at hand. Should you want to recycle an article already written, the file will be the obvious source for fresh anecdotes among those you decided not to pack into your original. Space doesn't permit us to store bulky files forever, but we can usually find enough for them for a couple of years at least. Here, the personal computer can be useful for filing both research material and original stories on disk.

• File away clean copies of every manuscript you write, not only for recycling, but in case you want to reuse a part of one story in another. And by occasionally reviewing old work, as I still do, you'll get a clear sense of if or how you have improved and what you can still do to make your writing better.

If freelance writing is to be a full-time profession, it deserves a full working day. Allot a specific number of hours to it daily – as would be expected of you if you were employed as a staff writer for a newspaper or magazine. Novelist Arthur Hailey, who lives in the Bahamas, showers, shaves, and has breakfast, then puts on a suit and tie and goes to work in his office in his house. "I like to feel I'm going somewhere else to write," he says. "It helps me take hold of myself and reminds me that it's a bit more than just a hobby."

Not all of us are expected to go that far. (I've done some of my best writing in my pyjamas.) If we want to be published regularly, however, we must work on a daily basis and take the job seriously. You may not always feel like working hard, and you don't always have to; writer's block means that we often *can't* write or shouldn't. But there are so many other things to do, even if it's only cleaning out a desk drawer or stacking up old newspapers and magazines so they no longer impede the way. By being in your office during regular hours, you'll be there if the phone rings, as it surely will.

• Be part of the entire media spectrum. Listen incessantly to intelligent radio and watch high-quality television programs. Above all, listen to the news and read what's behind it. Insular people do not make writers, let alone successful freelancers who must constantly search for new ideas. If most of the young writers I've counselled over the years had a fault in common, it was that they were making no efforts to become "worldly." Obviously, we can't expect people in their early twenties to have solutions to all the world's problems, but is it too much to expect them to know just what those problems are and how they came about? Few of them do, and it will hamper their careers.

• Maintain good, up-to-date records of phone numbers and addresses of all people you've mentioned in your work, however insignificantly. You never know when you may want their help again. In time, you'll be surprised to find that some people you interview – even star entertainers who guard their privacy zealously – will recognize your seriousness and trust you with their unlisted home phone numbers in case you need to contact them for extra information. You could eventually accumulate a gold mine of sources that is always at your fingertips: stage performers with good stories about others you may think of profiling, or scientists with expert opinion relating to something else you'll be working on. Heinz Lehmann has actually called me with two story ideas.

• Keep a good supply of dictionaries, thesauruses, and other word-finders. As time goes on, you may also want to collect reference tools like encyclopedias, more specialized dictionaries – certainly one in French, by the way – and books of quotations.

• Save money by doing all writing except for the final draft on scrap paper. I've been known to transcribe research onto envelopes, restaurant place mats, even pieces of wallpaper chopped small enough to be fed into the typewriter. When building early drafts or moving blocks of research around, remember that staples are less expensive than Scotch tape.

• Ensure that your manuscripts are legible and complete – nicely typed on good, white bond paper. Margins need to be wide enough for editors' notes. Book manuscripts should also include everything from the dedication and acknowledgements to a list of chapter titles and, if necessary, a bibliography. Pages that have been radically cut and pasted may need retyping; any handwritten inserts must be in upper and lower case lettering, not capitals. When in doubt, retype "dirty" pages and make the editor's work a little easier.

• Freelancers usually maintain a supply of postage stamps. Smaller magazines tend to expect writers to accompany unsolicited work with a stamped and addressed return envelope.

• Keep tear sheets of all your stories so you can show editors and publishers examples of your work. In their contributors' guidelines, more and more magazines say they welcome suggestions from new writers but all will want to ascertain whether their writing styles are "suitable" before giving them assignments.

• A story's deadline is one thing to consider; another is lead time. This is the period needed to put a story through its first editing, then fact-checking and copy editing, and into the art department for illustrations – not to mention proof checking and any last minute trimming that may be required to make it fit into a page layout. Though some of this work can be, and is, carried out simultaneously, from the moment a manuscript arrives, it takes a large magazine about four months to process it completely and properly for the printer. Publishing houses always need a lot longer, sometimes as much as a year, which is why they, more than magazines, ensure that deadlines are stipulated in contracts.

It's a good idea to get to know lead times so that when an editor asks for a piece for the Christmas issue to be delivered by mid-August, you'll know why. You should also be constantly aware how lead times can all too often outdate stories, particularly those intended for news magazines.

• Some editors believe, and not without good reason, that photocopied manuscripts are such because they are being offered elsewhere simultaneously. For this reason, they are sometimes unwilling even to read them. It's as well to keep in mind that, as a rule, editors prefer receiving original drafts, though for assigned pieces it's usual to keep the original safely in a file and mail a copy. I nearly always add a note saying, "I'll send the original if you want it." Before submitting work, it's always both useful and tactful to check this point out. When recycling the same story to several magazines, however, sending photocopies is quite acceptable.

• Although the word processor ensures clean, professional manuscripts, it's unwise to rush out and buy one until you are fairly sure you can sell articles regularly enough to be able to make it pay. And remember that the word-processing software, the disk you insert into the computer to enable you to work, is far more important than the computer itself. To be able to produce manuscripts that will be acceptable to good magazines and publishing houses, you will need to underline to denote italics, have available foreign accents and currency signs and, of course, use upper and lower case lettering.

I point this out because some cheaper word-processing packages sold with less expensive personal computers are too basic to include these vital features. Nor are the computers themselves always offered with easy-to-use keyboards and good, high-resolution screens – extremely important factors to consider for personal comfort, if nothing else. So before investing in a word processor, make sure that it will quickly earn its place in your office, and ask professional, long-distance writers – not sales clerks who have probably never written professionally – what type of computer and software they think will best suit your needs.

• By far the better investment for any beginning writer is a telephone-answering machine that will record messages during absences. I bought my first one back in the early 1970s, when they cost considerably more than they do today. But it paid for itself within a matter of only days. Among my first dozen messages were two left by editors at *Maclean's* and *Canadian Business*. Both led to assignments together worth far more than what the machine had cost me.

• Freelancers new to the business are constantly asking me how they can find an agent. My answer is usually, "Don't waste time, energy, or money in stamps or phone calls unless you really feel you're writing a lot of material of interest to the American market." In Canada, we don't need agents. Our country may be large in size, but our magazine industry is relatively small, and news of a competent freelancer spreads quite quickly. Usually writers are quite successful in selling their own work. In any case, no agent has a magic wand that will sell unwanted work when waved; he or she will invariably want proof that your articles or books are so saleable that taking you on as a client will be a profitable arrangement for both of you.

Until writers have sold at least several articles and a book on their own, in fact, it's very difficult to find a reputable agent willing to handle their work. It's also hard to find competent critics willing to give honest critiques of writing for reasonable fees. The best nonfiction criticism comes from journalism teachers in our universities and colleges, or from good writers themselves. Agents will often require these opinions of a potential client's work before even considering representing him.

Good financial management is a part of any successful business, and freelance writing is no exception. Working in a buyer's market means that the freelancer must constantly look for ways to save money, conserve it, and administer it.

• Each year you'll need to be your own bookkeeper. You won't need talent in this field simply to keep track of what you spend and what you earn, just good records. Some magazines may not send you Federal T4A slips to support payments for articles, thus leaving you on your honour to declare these earnings to Revenue Canada.

The Income Tax Act has been fairly good to writers. You may reasonably deduct against income anything you spend on stories: parking, air and rail fares, office rent (or a portion of the costs of your home), postage, your telephone, photocopying, some meals, and membership dues to such organizations as the Writers' Union or the Periodical Writers Association of Canada. Secretarial help, newspapers, journals, and magazines are also tax deductible.

• When on assignment, keep receipts of all expenses incurred. Larger magazines nearly always reimburse writers for travel and lodging the moment their editors receive the manuscript. These expenses, however, cannot be included in an honest tax return.

• To avoid misunderstandings, always ask an assigning editor to send you a letter outlining the terms of the agreement. Some magazines send contracts; others merely set out the conditions by phone. This is not always good enough. The writer needs to know how much he or she will be paid, how many words are expected, and by what deadline. The letter should also say if there'll be a "kill fee" if the piece doesn't pan out and whether or not the writer will be reimbursed for travel expenses.

• Some magazines pay only on publication. Find this out early. If they want your article badly but can only schedule it several months down the line, you'll have to wait several months for payment. Unfortunately, many magazines genuinely have cash-flow worries, and need all the understanding they can get. Other publications, though, take advantage of being the purchaser in a buyer's market and pay on publication so they can "borrow" money interest-free from those people who can least afford to lend it. Check them out, and remember that by having to wait so long for your piece to appear in print, you may be restricting your chances of recycling it, particularly if it has been pegged to a time frame.

During preliminary research for a story proposal, a writer must often interview an expert and admit to being unfamiliar with the topic. It's always best to explain that all research must start somewhere and that yours will continue. When writers are honest, people automatically warm to them.

Among literally hundreds I have interviewed by telephone as I embarked on a story idea, was soprano Joan Sutherland. I wanted good stories and an assessment of Luciano Pavarotti, which she gave willingly, referring to him constantly as "Big P." Conversely, there were times when people weren't forthcoming at all, fearing I was about to blow open their personal lives. Things were different, however, when I told them the *type* of story I was writing and how I felt they could help. Sound honourable and they'll speak. If the magazine you're writing for has integrity, your job will automatically be easier. Let people check you out if they want to. It's their right. They don't have to speak to you about anything.

• There are ways to encourage characters in important stories to co-operate. While doing a piece on a tornado which ripped through Woodstock, Ontario, I wanted to incorporate a note of heroism – the bravery of an eighteen-year-old woman who had shielded her young nephew as the storm bore down, losing a leg doing it. But she refused to meet me. She'd never spoken to a journalist, she told her mother, and didn't want to in case she was trapped into saying something she didn't mean.

I set about researching the story anyway, and eventually visited Woodstock. Back in my motel room one night after interviewing eyewitnesses, I telephoned the woman again. This time I explained my motives to an understanding brother-in-law. He convinced the woman she should talk to me and, within an hour, drove her to meet me. Relatives can often be extremely useful in helping writers break ice to reach valuable sources.

• Sometimes, a person wants to be reassured that something said outside the interview won't be used in case it embarrasses others. You can discuss this, which should suffice. The moment we let the public edit or censor our work, freedom of speech will deteriorate. Let writers write, editors edit, and readers read. I have, however, been known to recite to sources sections from an unusually intricate scientific or medical story, purely to check for accuracy. You might find this a good policy, too.

• When interviewing, you'll frequently discover that people will be prepared to give you information only if you promise not to mention their names. If you make such a promise of non-attribution it's one you *must* keep. This will require you to use vague labels like "an Ontario heart specialist" or "a Calgary businessman." But these are not very satisfying and an article fairly scattered with them immediately loses impact and authenticity. Never submit an article containing more than three of these and don't use two back-to-back.

• A gentle caution about tape recording telephone conversations during research. According to the Criminal Code, there is absolutely no need to tell interviewees that you are recording their words. So long as one person agrees to the idea – and, says the law, that one person can be yourself – no offence has been committed. It is, however, honest and ethical to warn other people when you have attached a recording device to the telephone line. You should do this before starting your interview. From my experience, people who anticipate the nature of the questioning and why it is being done, will be only too pleased to agree, for accuracy's sake.

• When striving for geographic spread, you'll need to interview people by letter. Write to about three times as many prospective sources as you have room to quote. From my experience, I found useful replies were returned by roughly one in three. Begin each letter by saying exactly what your topic is and explain what publication you're writing for. You must then say where you got the source's name and how you think he or she can help you. When asking your questions, make sure that they can all be answered in one or two sentences. Never put the kind of question that requires an essay in reply – "What do you think about capital punishment?" This will both baffle and annoy any busy recipient and your letter will end up in a wastepaper basket.

Even though you'll expect only short replies, many people won't be able to resist writing several fact-packed pages. Be grateful and acknowledge their effort.

• Obviously, any person you quote should have some evident expertise in your topic. When writing about an aspect of health, for instance, you will probably need to seek out medical doctors or experts in related fields. They need not *all* be nationally known and reachable only by costly long-distance phone calls. Men and women in your home town can serve your purposes admirably, as long as they don't dominate your manuscript.

There are many ways to find them. A good way to contact doctors is to call the nearest large hospital and ask for either the publicity or press relations director. Almost every medium-sized organization has such a person on its staff whose job it is to get the organization, its people, and its accomplishments into the media. Simply explain the subject of your article or book and ask to be directed to a quotable source.

Don't expect expert opinions of your work from people who know absolutely nothing about the business. A critique from someone who understands what your assignment was and what it's expected to yield is different. But generally speaking, you can't hope for friends, neighbours, and uncles to suddenly assume the editor's role if they work in completely unrelated areas. They may think otherwise, but don't listen.

Some years ago I was entrusted, as an editor-cum-ghost writer, with the job of helping Governor General Jules Léger write an article called "Memories of My Father" for *Reader's Digest*. Through an aide, the Governor General said he wanted to try the first draft himself. When it arrived on my desk, however, everything that could have been wrong with it was. It might have been acceptable as a quick newspaper feature, but as a magazine piece it left a lot to be desired. The writing was lucid enough, but the topic lacked both focus and anecdotes. Besides this, the chronology of the subject's life was disjointed and there weren't nearly enough examples of what he had come to mean to his son, and how he inspired him – the very purpose of the piece.

It fell to me to tell Léger that his work was not quite what we wanted, that it needed to be completely recast. "But I showed this to my friends," he said, taken aback, "and they think I've really caught the spirit of my father and described him well."

"With respect, Your Excellency," I said boldly, "I don't think you have! You're writing for people who've never met your father and know nothing about him – like me. I don't see him at all. I don't see him physically, don't hear him speak, don't get a feeling for what he felt or thought, and I certainly don't have a sense of how important he was to you and how he shaped your life."

Léger looked stunned, but only for a moment. "All right," he said finally. "Then we must do something about it, mustn't we?" The outcome was a complete and amicable overhaul of the manuscript, with Léger plucking out anecdotes completely at will, and me slotting them into the text. But the extra work and the initial tension between us could have been avoided had he sought opinions not from friends, but from Government House journalists.

• It's often unwise to share a manuscript with *anyone* before it reaches the editor – particularly a key person in a story. This can lead to a showdown. We rarely see ourselves objectively, so why should we expect anyone else to? Usually then, the subject of a profile will want to make changes that are not always practical. That's not to say the writer has been inaccurate; it simply means that the subject wants his age omitted, say, or the town in which he lives – details that might be integral.

A word about rejections. If you go about writing as a professional, with a good idea, a story proposal, copious research, and deft writing, you'll get fewer and fewer of these. There *will* be times, though, when you'll be disappointed. We all are from time to time. But don't give up. Even though you may get a brief note carefully evading reasons for the rejection, consider the mathematics. If every story suggestion were acceptable, magazines that normally publish twelve times a year would need four times as many editions! It's better to think that your idea was probably a good one, but that editors felt it was too similar to another they had recently commissioned.

Or their editorial "bank" may be full of articles that must be used before more are assigned.

Always ensure that you have several proposals or manuscripts for recycling circulating at one time, preferably all on different topics. The logic is that if one or two are rejected, others remain alive. Keep writing without becoming hopelessly dejected. I've had as many as six pieces and two book proposals simultaneously doing the rounds; whatever isn't turned back sustains my hope. And without hope in writing, you might just as well give up. So list all your ideas as and when they occur, then assign a little corner of your week to reading through lists of magazines to find each a likely market. You'll be surprised to discover that your chances of selling your work are quite good.

17. Crafting the Speech

Length / structure / corporate speeches / theme / focus / brevity / different types of speeches

"There are three things to aim at in public speaking:
first to get into your subject,
then to get your subject into yourself,
and lastly, to get your subject into your hearers."
BISHOP ALEXANDER GREGG

At some time in our lives, most of us are called upon to give a talk. There may be occasions when, like a lot of freelancers, we'll be asked to write a speech for others. They may have confessed to not being good at speaking in public; our job will be to assist them. Nothing, of course, can be done to rectify a voice that squeaks like a hinge or gurgles like bathwater, and only experience will help an orator conquer nervousness. But crafting speeches reaches far beyond this.

Like any kind of writing, a speech (an average twenty-minute one runs to about thirty-five hundred words) is not particularly mysterious. To be interesting, it needs a healthy mixture of information, ideas, impressions, and opinions, and must be attractive to listen to. It should follow closely the kind of structure you would use for crafting a magazine piece – touching on all the topic's pulse points. These should be embraced in an arresting opening, a middle that backgrounds the topic, and an ending that leaves listeners with a lasting impression.

Given once again, however, that the written and the spoken word are two entirely different things, the speech must be looser. You can't expect anyone to stand up and read a magazine article because it would sound just that – a piece of writing that was originally intended only to be read. Ideally, then, a speech is built to have room within it for the odd off-the-cuff remark or the occasional dramatic pause, a speaking technique passed down from the theatre.

In general terms, says a CN executive who assigns speech writers, "a speech needs a loose front end, a tight middle in which you get down to the nitty-gritty, and an upbeat ending – a classic finale in which the speaker urges his audience into action even if he himself doesn't have all the solutions." Air Canada's senior speech writer puts it another way: "Tell 'em what you're going to tell 'em; tell 'em; then, in a summation, tell 'em what you told 'em."

A good piece of advice is to research the topic fully then, armed with what you know, insist on interviewing the person for whom you are writing the speech so it may be written as he or she would normally speak. This collaboration is critical to turn a struggling orator into one who sounds comfortable, knowledgeable, and committed to his topic. It goes without saying, of course, that crafting the right words is crucial. But so is a strong partnership between speaker and writer who, while providing his specialized skill and service, becomes something of a confidant and adviser. Ultimately this involves a little giving on both sides. For all this, many senior executives find themselves too busy to grant speech writers time, then wonder why they aren't as effective in public as they'd like to be. Yet corporate speeches are important because they are most often intended to reach well beyond the room in which they are delivered. Ideally, they carry messages strong enough to be of interest to the media at large.

Just as he must have access to his speaker, so it is vital for the writer to know who will be in the audience. You can't hope for a speech prepared for the Conference Board of Canada to appeal to the Lion's Club in Edmundston, New Brunswick, any more than you can expect to enthral a group of Prairie model-railway enthusiasts with a talk aimed at a breakfast meeting of Federal Government transportation experts. The speech writer's job is to find and set out entertaining, informative, or helpful words that will be easily understandable to a specific audience.

The best speeches are a pleasure to listen to because they're interesting and sparkle with crisp, clear language. The worst drag on forever, it seems, because the topic hasn't been made appetizing with stories or analogies, or the words they use are cumbersome or unfamiliar. It has always seemed a great pity to me that so many corporate speakers with something important or interesting to say have inadvertently "distanced" themselves from their audiences so effectively with jargon and pompous language that you immediately suspect it was done purposely. Unfortunately, some executives *insist* on jargon, claiming that it *is* familiar language. This is a writer's dilemma, especially if he has high standards and feels that this kind of language will deaden the speech. All he can do is try to persuade the executive to avoid it, and remind him or her of the English writer Sir Alan Patrick Herbert's famous words – "A dull speaker, like a plain woman, is credited with all the virtues, for we charitably suppose that a surface so unattractive must be compensated by inner blessings." The writer should then explain that wading through corporate verbosity to find meaning and inner blessings can, for many audiences, be too much hard work.

This raises another point. Successful speeches usually focus on a main theme and include one subordinate theme at most. A speech can't hope to document fully all a speaker's opinions or theories in a single shot, only those that can be explained well within an allotted time. "The simple measurement of a good talk," says another corporate executive, "is if it can be easily summed up afterwards by a listener. He should be able to explain the gist of it to anyone who wasn't there, in just five or six sentences."

Common to nearly all corporate speakers is the challenge of having to tell audiences what they would too often prefer not to hear – a forecast of higher interest rates, say, or severe financial cutbacks that are almost certain to translate into job losses. Very often they must tackle "dry," complex topics, or argue against what their audiences believe. When they do, they need to work on one simple principle – that they must win listeners' approval the moment they start speaking. "You have to say enough acceptable things before venturing into the controversial stuff," says the CN executive. "You have to get heads nodding and people saying, 'He's right,' very early on. You need to get them applauding. You must sound as if you're in their corner before saying all the things that are likely to be challenging to them. That's how you build the bridge of credibility."

Many speakers think they achieve this best by taking a splash of gentle humour to the podium, or by showing some previously uncovered human quality about themselves. I've known some of the country's most senior bankers to begin speeches on how the budget will affect business by talking about the Stanley Cup play-offs, or inanely comparing "windy times" ahead to the junction of Winnipeg's Main and Portage streets, said to be Canada's windiest corner. Journalistically, however, these introductions are too often condescending and trite – silly attempts at winning listeners' hearts by striking at those things that are likely to be of immediate interest to them.

Usually, such opening sentences are not an experienced speech writer's work at all, but an executive's additions to the text. However good a speech may be, the person giving it will almost certainly edit in the odd personal touch, which is his privilege. He must feel comfortable with what he reads, and it must flow from him naturally. The writer's task, then, is usually to provide the body of the speech, leaving the opening remarks to the speaker's discretion – according to how, on reaching the podium, he or she has assessed the audience's mood.

The best speech writers, though, particularly those who work for our senior politicians and best corporations, craft *all* of a talk as it will be delivered. They ensure, as they would in a magazine piece, that any attempts at humour in the beginning always bear a strong and direct relationship to what will follow. A fine example of this was the opening of a speech made by a man trying to raise money for his church. Compared to the kind of problems contemplated by the Conference Board, his might be considered inconsequential. The signpost at the beginning of his talk, nonetheless, remains a superb example for speech writers everywhere.

The man chose to tell a story about a burglar entering a house one night, tripping over a chair in the darkness and waking from sound slumber the person who lived there – the amiable old vicar. "If you cry for help," the burglar threatened, brandishing a knife, "you're dead! I'm looking for money."

"If you'll let me get out of the bed and light a candle," the vicar replied, "I'd be more than happy to hunt for money with you."

His point concisely and astutely made, the speaker – his audience in his pocket – went on to explain the dreadful state of church finances and what could be done to improve them. His introduction had worked well for him and his listeners alike.

United States president Calvin Coolidge was, by all accounts, a master at setting tone and indicating the subject of a speech in a bright, appropriate opening. Called upon to give his address at a

Washington state dinner, he took the old advice, "Get up, speak up, and shut up," literally. He rose with dignity, sipped some ice water and shuffled his notes. "My address," he said finally, "is the White House, Pennsylvania Avenue, Washington, District of Columbia, U.S.A." – then sat down. The laughter was predictable. In seconds, Coolidge stood up again to deliver a light speech which poked fun at foreign diplomacy.

Before writing any speech, it's imperative to ask yourself why it is going to be delivered. Is it for a speaker to thank associates? Is it to sell a proposal, launch a plan of action, explain a concept, or commemorate an occasion? Each will require an entirely different approach. An advocate can be a compelling speaker, a lecturer a fascinating one. But there can also be a special poignance in a simple eulogy or dedication, lifting a speaker to rare, nostalgic eloquence.

On the surface, these may seem like easy little speeches to write. But they aren't. Too often they have tended to snare orators, causing them to spout clichés and boring banalities, or make statements that smack of over-sentimentality. As in the case of the short magazine piece, they are extremely tricky for the writer, and must be carefully prepared and stitched together. Research all the facts that must be introduced, study the character of the event, person or institution your speaker will salute and, above all, resist the temptation to let him or her be unnecessarily wordy. A New York advertising executive named Bruce Barton used to contend that "there was far too much speaking in the world, and almost all of it too long." He cited *The Lord's Prayer*, *The Twenty-Third Psalm*, and Abraham Lincoln's *Gettysburg Address* as three great literary treasures that would last forever, even though none was more than three hundred words long. "With such striking examples of brevity," Barton added, "it's amazing that speakers never learn to be brief."

There's often no need to be otherwise. You may find you are writing a speech for a moderator, whose job it is to keep a discussion running smoothly, building bridges in words that will swing from one speaker to the next informatively and sometimes entertainingly. A good moderator is expected to give a quick, thumbnail sketch of the various people who are appearing on his panel, first at the outset when opening the proceedings, and later as each person is about to speak.

Unlike the moderator, the introducer at a dinner or ceremony emerges smartly to tell the audience about the main speaker. His words must be few and well-chosen. The late American diplomat

Adlai Stevenson, one of the finest political speakers ever to grace a platform, once likened one speaker's introduction of another to a fan dance. "You cover the subject only enough to make it tantalizing," he said.

Again, the secret to preparing this sort of speech is research, and distilling it sufficiently well that the introduction is brief and succinct and does not spoil what will come. And never write an introduction which overpraises the speaker. It immediately promises the audience more than he or she may be able to deliver.

A few years ago, I was invited to talk to an association of school principals on my early education and career. The man who introduced me spent seven of the thirty minutes allotted to me, reading from my curriculum vitae, which he drew like a sword from his inside pocket to view for the very first time just moments before I rose to speak. Fortunately for me, he pronounced several words incorrectly, prompting hoots of laughter and inadvertently "warming" the audience. But I often think how much tidier the occasion would have been had he distilled my background first, jotted down a few pertinent and appealing facts, then spoke for no more than a minute.

I was lucky, it seems. Broadcaster Clyde Gilmour tells how he was once invited to speak to a group of music lovers where the introducer sauntered to the microphone, cleared his throat and said, "I now call upon Mr. Gary Gilman who will speak about . . . er . . . his . . . er . . . his address."

The most difficult speeches to craft are those expected of people who are being honoured. Imparting feelings of gratitude without being patronizing, condescending, or glib, is also tricky. The perfect ploy for the honorand is to switch the focus of attention from himself back to the audience with a little humorous aside which may well be pre-arranged, but nonetheless appears natural. This device provides a sure-fire guarantee that the speaker will endear himself to his listeners. Take a tip from another professional. A woman called upon to introduce Winston Churchill at a dinner where honours were being poured upon him for his years as Britain's war-time leader and for later academic work, began, "It must be very pleasing for you to know, Mr. Churchill, that whenever you speak, there is always a large attendance." Churchill rose and thanked the woman for her generous introduction. Then he said, "Think how much larger this audience would be if I were about to be hanged."

Just as books and magazine articles need case histories, examples, and anecdotes, so do speeches. After spending more than thirty-five years as a photojournalist exposing consumer fraud, Gene Selig, a member of the Blue Flame Toastmaster's in Irvine, California, was kept busy giving lectures and seminars to all manner of groups from police departments and insurance companies to retail management teams and service clubs.

He always made a point of designing his talks to be factual, yes, but interspersed with anecdotes so he could turn a tragic or serious event into a humorous one. "The reward," he said, "is that the majority of the audience always comes forward afterwards to shake my hand and say that what I said was funny, interesting, and informative. Life is, after all, a one-way street. So why not laugh a little, even in the face of all the bad around us? At lectures and seminars we have a perfect podium to practise that philosophy and I do it all the time."

18. The Freelancer's Market

Books / consumer magazines: children's, general-interest, "specialty," news, women's, travel, sports, and outdoors / trade magazines

"In Canada, the standard magazine page is 4,800 kilometers wide, with the right-hand margin on the east coast, the left-hand margin on the west coast and the trim line at the United States' border."

MAGAZINES CANADA

Much has happened since the pugnacious Joseph Howe began editing his *Novascotian* back in the 1820s. Publishing houses – large and small – have never stopped sprouting up, giving Canada a print industry second to none. Today, we have well over three hundred book publishers, of which about two-thirds are either partially or wholly Canadian-owned. More than a hundred and twenty of these are members of the Association of Canadian Publishers, formed in 1971 to encourage writing, publishing, and the promotion of books written by Canadians. A further fifty are represented by the Canadian Book Publishers' Council, established in 1910.

Together, these publishers are responsible for ninety per cent of all our home-grown literature. They range from determined little rural presses turning out two or three books a year, to large Toronto-based companies launching as many as thirty – novels, dictionaries, biographies, guides, and handbooks on every topic imaginable.

To be painfully honest, however, the chances of freelancers new to the business seeing their book in print, are slim. The average large house receives nearly two thousand suggestions and unsolicited manuscripts each year, of which fewer than one per cent are successful. No one should ever stop sending off book ideas, but freelancers would be far better off mastering the article and trying to conquer a magazine market which, in recent years, has exploded farther and wider than we ever thought it would.

In the late 1960s, Canada had a mere forty-six consumer magazines – some monthly, some only quarterly – distributing an average of six million copies per issue. But despite their sparseness, they combined to create an important national voice. Pierre Trudeau's ideas on French Canada's place in Confederation were first expounded in a Montreal magazine called *Cité Libre*. From his cluttered office at the University of Toronto, Professor Marshall McLuhan began spreading his theories on communications in the on-campus publication, *Explorations*. Just a few blocks away, meanwhile, *The Tamarack Review* was giving important writers like Mordecai Richler and Alice Munro the opportunity to reach their first appreciative audiences.

Sadly, these magazines are no longer with us. Others, however, have sprung up in their place. By 1980, and despite precarious economic times, the number of Canadian consumer magazines had grown to 318, together distributing thirty million copies per issue. Now, as Canadians read more about themselves, their neighbours, hobbies, work and aspirations, there are nearly five hundred such magazines with a combined per-issue circulation of some eighty million copies. "The wide range of Canadian consumer magazines," says the *International Report on Periodical Publishing*, "makes them appealing to an equally wide range of Canadian consumers."

It does. The self-interests of twenty-five million people, somewhat diverse in attitudes and values "as affected by regional disparities, ethnicity, lifestyle and language," says Magazines Canada, a non-profit organization toiling hard to promote our periodicals, "are easily met and accommodated by the many different kinds of magazines available."

The choice is eclectic indeed. There are magazines for every subject you and I can think of from stamp collecting, gardening, and astrology, to organic farming, knitting, and the monarchy. Some are large and national, but the majority are small and regional, like Saskatchewan's *Briarpatch* and Nova Scotia's *The Pottersfield Portfolio*. More and more are local. The glossy *Windsor This Month*, *Key to Kingston* and *Montreal Magazine* are typical of an increasing number of city publications that offer readers information on wines, food, fashion, events, and people. So is Toronto's *Now*, a weekly aimed at an audience of active young adults. It carries pieces on film, music, theatre, local personalities and issues, and publishes special supplements on books, art, fashion, and travel.

Our children have their magazines, too, from *Crackers* and *Jam* to the Young Naturalist Foundation's *Chickadee* and *Owl*, which, through informative, educational stories aimed those aged between seven and twelve, have posed such questions as "How can a fly walk on the moon?" and "What's winter like on Mars?" – then supplied the answers.

With unprecedented public awareness for all that improves the quality of community life, news and opinion magazines have never fared better. In Halifax, the *Atlantic Insight* thrives; in Toronto, *This Magazine* has won public acclaim, plus four National Magazine Awards, for the provocative, informed way it has challenged "the mainstream" with solid investigative articles on culture, politics, labour, and international affairs. Among its admirers is *Toronto Star* columnist Richard Gwyn, who says it has accomplished "some of the most energetic political commentary in the country." A spirited and attractive national feminist magazine called *HERizons*, published in Winnipeg, offers a comprehensive overview of such critical women's issues as health, childcare, and employment, as does *Kinesis*, published by the Vancouver Status of Women. This journal includes analytical, provocative pieces on politics and pornography, as well as regular columns on music, small-press poetry, theatre, dance, photography, and women's art.

Our largest national all-news magazine is *Maclean's* which, in 1975, began a careful transformation from being a general-interest monthly to one that incorporated issue pieces, political profiles, and on-going regional stories, and published every two weeks. By 1978, the change-over was complete and *Maclean's* became Canada's answer to *Time* or *Newsweek*, appearing on our newsstands every Monday and soon building up a paid circulation of 650,000 loyal readers.

Like *Time* and *Newsweek*, *Maclean's* relies on freelance correspondents with news-gathering experience. When a big national story breaks, freelancers immediately dash into the field in their own areas, building up files of facts, quotes, and anecdotes which will give the subject its geographic spread. The files are then fused into one large piece by an experienced staff writer who could be at either the magazine's Toronto headquarters or in any one of its news bureaus in Vancouver, Calgary, Ottawa, Montreal, and Halifax.

The quality of the final story depends on how well a news file is compiled. Making one rich with good information is work for an energetic, perceptive freelancer who enjoys news, can build up useful contacts, and work quickly and thoroughly against intense Friday deadlines.

General-interest magazines remain fairly healthy in Canada. Beyond the best-known, *Reader's Digest*, *Equinox*, and *Saturday Night*, there are others Joseph Howe would never have envisioned. With sophisticated air travel came sophisticated in-flight publications – Air Canada's *enRoute* and CP Air's *Empress*, among others. Both provide good markets for quality pieces written to give travellers fresh insights into such topics as business, the arts, inventions, or technology. An *Empress* editor neatly defines the types of articles in-flight magazines expect when she says, "We want pieces that have some connection with the movement of people or goods."

Travel is obviously a favourite with all general-interest magazines. But be careful here. Good ones don't want travelogues that deal exclusively with a destination's touristic aspect. "We *never* write about a place just because it might be a nice place to see," says an *Equinox* editor. Neither does *enRoute* or *Empress*. They look for travel articles that give unusual glimpses into an area or country, but always with a theme – be it business, cultural, historic, sociological, or sporting. In-flight magazines want a country or region to interest readers who may never intend to visit it.

Among other magazines using travelogues is Vancouver's *Great Expeditions*, which combines a mixture of useful travel tips and ideas for unusual vacations via first-hand accounts of far-off destinations by writers who have been to them. The magazines will take you down the Zambezi River on a steamer, for instance, birding in India, or on a villa holiday in Jamaica.

So will *Doctor's Review* of Montreal. But why would a magazine aimed at medical practitioners want to give its readers travelogues? "Why not?" says the publisher. "We're not a clinical journal. We try to help busy people climb out of themselves. Feeding them nicely written travel pieces is one of the best ways of doing it." He started his magazine in 1983 simply to give physicians good, leisure-time reading. But to find out who they were exactly, and what they wanted, took two studies. Both involved polling physicians every three months for two years, asking them what subjects they most enjoyed. Travel headed the list, followed by food and drink, hobbies, business, art, literature, profiles of successful Canadians, and humour. The studies also showed that the doctors were so used to confronting solid, hard facts in their medical reading, that they expected them in their spare-time reading too, even when it was general-interest.

By far the biggest growth in Canadian magazines has been spurred by readers' special interests. These – the so-called "specialty magazines" – include *Continuo* for music lovers, *Discovery* for retirement-age people, *The Canadian MoneySaver*, a consumer's guide to personal finance and investment techniques, and *Gardening & Leisure Living*, whose how-to and when-to articles are designed to help Ontarians get more from their flower beds and vegetable patches.

There is also the lively nature and ecology magazine *Wildlife Review* of Sidney, British Columbia, Calgary's *Explore* for those of us who thrive on both the challenge and excitement of the outdoors, and *Select Homes* of Toronto and Vancouver, which satisfies interests specific to home ownership – mainly interior design, renovation, and maintenance. The magazine's news column about new products, mortgages, and insurance, says the editor, "is an excellent market for freelancers starting out."

Predictably, dozens of Canadian periodicals have been spawned by trends. They range from the top-selling *Videomania* and *Sound & Vision*, to *Ontario Craft*, and *Canadian Bluegrass Review* for old-time Country music enthusiasts. Those who buy dreams enjoy *Lottery & Gaming Review*, which offers "winning" formulas to serious casino players and those who gamble socially. And with the national keep-fit bent well and truly rooted, sports magazines thrive – *Ski Canada*, *Soccer News*, *Racquets Canada*, and *Athletics*, established in 1976 to promote family participation in track, cross-country and road running.

Canadians' entrepreneurial spirit is encouraged by *Small Business*, their need for wise investing by *Your Money*, a snappy little magazine that has provided good opportunities for writers able to explain the intricacies of personal finance in layman's terms.

While trends come and go, old values stay. Hence, in the true spirit of kinship, *Legion Magazine* keeps war veterans and their families in close touch country-wide while covering issues integral to an aging society. News, views, and articles on physical rehabilitation for both the professional and the disabled person are contained in *Rehabilitation Digest*, first published in 1969. And *Dogs in Canada* continues to inform and advise pet owners, as it has since it was launched by the Canadian Kennel Club in 1889.

That year, by the way, a Scots-Canadian novelist named Robert Barr complained, "The bold truth is that Canada has the money but would rather spend it on whisky than on books. It prefers to inflame its stomach rather than inform its brain!" How wrong he was. The two-year-old *Saturday Night* had begun its long climb to international acclaim and within four decades, such stalwarts as *Maclean's*, *Chatelaine*, and *Canadian Author & Bookman* were born, as was *The Canadian Forum*, established in 1920. Since then, says one critic, *Forum* "has, in a dignified way, cocked some considerable snooks at the business and political establishments."

As the upsurge in Canadian periodicals gained momentum with unprecedented vitality in the 1960s, there appeared in our mail boxes the first of several controlled-circulation – or give-away – magazines. Many, like *Quest*, have since died. Perhaps the most durable, however, is *Homemaker's*, born on a pleasant October day in 1966, and which has never altered its mandate. As then, it still aims to inform and entertain women aged between twenty-five and fifty-four.

Regular columns on health, finance, fitness, fashion, food, cooking, beauty, and decor – all vital components of each issue – are handled at *Homemaker's* by freelance contributors with expertise in those areas. But the magazine offers opportunities for other freelancers, primarily through pieces that put a strong emphasis on women in their communities, their relationships – and important aspects of family life like sex, bringing up children, coping with teens, and learning. You don't have to be a woman to make editors happy here. I've done it several times.

As *Homemaker's* blossomed, so literally dozens of magazines directed solely at the workplace appeared, all catering to specific industries, trades, and professions. These are Canada's business and trade journals. We have about two hundred of them, some owned by societies, government agencies, Crown corporations, or large businesses, many published monthly by Toronto companies like Maclean-Hunter, Southam Communications, and Wadham Publications. They combine with book publishers and consumer magazines to give Canadian freelancers roughly a thousand markets for their work.

We've already met two trade magazines that frequently buy freelance material – *Canadian Doctor* and *Hardware Merchandising.* Others show the diversity of a market many writers too often omit to tap: *Canadian Secretary*, *Baker's Journal*, *Mining Review*, and the *Canadian Footwear Journal*. There are, in fact, publications satisfying every section of the work force you and I can think of – cars and transportation; beauty, dentistry, health, and pharmaceuticals; building, heating, and plumbing; accounting; business and civic; chemistry; farming; fisheries; nursing; forestry; food and hospitality; hardware; garden and sporting goods; mining; office equipment and administration; teaching; travel. The list goes on and on.

Most of these publications – or "the trades," as they're affectionately called – are neither slick nor attractive. They don't have to be, because they have captive audiences who share one common interest and for whom gloss and page-design are of little or no concern. They are, however, professional magazines. And considering that most assignments they hand out generally pay around two hundred dollars and can be done in a couple of days, they pay reasonably well.

The basics for selling to trade journals are similar to those you would use to place an article anywhere: Acquaint yourself with both the publication and its readers, then find ideas you think will apply. Remind yourself constantly, though, that the market is not as easy to penetrate as it may appear. Trade magazine staffs are usually too small to afford the time to read unsolicited manuscripts. Their needs are so specialized anyway, that what we may consider the best ideas often won't come close. The quickest way to make the editor of the bi-monthly *Heavy Construction News* happy is not with graceful, anecdotal writing, but with solid, hard facts – "the meat and potatoes," he calls them – on the engineered construction of our roads, bridges, dams, power stations, quarries, and pits. His readers, he knows, are more informed about the methods and types of equipment used in such engineering than you and I could ever hope to learn in a lifetime.

If, like me, you enjoy working in French, there are the Montreal-based magazines *L'Actualité*, *Les Affaires*, and *Vie des Arts*. Each is among a healthy breed of Quebec publishing enterprises which, in recent years, has gained national and international recognition.

You should be aware by now, however, that there's a market for almost everything you will ever want to write, but that you must find it. The secret to breaking in lies largely with never shunning a magazine because it appears small or grey; freelancers new to the business should be grateful for the chance to write for anyone. The more you turn your hand from one magazine to another, trade or consumer, you'll gain practice, skill, and experience, as well as pay the rent.

That's how I reached out. While at the *Sheerness Times-Guardian*, I sold little stories to London's *Evening News* and *Evening Standard*. Fleet Street then beckoned, and I couldn't resist it. Working for such giant newspapers as the *Daily Express* and the *Daily Mail* taught me that, however complex a story might be, it can and must be explained simply. With the security of being a full-time reporter, I freelanced in London for whatever magazines would accept my work, and when I emigrated to Canada in 1963, I found jobs on five different newspapers, including the Hamilton *Spectator* and *The Globe and Mail*, while quietly establishing myself as a freelancer who would one day be self-employed.

I eventually was, of course, but at the outset it was hard. Throughout the mid-1960s, and at last on my own, I sold five-paragraph pieces to a Toronto trade paper which extolled the virtues not of good writing, but of translucent plastic panels. "They've just built another john!" the paper's publisher would say with enthusiasm. "Can we get the story?" Camera in hand, I would rush off to a local park to write another piece – for twenty-five dollars. I have photographed and written about more toilets than any other person I know.

I wrote articles for theatre programs, trucking journals, and a little paper published by a group of funeral directors. Then *The United Church Observer* began assigning me two-page articles – for thirty-five dollars each. You don't have to be a church-goer to find the religious dimension in a serious social problem. I rose to the task willingly and it paid off. In 1968, the late Fiona Mee, editor of the book trade's bible *Quill & Quire*, invited me to lunch and offered me seventy-five dollars to interview Mordecai Richler, with the promise of more assignments later. I was over the moon with joy.

Nonetheless, I continued to suffer long, impoverished years I wouldn't want inflicted on anyone. "You must be starving, dear," my grandmother wrote – and mailed me a bread pudding. It was inedible when it reached me because she forgot to affix airmail stickers and the parcel took six weeks to come by sea. Around that time, *The Spectator* assigned me to write a freelance piece on the plight of

Hamilton's welfare recipients. Without exception, all those I interviewed had better monthly incomes than I.

Through the worst of it, I stayed debt-free, took odd jobs, gave guest lectures, and spoke to women's groups, mostly without payment, to get myself known. Eventually, by picking saleable subjects and refining and proposing them in a professional way, I was able to penetrate the larger magazines – *Weekend*, *Maclean's*, *Chatelaine*, *enRoute*, and *Canadian Business*, and earn fees of hundreds of dollars for each piece.

By the early 1970s, I could completely sustain myself by freelance magazine writing, crafting original pieces then recycling them with a vengeance. A fairly steady income now allowed me to start writing books – my first four within only two years. In 1975, the *Reader's Digest* began using my work regularly and paying me fees that stretched into the thousands. Everything had at last come together.

It was strenuous but rewarding, and if I could choose my destiny again, I'd probably select the same path with those same struggles. Struggles, after all, are the very things of which writers are made. You learn to shrug off disappointment, repel writer's block, chuckle at rejection slips, and become impervious to useless criticism. "Why waste your time on that?" a colleague said while I was writing *Theatre on a Shoestring*. "You'll never get it published."

"Maybe not," I said. "But it's something I've got to do." And it was – if only to prove that colleague wrong.

If I never type another word, shape another sentence, or wield a pencil through another sloppy paragraph, I can honestly say that writing has been good to me. Learn the craft, study the market, and administer writing like a fully-fledged business, and it can be good to you, too.

I truly hope so. Work well, meanwhile – and above all else, try to have fun.

USEFUL ORGANIZATIONS FOR WRITERS

The Alberta Publishers' Association,
10022-103rd Street, Room 102,
Edmonton, Alberta
T5J 0X2

Association of Book Publishers of British Columbia,
1622 West 7th Avenue,
Vancouver, British Columbia
V6J 1B5

Association of Canadian Publishers,
70 The Esplanade, 3rd Floor,
Toronto, Ontario
M5E 1R2

Atlantic Publishers Association,
Killam Library,
Dalhousie University,
Halifax, Nova Scotia
B3H 4H8

Canadian Authors Association,
24 Ryerson Avenue,
Toronto, Ontario
M5T 2P3

Canadian Book Information Centre,
260 King Street E.,
Toronto, Ontario
M5A 1K3

Canadian Book Information Centre (West),
1622 West 7th Avenue,
Vancouver, British Columbia
VJ6 1B5

Canadian Book Information Centre (East),
Killam Library,
Dalhousie University,
Halifax, Nova Scotia
B3H 4H8

Canadian Book Information Centre (Prairies),
374 Donald Street, 3rd Floor,
Winnipeg, Manitoba
R3B 2J2

Canadian Book Publishers' Council,
45 Charles Street E., 7th Floor,
Toronto, Ontario
M4Y 1S2

Canadian Copyright Institute,
34 Ross Street, Suite 200,
Toronto, Ontario
M5T 1Z9

Canadian Periodical Publishers' Association,
2 Stewart Street,
Toronto, Ontario
M5V 1H6

Freelance Editors' Association of Canada,
34 Ross Street, Suite 200,
Toronto, Ontario
M5T 1Z9

The League of Canadian Poets,
24 Ryerson Avenue
Toronto, Ontario
M5T 2P3

Literary Press Group,
70 The Esplanade, 3rd Floor,
Toronto, Ontario
M5E 1R2

Magazines Canada,
250 Bloor Street East,
Toronto, Ontario
M4W 1E6

Periodical Writers Association of Canada,
24 Ryerson Avenue,
Toronto, Ontario
M5T 2P3

Playwrights Union of Canada,
8 York Street, 6th Floor,
Toronto, Ontario
M5J 1R2

Prairie Publishers Group,
374 Donald Street, 3rd Floor,
Winnipeg, Manitoba
R3B 2J2

The Writer Federation of Nova Scotia,
P.O. Box 3608,
South Post Office,
Halifax, Nova Scotia
B3J 3K6

The Writers' Union of Canada,
24 Ryerson Avenue,
Toronto, Ontario
M5T 2P3

USEFUL BOOKS FOR WRITERS

A Manual of Style, (12th edition, revised), University of Chicago Press, Chicago, 1974.

Burack, Sylvia K., ed. *The Writer's Handbook*, The Writer, Inc., Boston, 1982.

Bernstein, Theodore M. *The Careful Writer*, Atheneum, New York, 1965.

Bernstein, Theodore M. *Miss Thistlebottom's Hobgoblins: The Careful Writer's Guide to the Taboos, Bugbears and Outmoded Rules of English Usage*, Simon and Schuster, New York, 1971.

Bernstein, Theodore M. *Watch Your Language*, Atheneum, New York, 1976.

Kernaghan, E., Kernaghan, P., and Surridge, E. *The Upper Left-Hand Corner*, J.J. Douglas, Vancouver, 1979.

Messenger, William E. and de Bruyn, Jan. *The Canadian Writer's Handbook*, Prentice-Hall of Canada, Ltd., Toronto, 1980.

Miller, Casey and Swift, Kate. *The Handbook of Nonsexist Writing*, Lippincott & Crowell, New York, 1980.

Molinaro, M. and Wilson, M.C. *A Writer's Contract*, Canadian Speakers and Writers' Services, Toronto, 1979.

Peterson, Franklynn and Kesselman-Turkel, Judi. *The Magazine Writer's Handbook*, Prentice-Hall, Inc., Englewood Cliffs, N.J., 1982.

Shaw, Harry. *McGraw-Hill Handbook of English*, (2nd edition), McGraw-Hill Company of Canada Limited, Toronto, 1970.

Strunk, William Jr. and White, E.B. *The Elements of Style*, (3rd edition), Macmillan Publishing Co., Inc., New York, 1979.

The Canadian Style, A Guide to Writing and Editing, Dundurn Press Limited, Toronto, and the Canadian Government Publishing Centre, Ottawa, 1985.

Woolfolk Cross, Donna. *Word Abuse*, Coward, McCann & Geoghegan, Inc., New York, 1979.

Words into Type, (3rd edition, revised), Prentice-Hall, Inc., New Jersey, 1974.

Zinsser, William. *On Writing Well*, Harper & Row, New York, 1980

Zinsser, William. *Writing with a Word Processor*, Harper & Row, New York, 1983.

Dictionaries and Thesauruses

Chapman, Robert L., ed. *Roget's International Thesaurus*, (4th edition), T.Y. Crowell, New York; Fitzhenry & Whiteside Ltd., Toronto, 1977.

Copperud, Roy H. *A Dictionary of Usage and Style*, Hawthorn Books, Inc., New York, 1967.

Fowler, H.W. *Dictionary of Modern English Usage*, (2nd edition), edited by Sir E. Gowers, Oxford University Press, Oxford, 1965.

Hayakawa, S.I., ed. *Funk and Wagnalls Modern Guide to Synonyms*, Funk and Wagnalls, New York, 1986.

Funk and Wagnalls Standard College Dictionary, (Canadian edition), Fitzhenry & Whiteside, Toronto, 1976.

Oxford American Dictionary, Oxford University Press, New York, 1980.

Oxford Dictionary for Writers and Editors, Oxford University Press, Oxford, 1984.

Reference Books and Magazines

The Book Trade in Canada, published annually by Ampersand Publishing Services Inc.

Canadian Author and Bookman, published by the Canadian Authors Association, at 24 Ryerson Avenue, Toronto, Ont. M5T 2P3.

Literary Market Place, published annually by R.R. Bowker Publishing Co. Ltd.

Sources, The Directory of Contacts for Editors, Reporters and Researchers, published twice yearly at 9 St. Nicholas Street, Suite 402, Toronto, Ont. M4Y 1W5, as part of *Content Magazine*, and circulated to almost 12,000 newsmedia personnel.

The Writer, 8 Arlington Street, Boston, Massachusetts, 02116.

Writer's Digest, published by Writer's Digest, 9933 Alliance Road, Cincinnati, Ohio, 45242.

Writers' and Artists' Year Book, published annually by A. & C. Black.

* significance

- interesting people / backgrounds
- action - sustained action
- lasting interest (years)
- imp. to human life / substance / human value
- combines human drama w/ practical information
- examples / solutions // shows ups & downs

- to entertain & to inform

→ think of your readers: who is this piece likely to appeal to?

→ READ magazine articles: ① find out how they're written
② " " what particular editors like
③ " " what's already been done recently